RIGHT
vs.
WRONG

Harry and Betty Dent

THOMAS NELSON PUBLISHERS
Nashville

Published in Nashville, Tennessee, by Thomas Nelson, Inc., and distributed in Canada by Lawson Falle, Ltd., Cambridge, Ontario.

Unless otherwise noted, Scripture quotations are from the NEW KING JAMES VERSION of the Bible. Copyright © 1979, 1980, 1982, Thomas Nelson, Inc., Publishers.

Scripture quotations noted NIV are from The Holy Bible: NEW INTERNATIONAL VERSION. Copyright © 1978 by the New York International Bible Society. Used by permission of Zondervan Bible Publishers.

Scripture quotations noted J. B. Phillips are from THE NEW TESTAMENT IN MODERN ENGLISH, Revised Edition. Copyright © J. B. Phillips 1958, 1960, 1972. Used by permission of Macmillan Publishing Co., Inc.

Library of Congress Cataloging-in-Publication Data

Dent, Harry.
    Right vs. wrong : solutions to the American nightmare / Harry and Betty Dent.
      p.   cm.
    Includes bibliographical references.
    ISBN 0-8407-3438-7 (pbk.)
    1. Christian ethics. 2. United States—Moral conditions.
  3. Dent, Harry. 4. Dent, Betty. I. Dent, Betty. II. Title.
  III. Title: Right versus wrong.
  BJ1275.D46 1992
  241'.0973—dc20   92–18657
                                            CIP

Printed in the United States of America

1 2 3 4 5 6 7 — 96 95 94 93 92

To
The late Lt. H. N. (Fritz) Dent, Jr., age 24,
and The late Lt. Richard Clayton (Jack) Dent, age 22

These brothers made the supreme sacrifice in World War II so that others could enjoy the blessings of liberty in America, a land blessed by God as none other in the history of the world. They did the right and responsible thing.

May we do likewise!

Contents

Foreword by
Dr. Richard C. Halverson

It is important that the readers of *Right vs. Wrong* know the great experiences and the sincere heartbeat of these two authors so you can know what is behind and inside this most timely, vital, and compelling book on my favorite subject and country: righteousness in America. *Right vs. Wrong* is the product of a lifetime of searching for right over wrong by the products of two dysfunctional homes who have been able to live the American dream and now discern the coming American nightmare for our posterity.

Harry and Betty Dent point to the rising problems for our beloved America, but they provide answers for turning America back to what they call the right thing and the real thing, meaning God's Will and the righteousness of Jesus Christ.

The answers come out of the Holy Bible, from their study of hundreds of Christian and secular works by renowned experts, and from their rich store of varied and valuable experiences. This couple has poured their open hearts of concern and their knowledge, wisdom, and understanding of the ways of God and the ways of man onto these pages. Here is a couple who have matured as mates, parents, grandparents, and Christians. They know the vast gulf between man's spiritual lostness and God's aim for all of us to come to Christ, to grow up in Christ, and to go out into the world for Christ as lay witnesses and ministers for righteousness.

Like Paul, they have run the race, but unlike Paul they have not finished their course. Their aim before passing on is to be a key part of waking and shaking the land and people they so love. They hope that America might be saved from moral and financial wrongdoing and used of God to be the beacon light of righteousness for the world to emulate at this most critical time in history.

Once lay people taste of the truth of God's Written Word and God's Living Word they experience the imperative of finding their place in God's Plan. The Dents present what they have discovered about God's Plan, which they are now implementing in a full-time

Christian lay ministry across America and around the world. You will find yourself being challenged throughout this book to examine your life and to get with God's program NOW!

This quest began with a "good" boy and a "good" girl growing up in two dysfunctional families fifty years ago. Both were looking for a better life and the Right way of life for themselves and their future families, not knowing that their individual quests would become their joint quest.

The two searchers were reared in the old Bible Belt of the Deep South. The Dents were married for almost three decades before they sensed the reality of their place in God's master plan as the answer to the Right Thing and the Real Thing. They closed the door on Harry's practice of law and politics; they had no retirement program, except for the one Harry calls "out of this world." They literally operate off of their back porch in Columbia, South Carolina.

Their full-time Christian lay ministry is called "Laity: Alive & Serving." It has taken them into more than seven hundred churches and into schools, homes, civic clubs, prisons, and on Billy Graham Crusades. On motion of Charles Colson and God they have reproduced other lay ministers.

Harry has had a wide variety of rich experiences in life. He began as an Army officer in the Korean War; then he worked as a Washington newsman, chief of staff to United States Senator Strom Thurmond of South Carolina, chairman of the South Carolina Republican Party, a businessman, attorney, and special counsel to President Richard Nixon and to Republican National Chairman George Bush. He also served President Gerald Ford and President Bush on presidential commissions.

Harry also has worked for broken people in prison, divorce courts, and mental institutions. He has ministered to all kinds of people in varied circumstances. Having fought communism in politics during his political career, Harry began ministry behind the Iron Curtain as soon as the walls of communism began crumbling under the hand of the Real Thing.

Not only has he represented and/or ministered to people up against the wall in life, but he has been there himself. His quest for understanding has taken him beyond a year of graduate study in the Bible to a study of hundreds of Christian and secular books and the writing of four books.

Betty has served for more than forty years as the strong rudder for what is the Right Thing in the Dent family. She has reared four children, two boys and two girls. All are married and have given Harry and Betty what the Dents call their posterity: seven "perfect" grandkids.

While Harry had his enemies in politics, Betty has always had nothing but faithful friends. She disliked politics and kept trying to extricate Harry from the political life. She believed that only God, not man, had the answers to life's problems. Friends of the Dents will tell you that next to salvation, Betty is the best gift God has bestowed on Harry. While he juggles the big picture, Betty makes sure the bits and pieces fall into their rightful places.

Betty has spent her spare time in leading and helping with many charitable causes and Bible studies. For her good works she has been honored as one of Columbia, South Carolina's most outstanding ladies. The Dents are alike and also very different. But they mesh together as a strong team with mutual submission to God and to each other. I know, for I have ministered with them.

The Dents show that it is possible to come from dysfunctional families and still experience and enjoy a life of meaning and purpose which leads to fulfillment. They also demonstrate how it is possible to come alive spiritually "in Christ" after being involved in the church for years with good intentions. This is a prime solution trumpeted in this book.

Harry and Betty confess that they have found the major problem to be that there are too many "old" Harry and Betty Dents in America who mean well, don't know well, and thus do not do well.

The Dents demonstrate in this book and in their lives today that it is possible in this lifetime to move from being a part of the problem to being a part of the solution to the problem in America, the family, the church, education, the workplace, and even in politics and government.

The ultimate answer the Dents see is getting the "old" Harrys and Bettys into God's Master Plan and getting God's Master Plan into the "old" Harrys and Bettys. Good intentions must be transformed into implementing the right things in this world for the Real Thing, Jesus Christ. This is how to save America from immaturity and the things of the world.

The Dents are not pessimists about the future of America and the world. They are realists. I join the authors in believing that as America goes so will go the rest of the world in these perilous times of such rapid deterioration of our morals and values. Yes, the answer does lie directly in reviving and changing the Church of Jesus Christ to be used of God to save America!

What America needs today is more "new" Harry and Betty Dents!

Dr. Richard C. Halverson, Chaplain,
United States Senate
April 1992

CHAPTER ONE

Superficial Christians

Methodist leader E. Stanley Jones described slightly religious people by saying they had been inoculated with a mild form of Christianity and thus rendered immune from the real thing.[1]

There are cataclysmic experiences in life that can shake the foundations of our lives, especially if the experience is concerned with the charge of being caught doing what is wrong. When we do the wrong thing we usually reap adverse consequences. When we do the right thing we usually reap good consequences. The bad consequences can spell defeat, divorce, death, bankruptcy, personal injury, or even time in jail. All of these bad consequences rate high on the scale of human trauma.

The first major trauma I remember experiencing was as a rising senior in my small high school in 1946. My four older brothers had all been elected president of the student body, and I was the vice president awaiting my turn at this high honor. This was my first major political campaign challenge, as I had won all other previous school leadership positions without having to campaign. This time I had to strategize and implement my plan to assure my almost assured election. I was my own strategist and campaign manager.

The campaign was flawless until the final days when I handcrafted 150 campaign leaflets which proclaimed: "Vote for Dent or Repent!" After the ballots were counted there was only one person repenting in St. Matthews High School: Harry Shuler Dent. I lost an easy race by a few votes and a faulty strategy. I had done the wrong thing. So at age 16 I experienced the biggest shock and defeat of my young life. I remember believing this was the end of the world for me.

Twenty-six years later I received the second major shock of my life. In that period of time I had become a very successful political operative in college and national politics as a strategist and implementer of my own strategy. But at midnight on June 20, 1972, I was awakened by a ringing telephone. On the other end of the line was

Washington's leading reporter of scandal, Jack Anderson. He informed me that he had confirmation that I was the Nixon White House official who had ordered the June 17 break-in at the offices of the National Democratic Party staff headquarters in the Watergate complex.

I could not sleep. I knew that this information was wrong as far as I personally was concerned. However, the information he was giving me indicated that one of my best friends and also one of my assistants in the Nixon White House were connected with what was becoming the biggest political scandal in American history. By implication I would become a part of that scandal and might not be believed in all of my denials because of my role in the White House as political coordinator. Also, my friend, now the late Manuel Giberga, was a Cuban freedom fighter who would give his all for any cause he considered to be the right thing. He was a strong Republican Party activist who relished covert assignments for good causes. And some of his Cuban freedom-fighter friends had been arrested in the Democratic Party offices.

Before Anderson could get his story out to the hundreds of newspapers who use his column, I was able to discover that Manuel was innocent, and my trauma eased.

Another Watergate Shock

Several months later, in the spring of 1973, a third shock wave hit me at 5:00 P.M. in my law office. This was another of many phone calls I had been receiving about this Watergate scandal that was then being investigated by the United States Senate. This call was from an assistant to Sam Donaldson of ABC-TV. I was informed that in one hour Sam would be reporting on national television that Charles Colson and Harry Dent were the two principal White House culprits behind White House dirty tricks and the break-in at the Watergate complex. He had information that a confessing Watergate witness, James McCord, had so informed the Senate committee behind closed doors. The query was whether I wanted to affirm or deny the allegation. Shocked as I was, I nevertheless yelled out a loud denial. Then I had to go home and view Sam on TV with Betty. I had assured her there would be no Watergate problems for her husband and family.

Knowing the report was wrong, I traveled to Washington looking for someone to correct the bad information. The problem was that no one on the investigating committee could talk to me because Mc-

Cord's testimony was secret. Now the focus of Watergate was on Harry Dent, and I could get no relief from my trauma.

Finally, after three weeks, Senator Howard Baker of Tennessee, a friend and vice chairman of the committee, called in Sam and assured him that the information he had was false. I was relieved when Sam then apologized on national television for his mistake regarding me. He did the same thing in his 1987 book, *Hold On, Mr. President!*[2] Sam also wrote that a committee member falsely denied giving him the bum information. That Republican Senator had a grudge against Colson and me. It was his way of playing a dirty trick himself.

Finally, the biggest trauma hit me in 1974. I received a subpoena to appear before the Watergate grand jury. The Special Watergate Prosecution Force had received approval to go back beyond the Watergate crimes and into the entire first term of President Nixon. They had gotten access to all of our secret memos and our secretly taped telephone conversations. None of us in the White House knew we were being taped, except for two staffers and the president. They must have forgotten because one of the two staffers, Chief of Staff Bob Haldeman, and the president engaged in incriminating conversations while their tapes were running in the Oval Office and other key locations, as well as phone conversations. This cost Haldeman jail time and Nixon his presidency.

You can imagine the kind of trauma I experienced this time. What did I write in those memos and what did I say in all of those taped conversations, all of which we had been assured were protected by the principle of executive privilege? This meant that we did not have to answer for our communications with the president. By this time it was apparent that while executive privilege had been initiated by George Washington and been upheld for all presidents since his time, it had now all ended with Richard Nixon and his staff by order of the United States Supreme Court. The justices made an exception to the privilege because criminal activity was suspected.

No one had written more memos to the president on politics than Harry Dent. I was the political liaison for the president with all political entities of the Republican Party. In the minds of inquiring news people, they could not understand why I was not in the center of the scandal because of my position in the White House. Nor could the prosecutors, many of whom were ex-Kennedy staffers or friends, including the chief prosecutor. I was up against the wall and my wife, Betty, was too.

I prayed and prayed for relief. Finally, I got relief, not total relief, but substantial relief. I came to realize that I could have been at the center of the Watergate scandal had I not been vetoed from being the executive director of the 1972 presidential re-election campaign. What had been the biggest disappointment of my life turned out to be my best fortune up to that point in time. The late John Mitchell, then the Attorney General, had asked me to be his campaign manager, as he would soon become the chairman of the Nixon re-election campaign. This is what I had wanted to do most in life. I had run two presidential campaigns in the South, but not at the national level. This was to be my moment in my number-one preoccupation: politics!

Two months later I was told that this would *not* be my moment. Indeed, I had told Mitchell that I would be vetoed by the chief of staff because of my refusal to carry out many orders that I considered "political dirty tricks." Mitchell knew that I had used him to defuse some of these orders because of his very close personal relationship with his old law partner, President Nixon.

Too Much of a Boy Scout

Two years later, my best friend, the late J. Fred Buzhardt, Jr., who was Nixon's Watergate lawyer, informed me that he had turned over to the prosecutors a memo from Haldeman to Nixon stating that he was vetoing Harry Dent from running the re-election campaign because "Harry is too much of a Boy Scout."

Just as I had prophesied to Mitchell, my good friend Jeb Magruder, a Haldeman staffer, was selected to take what could have been my glorious job. This turned out to be Jeb's infamous job because he was the one who had to give the orders to the Watergate break-in team to go on the illegal and covert search operation in the Democratic Party offices. That would have been my duty. Jeb was the first key White House staffer that the prosecutors arrested. After pleading guilty to obstruction of justice charges Jeb was forced to be a prosecution witness and thus was permitted to stay out of prison for a year. During that time I helped him get a job with a South Carolina friend so he and his family could pay the home bills and the lawyers.

I look back over my shoulder from time to time and shudder to think that I could have been at the very eye of the Watergate hurricane like Jeb had I not had great Boy Scout training by my scoutmaster, the late L. Roger Kirk, Sr., and a boyhood friend, the late David Banks, Jr. They saw to it that I became an Eagle Scout. Indeed, before Mr.

Kirk placed that Eagle badge on my chest he required me to pledge to two commandments from him:

> Harry Shuler (as I was called in St. Matthews), there are some things you can never do as an Eagle Scout, and there are some things you must always do as an Eagle Scout. Do you pledge on your Boy Scout honor to always live by these two commands?

I responded in the affirmative, and I never forgot what my old scoutmaster required of the youngster he had determined to impact for the good and the right for the remainder of my life.

Later as chief of staff to U.S. Senator Strom Thurmond of South Carolina I had learned to live by two maxims. The senator had been given these for his life by his parents.

> (1) You must appear right as well as be right.
> (2) If you do what is right, things will turn out right.

I have never forgotten the two Kirk commandments and the two Thurmond maxims for life. They worked for me as I did what I could to avoid doing the wrong things in life. Yet I did get hooked on a mistake that was just what the prosecutors needed to score another win. I had provided the political intelligence information and recommendations for dispensing campaign funds to candidates the president wanted to support in the 1970 off-year elections across the country. I did this for the president on all campaigns, even down to the level of local elections. The fundraiser made the mistake of receiving a million dollars worth of stock as a contribution to be passed on to some of the candidates of our choice. This individual was only to be the conduit, not the possessor or custodian of the campaign contributions. The prosecutors determined that when he cashed in the stock and put the funds in a bank account that made him and those allied with him accountable to publicly report these funds. He never informed me of this account.

The prosecutors elected me for membership on a committee of several people that they maintained had the duty to report these contributions. The hand of one was the hand of all. I pleaded guilty to a misdemeanor as being a part of this small group. Upon hearing my testimony, U.S. District Court Judge George Hart in Washington, D.C., sentenced me to thirty days of unsupervised probation and declared from the bench, "It does appear to me that Mr. Dent was more of an innocent victim than the perpetrator."

Finally, I got relief. Senator Thurmond placed in *The Congressional Record* on January 16, 1975, thirteen newspaper and television editorials which raised questions about the prosecution of the case and sympathized with the innocent victim. Subsequently President Gerald R. Ford appointed me to a White House Commission in his effort to provide a pardon for something for which there is no pardon, a misdemeanor. Even Jack Anderson tried to help me.

Subsequently I thanked Bob Haldeman for vetoing me. I hope I would have refused to implement the order that Jeb felt compelled to execute. But when higher officials tell you that the outcome of this election can determine the outcome of national and world events for good, the urge becomes very compelling.

Jeb is one of several people who came through the Watergate tribulations to become one of God's servants on a full-time basis. He is the pastor of First Presbyterian Church in Lexington, Kentucky. Previously in Columbus, Ohio, he headed a city-wide campaign to improve the moral climate in the city. Jeb is dedicated to doing the Right Thing and has a much better understanding of right and wrong, as do I today.

Doing what is Right as opposed to what is Wrong was once a most hallowed character trait in the Bible Belt. Betty and Harry Dent grew up in the South looking for "the Right Thing" and "the Real Thing." We were convinced that the entry door to doing right, whether this meant in accordance with stupid mistakes such as my high school election or violations of etiquette or law, was wrapped up in having "good intentions" and doing "good works."

To us good old Southern boys and girls back in the 1930s and 40s, "good intentions" and "good works" meant that the Right Thing to do was to be in Sunday school and church on Sunday morning. That was a key teaching in our culture.

Where I Got My Values

World War II seared into my heart tremendous respect for my country and thus my culture. Two older brothers were killed in the war. A third brother was seriously injured in piloting his Army Air Corps plane. My family came to know the value of a country that would require the blood of three of the five Dent boys. The Right Thing we had in America was worth that much blood and more. Patriotism was the order of my young life and continues to be important today.

The Boy Scouts and my experiences in those early years taught me to love my country and to have reverence for my God and what He saw as the Right Thing. The Boy Scout Law says that a Boy Scout is first to be trustworthy and, after reciting a litany of other Right Things, concludes with "and reverent." To make sure that we were "reverent" our scoutmaster induced us to attend the Methodist Youth League services he conducted every Sunday evening. (His bait was the pretty girls in town, like Betty.)

At Presbyterian College I was a good student trying to do the Right Thing. So the students and faculty awarded me their highest honor at graduation: the Founder's Medal as "that member of the graduating class most nearly approximating this institution's ideals for young manhood." When I received my second lieutenant's bars through the Army R.O.T.C. program I was ready to follow my brothers in laying down my life for my country in the Korean War. That meant also for my God. Somehow "God and Country" meant one and the same thing to us good "ole" Southern boys back in that wonderful time following World War II.

I worked so hard to be a good guy who wanted to do the Right Thing that I became a workaholic. I vowed as a little boy growing up under an alcoholic father to never become an alcoholic. Little did I realize that in seeking to do the Right Thing and not the Wrong Thing I could get caught up in being another kind of "holic." A workaholic also can destroy his family and home.

Betty's Story

Betty says that good intentions were her motivation as a little girl growing up in a home with a runaway father who evidently rejected not only Betty's mother but his six-year-old daughter. Little Elizabeth Inez Francis did not rebel and become a bad girl, as happens in many similar situations. She just wanted to do the Right Thing in this life and provide a better life for her future family. Her intentions were so good that she embarked on a search for another father—a heavenly Father—in a Methodist Church that catered to children. She found a "Survival Kit" in her heavenly Father in church. After she and her mother were burned out of their rented flat in Orangeburg, they moved fourteen miles north to St. Matthews.

When Betty arrived in St. Matthews she joined St. Paul's Methodist Church so she could continue her relationship with her heavenly Father. She had no ideas about prosperity or success because she had not tasted of these delicacies that are part of the American Dream. She and her mother and older sister, Marie, were glad to survive and subsist. As a teenager Betty began a quest to find a young man who also wanted to do the Right Thing.

In particular, Betty wanted her man to be a good husband and the spiritual leader for her next family. She craved the kind of love she missed as a child. Betty had seen what did not work in a marriage, so she wanted her children to have a good father.

Soon after her arrival in St. Matthews she attended a high school dance that featured three dance contests. It was at this dance that I met a girl who shared my yearning for doing the Right Thing. Upon hearing that this new girl could "cut a rug" on the dance floor, I tried her out on the slow dance contest. We won. So we danced on through the square dance and the shag dance, winning all the way.

From that evening forward we started dancing through life together as boyfriend and girlfriend and subsequently as husband and wife, father and mother, and grandfather and grandmother. We knitted together very well because we both had good intentions, and we both wanted to do the Right Thing in life—whatever that was.

I usually tell people that "I've been dancing to her tune ever since." But that is not exactly the way things worked out in our life together. I came to believe that the Right Thing in life was success. It seemed to come so easy to me as a workaholic. I found myself outworking my competitors in most instances. I realized that I could outthink many of my competitors, even those with higher IQs. While their minds were out of joint with alcohol or other brain-killers, my mind remained turned on. I tell people that I came out of the womb with a "To Do" list and a sense of urgency. While others were busy wasting time I was thinking, planning, and strategizing how to win and come out on top for my idealistic causes.

For Betty, success was not a priority. She wanted the Right Thing in our home. She even believed that it was connected to the Real Thing, the God and Creator of the universe to whom I had been paying tribute in the Boy Scouts, Sunday school, and church. She never forgot all the mercy and grace she had experienced from her "Survival Kit" Father.

The big question I wanted answered in this life was this: Why are people so irresponsible and unrealistic that they shoot themselves in the foot, like our fathers did? Why can't people see that life on planet Earth is all about having good intentions that are translated into doing what is Right instead of what is Wrong? Don't they know Right from Wrong and reality from unreality?

Betty shared my concerns. Our only problem was that Betty had a different view of the Real Thing. She believed this was Jesus. I paid obeisance to Jesus, but I gave my obedience and life to the ideals of man's politics and success.

Our marriage got off to a fair start. We had not been trained in how to do the Right Thing in marriage or in rearing our four children. We were winging our way through life with good intentions. We both handled many jobs in the church. We were being and doing better than most of our neighbors and friends in our family life. As Betty testifies, we certainly were doing better than the two families from whence we had come.

Betty's view of the big problem in life is that people seek to live out life according to the world's standard rather than God's standard. That is what we were doing.

Not Meeting Our Standard

It took some time before we realized that we were not even measuring up to our own standard of Right and Wrong. I became so enthralled with my work and schooling that I virtually abandoned my family, a little like Betty's father had done to her. I was a good husband and father when I was home. Even *Time* magazine certified this self-righteous nature of Harry Dent in 1969, printing that I "did not drink, smoke, cuss, chew or chase but one woman, my wife." This assured me that I was doing the Right Thing my way.

In working for eleven years in the United States Senate as the chief of staff for U. S. Senator Strom Thurmond of South Carolina and earning two law degrees during that time, I spent little time in my home. I convinced myself that I was doing the Right Thing for my family and certainly for my country. We were fighting for conservative political causes and the United States Constitution. We were the foremost opponents of world communism in the United States Senate. Could there be a more righteous thing than this? Not in "God and Country!"

How many of us ever dreamed that God might also have a plan for communism? I thought only we had the answer.

In the meantime, I was also touching bases with Betty's Real

Thing by being the co-founder and chairman of the staff prayer breakfast group in the United States Senate.

In 1965 I left Washington to become a practicing lawyer and the chairman of the South Carolina Republican Party. My aim was to help build up a two-party system in the one-party South. What could be more righteous than that? In the process I had a frank conversation late one evening with former Vice President Richard Nixon at the Columbia Airport. He had bailed our party out of debt by raising money for us at a dinner. When he told me that he was not certain about running again for the presidency in 1968 I offered an answer to his dilemma: Governor George Wallace of Alabama. Nixon believed that as a third-party candidate Wallace would sweep the South and deny Nixon the potential to break loose the Southern electoral votes that would be necessary for Nixon to win the presidency.

That one-hour delayed flight marked a turning point in my life and in the life of Nixon. While talking to Mr. Nixon I outlined a plan that became known as "the Southern Strategy" that nominated Nixon and then elected him in 1968 by less than a percentage point. That is the way the media recorded the story of the 1968 election. The key to the strategy was to use Senator Strom Thurmond of South Carolina to stiff-arm Governor Ronald Reagan for the nomination and then to block Governor George Wallace in the general election by getting across the message that "a vote for George is a vote for Hubert (Humphrey)." It worked, and the GOP Southern Strategy has worked in every presidential election since 1968 except when Georgian and born-again Christian Jimmy Carter pulled a reverse-Southern Strategy on President Gerald Ford in 1976.

There I was: doing the Right Thing again. Betty and I almost broke up over all of the time I gave to the 1968 election. I had abandoned my law practice. Then when she discovered through a third party that I was going to Washington with the new president, Betty lost faith in my understanding of Right versus Wrong. So I did wrong by determining on my own that I would commute back and forth to Washington. But I really thought that was the Right Thing also. I could not miss that great opportunity to serve the President of the United States!

Prayer in the White House

When I arrived at the Nixon White House in 1969 I was again doing the Right Thing. On motion of Dr. Billy Graham, I established the first prayer breakfast group in the White House. The noted world evangelist challenged me to repeat what I had done in the Senate. I quickly agreed to do so because when Billy Graham speaks Harry Dent listens. What could be more right than "God and Country" religion in the White House ?

In the Nixon White House we were also using man's politics to save our nation from world communism. We were fighting for many of the same Right causes that Senator Strom and I had championed in the Senate. Indeed, I was convinced more than ever that the answer to the problems in this world—unreality, irresponsibility, and irreverence—could be resolved through a good dose of man's politics.

I was the political liaison in the Nixon White House, and on the side I was the nurturer of the Southern Strategy. Politics had become the lord of my life. In this job I criss-crossed the U.S.A. telling audiences that the Nixon White House had the Right answers to the big questions in life, especially communism. No one believed this more than I. That is why I could speak with such sincerity and authority. The more I upped my "good ole boy" Southern accent the more came the applause and affirmation. To many Republicans the number-one enemy in the world was communism, not Beelzebub (Satan).

On the speaking circuit, people kept telling me that I was proclaiming the gospel of politics much like a Southern Baptist pastor preaching the gospel of Jesus Christ in a church pulpit. But I believed my mission was the more important one. I was convinced that I had the real answer—man's politics, especially the Grand Old Party variety. Doing the Right Thing was beating communism and Big Government and electing the right guys to be president.

In the re-election campaign of 1972, our campaign slogan was: "Nixon now, more than ever!" This was the Right Thing! We junked the 1968 slogan "Nixon's the One!" The enemies were using that one in pinning the Watergate scandal on Nixon.

The Most Important Man

For this "noble" cause I almost deserted my family. I commuted to the White House from South Carolina for three of my four years there. Determined to finally get my family together with me, I disrupted their lives, especially that of our three high schoolers, and moved them to Washington for the re-election year. But I deserted them again. This time I commuted back and forth again from my new home in Washington to speaking forays across the country. But in my heart, I knew I was Right again.

I traveled all over America campaigning as a substitute candidate for the president. I loved every minute of the campaign in doing the Right Thing for "the Right Man." Intertwined in my talks was the recurring theme of "God and Country." I felt I was in my best speaking form when I coupled these two winners together.

I had to make the most of this greatest time in my young life, my late thirties and early forties. These were great times because I was working for what I believed to be "the most important man in the world," the President of the United States of America. Surely this was the Right Thing and the Real Thing.

I soon realized that maybe this was not the Real Thing after all, even after my president won re-election with the largest number of votes anyone had ever received for president. Soon thereafter, what had been the Real Thing was drummed out of office and quite a few of my colleagues were being locked in jail, including my mentor, the late Attorney General John Mitchell. They put my friend in his own federal prison. Families and lives were being destroyed in the White House family. I almost joined them.

When I was sworn in to be special counsel to the president I had not envisioned this tragic twist to our great victory in 1968. Our 1972 re-election triumph garnered the most votes ever cast for a candidate for president. How could we be so Wrong as to come to this despicable demise when we were doing so much Right in the world and in America? This "cancer on the presidency," as John Dean had described the scandal, was breathing down my neck.

By the time that the Nixon Watergate scandal was being explored and exploited all over television and around the world, I was being forced to re-examine what the Right Thing was and who, not what, was the Real Thing: the most important man in the world or the One who created the most important man in the world?

Betty already knew what was the Right Thing and who was the Real Thing. The heavenly Father or her "Survival Kit" was the Real Thing and His plan as revealed in the Holy Bible was the Right Thing. She was committed in her trust of her heavenly Father and His Holy Bible. One day, however, she came to realize that she was not so literate in what she calls "God's Instruction Book."

It was about the same time that I accepted God's only begotten Son, Jesus Christ, as my Savior to ensure my place at Home Base in the event that the Bible was the Right Thing with the right message and promise.

I came to discern that I rejected Jesus as the Lord and authority in my life because I was obsessed with man's politics, and it was politics that dominated my heart and life. In making my way in the world, I had developed a good instinct for survival and success. I had become caught up in what Betty calls "the success syndrome." To me this was the American Dream.

In the practice of law, politics, news, and business I had encountered so many unrealistic, irresponsible, impractical, and undependable people that I was beginning to trust only in me. I now know that children of alcoholics tend to lose whatever sense of trust they may have had in people. Then I began to question myself.

What Is the Truth?

After four decades as a church member and leader, I stepped into the Bible as a lawyer looking for the truth—the whole truth and nothing but the real truth, so help me, God! And I found the Truth! When I plowed through the whole Bible for the first time in my life I realized this great truth:

**THE BIBLE IS A SUPERNATURAL BOOK
ABOUT A SUPERNATURAL GOD WITH
A SUPERNATURAL MASTER PLAN!**

This reality changed everything about my life and made me a traveling salesman, indeed, a circuit-riding "pewologist," for the message of this supernatural book and supernatural God.

Charles Colson's surprising testimony before my prayer breakfast group in the White House during the Watergate scandal served to shake me. So had a daughter in Young Life, a high school para-church organization. Ginny Dent became a born-again Christian although she was already a church member.

Ginny Dent won her boyfriend, Alton Brant, to the Lord as another born-again Christian. Both went to work on me. The consistency of Betty's steadfast faith and good works for her "Survival Kit" God also affected my life, as had the events of Watergate and the growing realization that maybe man did not have the answer about the Right Thing or the Real Thing.

In practicing law in Columbia, South Carolina, I found more and more human brokenness. I had experienced this in my home in St. Matthews. I was seeing it in my clients in prison, in their families, and in mental institutions, divorce courts, and then in the White House itself. Here were "the brightest and best" who certainly knew Right from Wrong. Most were lawyers. Many had been graduated from the White House to what the late Humphrey Bogart called "The Big House." Even a few years after the scandal I got heartburn when news reporters called. Maybe Harry had not found the Right Thing or the Real Thing after all.

My Self-ist Nature Ruled

As I looked into my own life, I sensed a selfish nature that I had seen all around me in others. Something inside was suggesting that maybe Harry was looking primarily after Harry and was perhaps bordering on being a self-ist. No one likes a self-ist, not even Harry.

I had these good intentions about wanting to be on God's side, but I wanted to do my own thing, regardless of the rules or the will of God: Man, not God, was at the center of my life.

In studying Genesis 3 and books about the theme of Genesis 3—the sin nature of humankind—I focused on my own problem. I was indeed a self-ist. All of us on planet Earth are self-ists who need supernatural help from Betty's "Survival Kit" God to become more and more like Him in unselfishness. In the remainder of the Bible I found that the answer is a spiritual transaction between God and man. This opens the door for supernatural help to fight the battle of spiritual warfare on Right versus Wrong. The transaction is that born-again experience I was beginning to see all around me. This is the real way to be able to do the Right Thing according to God's standard of righteousness.

For the first time in my life I discerned that while I might be able to bootstrap myself to the White House, I could not intend or work my way to heaven. The Apostle Paul instructed me that the Real Thing was strictly a free gift by the grace of God, and there was nothing I could do to earn it by my own good intentions, actions, or merits.

In the meantime Ginny had put a plaque under my pillow for witness purposes. It had this message: "The Purpose of Life Is to Serve God." I remember wondering: "Could this be the truth? Could it be that only God has the answer to the problems of life, and we are to let God use us to implement His purpose and plans on Earth?"

On a Sunday morning at a Methodist conference center at Lake Junaluska, North Carolina, I finally faced the ultimate question of whether I would continue "to be a part of the problem in this life" with my good intentions or whether I would surrender my life to Jesus Christ in order "to become a part of the solution to the problem in this life." Earlier I had finally committed to accept Jesus as the Lord of my life after discovering in my cover-to-cover study of the Bible the importance of having Jesus not just as Savior but as Lord (authority) and Savior.

Now I was receiving a summary of Jesus' Sermon on the Mount by a pastor-teacher whom I did not know. He was Dick Woodward of the Tidewater area of Virginia. Rev. Woodward was not issuing an invitation to walk down the aisle or to raise a hand. He was just throwing out the big question of Genesis 3, verse 9: "Where are you?"

I had no good or bad intention of doing anything that Sunday morning. But Genesis 3:9 had already given me an upper-cut to my volitional will center in my Bible study. The question in this abrasive Bible verse also confronted Adam and Eve as they were trying to hide and cover up from God their selfish, sinful desire to be the lords of their own lives.

When the speaker calmly asked the question, I found myself being raised up in the midst of a few hundred other Christians by what had to be the Real Thing—the Spirit of God—to do the Right Thing. I was raised up out of my seat. My right arm was stretched out and my thumb shot straight up in the air as my index finger was pointed like a pistol directly at the pulpit. There sat this speaker in a chair especially designed to support his crippled body ravaged by multiple sclerosis.

My tongue sent forth this strange statement: "Before my fiftieth birthday I'm no longer going to be a part of the problem; I choose to be with Jesus as a part of the solution to the problem!" My actions and words made me appear to be a fool for Jesus. Betty was shocked and amazed, as were most of the others, including Dick Woodward. Suddenly all of the eyes in Lambuth Hall were shifted from Dick Woodward to that old White House pol named Harry Dent. What in the world would happen next with these old Nixon hands? Was this another Colson experience, or what?

Time to Do the Right Thing

On the way back to Columbia that Sunday afternoon, Betty and I recognized that this must be the sign to close the law practice and pack up our political files. We knew that the Right Thing to do now was to pick up the practice of God's Law Book and to sell Jesus' brand of politics, the implementation of the Great Commandment and the Great Commission. We determined that we needed to be teaching people to be "salt" and "light" as Pastor Dick had just proclaimed and also to be unconditional lovers and servants for the glory of God and the good of all of mankind as commanded in the Great Commandment and the Great Commission.

Here we were at middle age. With good intentions I had missed God's message, my spiritual miracle, my moment for witness to a wounded president as Watergate began to ensnare him, and also my mission and purpose in this life. Now both Betty and I were getting tuned in to God's spiritual wavelength and work through His Word and His Spirit. We were now arriving at the tug and pull of our lives individually and collectively for all of these years, finally doing the Right Thing for the Real Thing.

The greatest years have been these final years, not my four years in the White House—as I had previously thought. What freedom, what joy, what consolation to find, with God's great help, the answers to the big questions that began haunting us in our childhood dysfunctional families. We know that these are the answers to the ultimate questions that really make the difference in this life and the eternal life to follow. We experienced satisfaction and fulfillment in the joy of knowing that we are enrolled in God's mighty program of that "so great a salvation."

The Beer Commercial Is Wrong

Some people think, "Life is tough, and then you die!" Unfortunately, this is coming to be the sign of our times. But our people, especially our young people, need to get hold of the greatest news that the beer commercial is all Wrong. We don't just go around once, we go around twice, and it is this second trip—called the Eternal Perspective—that really counts. Our time here on planet Earth is the warmup for our ultimate trip to eternity, forever and forever. There is hope! But first there is faith and then love—the real kind of love that shouts: "I love you anyway!!!"

This is what this book is about: What it really means to be an American, especially an American Christian. It reveals how we have twisted the flag around the church with a form of "God and Country" religion in the place of God's Plan as set forth in God's Instruction Book from Genesis to the Revelation of Jesus Christ.

The two great influences in this country are the American way and God's way. The American way is our system of man's government and the norm for our way of life. God's way is God's Government as exemplified in the flesh by God's instrument of salvation, the Spirit of Jesus living within real Christians who are spiritually alive and serving.

The big problem that blinded me to the Right Thing and the Real Thing for so long, and in spite of my good intentions, was the fact that I had unwittingly been part of the problem in this country. We have permitted our American culture to overrule and thus change the church to adapt more and more to our American way of life than to God's way of life for humankind. The American way has evolved into exercising our individual rights more than our individual responsibilities.

Now I understand the problem we have in America. I thought I was a highly educated man with three university degrees and a stint of duty as special counsel to the president. Today I realize that I was only an educated fool flying through life by the seat of my britches. Until we are learned in God's eternal perspective we will continue to be captive to the ways of the world and the things of the world because of our basic spiritual and emotional immaturity. This is what has spelled doom for civilization after civilization through the pages of history.

The key Bible passage for this book is found in Romans 12 at verses 1 and 2, according to the J. B. Phillips translation of the Bible.

> With eyes wide open to the mercies of God, I beg you, my brothers, as an act of intelligent worship, to give Him your bodies, as a living sacrifice, consecrated to Him and acceptable by Him. Don't let the world around you squeeze you into its own mold, but let God remold your minds from within, so that you may prove in practice that the plan of God for you is good, meets all His demands and moves toward the true goal of maturity.

Paul, writing under the inspiration and leadership of the Holy Spirit of God, commands God's people to be fully committed to God with everything He has placed before us and in us. He then warns that we be on guard lest we be squeezed by our culture into the mold of the world, man's standards, rather than the standards of God. Instead of

being changed by our culture, we are to be spiritually transformed by
the Spirit of God and the Word of God so that we become spiritually
mature and become God's change agents for the world. God's way
must become the American way instead of the American way being
substituted for God's way.

Paul concludes this instructive and vital teaching by admonish-
ing us that when we get this teaching applied in our lives we will then
find what Harry and Betty Dent finally came to discern: God's perfect
will for our lives—the Right Thing in this life and thus the ultimate
satisfaction and fulfillment of our quest and mission on planet Earth
and on into eternal life with God.

In His high priestly prayer, the greatest prayer in all of the Bible,
Jesus gave an accounting of the completion of His mission on planet
earth to His heavenly Father. This was a part of His farewell address
at the Last Supper. Earlier in the Gospels, Jesus had described the
purpose of His mission on earth in these terms: to do the will of His
heavenly Father who had sent Him, and to finish this work before
leaving earth; to be about "My Father's business," "to seek and to
save the lost," and "to give My life as a ransom for many." And Jesus
made it clear that He came out of love and as the "suffering servant"
prophesied by Isaiah.

THE KEY TO JESUS' MISSION, AND THUS
OURS IS TO: RESCUE THE PERISHING!

"God and Country" Religion

There is a place and purpose for "God and Country" religion, as
we will see in the pages of this book. It can be a stepping-stone to the
Real Thing or it can be a stumbling block that propels us to the Wrong
Thing. The key is finding and developing that righteous relationship
with the Real Thing, Jesus Christ. When we are in Christ and thus
Christ is in us, we will begin to march habitually in step with God's
way and against the things and ways of our culture.

Betty and I have discovered from the Scriptures that our mission
as Christians on earth is to be fully committed to the implementation
of Jesus' mission. He is to be our role model and the focus of our
worship and work. This is the meaning and purpose of life. This is
what we now mean by doing the Right Thing and knowing the Real
Thing. For Ginny was right: "The Purpose of Life Is to Serve God."
This is now the logo for our ministry.

After ministering in more than seven hundred churches and in prisons, civic clubs, and schools on five continents, Betty and I have learned so many great lessons. We have been able to better discern why the American culture is changing the church more than the church is changing the American culture. The heart of the problem lies in the hearts of the "old Harry Dents" in the pews. They mean well but do not know well and thus do not do well in implementing God's Master Plan. They are what Dr. George Gallup, Jr., calls "superficial" Christians. How many are there? Dr. Gallup says they predominate in the church. As the demon told Jesus in the country of the Gadarenes, "My name is Legion; for we are many" (Mark 5:9).

We must exorcise the demons of superficial Christianity if America is to be saved!

One of the strongest impediments to the implementation of God's Master Plan in America is the fallacious notion that good intentions and good works constitute the essence of God's plan. This is the conviction of most of the people in the culture, and, unfortunately, that of too many superficial Christians. Another term used is "culture" Christians. Paul used the terms "carnal" or "fleshly" Christians as contrasted with the "spiritual" Christians, and he calls the pagan out there in the culture "the natural man" (See 1 Cor. 2:14; 1 Cor. 3:1-3; 1 Cor. 6:19-20; 1 Thess. 5:23-24).

The natural man has never opened the door to the Spirit of God. He is centered totally in himself and thus is "prime beef" for Satan. The carnal or fleshly Christian has opened the door to the Spirit, but has not slammed the door that has been open to the "world" and the "flesh" for all those years. Therefore the world and the flesh are eating him alive on a daily basis, and he does not understand because he does not know the Bible or the Lord as he should. That was my problem—in spades!

The spiritual man is the model of Paul's description set forth in Romans 12:1-2. We also see him in Paul's description in Galatians 2:19-20 of the man who has died to the world and is now the place of habitation of Christ living in him. His body is the temple of the Holy Spirit. He is the spiritual man because the Spirit of Jesus Christ is the Lord and Savior of his life. He has done what the new Harry did; he has abdicated the throne of personal lordship in his life and invited Jesus Christ to come and be Lord of his life. This is a matter of surrender to accept supernatural help and love so that out of my life will flow supernatural loving and serving for the glory of God and the good of mankind.

What a difference!!! I continually thank God for knowing that difference. I never want to return to the past.

As a Sunday school superintendent and teacher, I remember ignoring the teachings on salvation by grace in the Sunday school lessons I was teaching. This is why I emphasize this critical truth in my speaking and teaching missions. Paul gave his head for this truth. In speaking and teaching in churches today it is evident that good intentions and good works salvation is the major problem in our churches just as it was in Paul's day.

Most people are living out their lives by their own hunches, superstitions, old wives' tales, and self-made rules regarding Right versus Wrong. This is a consequence of immaturity—mentally, emotionally, and spiritually—and addiction to what the Bible calls "the things of the world" and "of the flesh" and thus the ways of our culture.

The pagans are impacting us more for wrong than we are impacting them for right! Church members are being inoculated against the ways of God!

We are highly literate in "the land of the free and the home of the brave." Yet we can be educated fools, like I was, without a secure grasp of God's eternal perspective as embodied in God's Master Plan. No God-inspired writer of the Bible has been used to better set out for humanity the opening to God's Way in our lives than the Apostle Paul. He challenges us, especially those of us in the church of Jesus Christ, over and over again to examine our own lives, as I eventually did.

> Examine yourselves as to whether you are in the faith. Prove yourselves. Do you not know yourselves, that Jesus Christ is in you?—unless indeed you are disqualified. (2 Cor. 13:5)

Two of the biggest disqualifiers are good intentions and good works without spiritual transformation. Paul tells us why in a number of Scripture passages, but nowhere more eloquently than in Ephesians 2:8–10.

> For by grace you have been saved through faith, and that not of yourselves; it is the gift of God, not of works, lest anyone should boast. For we are His workmanship, created in Christ Jesus for good works, which God prepared beforehand that we should walk in them.

In another passage, 1 Corinthians 10:12, the apostle of grace and truth warns us further, "Therefore let him who thinks he stands take heed lest he fall."

Our principal concern today is the future fall of America. Why? After having so much exposure to God and benefiting more than any country in history from the blessings of God, this country has been paying Him obeisance rather than obedience, as I once did.

Russia and America

There was a time when Mother Russia was the foremost bastion of Christianity—for centuries. Then the ways of man began to become the ways of Russian culture so that the culture began to overcome the church. The people then fell into the trap of the most mammoth fraud of our day, another "ism," communism, which decreed that there is no God. For seventy-four years the people of Russia were forced to live with empty baskets, empty values, and empty lives. Now they have another opportunity to learn and to practice obedience over obeisance or outright blasphemy and Right over Wrong, according to God's view. Solomon warned us that: "Righteousness exalts a nation, / But sin is a reproach to any people" (Prov. 14:34).

In the Sermon on the Mount, which is all about righteous living in the Kingdom of God, Jesus tells us about *the* priority of life by equating righteousness with the Kingdom of God: "But seek first the kingdom of God and His righteousness, and all these things shall be added to you" (Matt. 6:33).

So it is not just the Russians and the people of the old Soviet Union who need to start all over again to get their priorities right with God. We Americans also must initiate a new beginning before we become cauterized and culturized by the same demons that sentenced the Soviet citizens to more than seven centuries on the road to nowhere.

Americans must come to realize that we are saved by the grace of God through our faith in Jesus Christ as Lord and Savior. John Newton, that ex-slave-ship captain, had his life turned around from being a pagan to being a spiritual Christian and was so amazed and gratified at his spiritual transformation that he captured his experience in the national anthem of Christians, "AMAZING GRACE." Grace means God's divine favor that is completely undeserved by man. God's mercy is closely related to God's grace. Actually, we need both. The devout German scholar Johann Albrecht Bengel distinguished between grace and mercy this way: "Grace takes away the guilt; mercy [takes away] the misery."[3]

The definition of faith that I see in the Bible is this: *Belief* in Jesus Christ plus *trust* in Jesus Christ plus *commitment* to Jesus Christ as Lord and Savior.

This is the heart of what it really means to be a spiritual Christian. I believe church members are in church because they have good intentions. A 1991 public opinion poll showed that 77 percent of people who attend church believe strongly or somewhat that "the Bible is the written word of God and is totally accurate in all it teaches." This same Bible clearly teaches that good intentions must be translated into faith, commitment, and good works. Once we are saved by grace through our faith, then will follow good works. And, finally, our good intentions will be transformed into witness and ministry for the glory of God and the good of all of mankind. This is the ultimate end of all Scripture:

THE WITNESS AND MINISTRY OF ALL OF GOD'S PEOPLE, THE 1 PERCENT IN THE PULPITS, AND THE 99 PERCENT IN THE PEWS.

But, here is the problem in the church and thus in America: There is a vivid and vast void between what people in the church believe about the truth and authority of the Bible and their translation of their good intentions into spiritual transformation and ultimately into spiritual action that is clearly and coherently commanded in the whole of the Bible. How far is the witness and ministry of Christians in America to go? Jesus commanded: Unto all the world! This includes the people in countries trapped for centuries behind the old Iron Curtain, who have thus had limited access to God's Master Plan. And what is the witness to be about? Righteousness, the very character of Jesus Christ. Righteousness in the Bible means spiritual maturity, holiness, godliness, and doing what is right in God's sight. So many people behind the old Iron Curtain do not know Right from Wrong in God's sight.

God's standard for every person everywhere is that we be like Him in holiness, righteousness, and godliness. "For I am the LORD your God. You shall therefore sanctify yourselves, and you shall be holy; for I am holy" (Lev. 11:44a).

The word *righteousness* appears in the Bible 302 times. *Righteous* surfaces 238 times, and *right* pops up 359 times.

One of the great men of God in this century, Dr. Richard C. Halverson, chaplain of the United States Senate, declares that "the biggest bottom-line in all of the Bible is righteousness, having the sterling character of Jesus Christ living in and through our lives."[4]

Where Are You?

The purpose of this book is to help in launching a turn to the right in America from the predominance of man's perspective to the predominance of God's perspective in the hearts and minds of Americans. The turning point must begin with the "old Harry Dents" who are still banking on their good intentions and good works without spiritual transformation.

The biggest impediment to the triumph of the church in implementing God's Master Plan in America is the superficial Christians or old Harry Dents.

God created us with the great gift and freedom of choice. Even in totalitarian countries people can choose to do Right or Wrong. They may pay a heavy price in making a choice, but that option is always available. James Russell Lowell turned a very eloquent and critical phrase when he wrote this challenge to Americans in Civil War days:

Once to every man and nation comes the moment to DECIDE, / In the strife of TRUTH with FALSEHOOD, / FOR THE GOOD OR EVIL SIDE. . . .[5]

I would add: "And for Right versus Wrong."

One of the greatest human writings I have studied is the classic work by Nobel laureate Aleksandr I. Solzhenitsyn entitled: *The Gulag Archipelago*. This mammoth and most powerful book shows how depraved one man can be in his treatment of another man—man's inhumanity to man. In all of his pain and suffering in the communist slave jail, Solzhenitsyn finally reflected on whether he would have done the same to prisoners had he been educated and indoctrinated in the NKVD school of his prison bosses.

If only it were all so simple! If only there were evil people somewhere insidiously committing evil deeds, and it were necessary only to separate them from the rest of us and destroy them. BUT THE LINE DIVIDING GOOD AND EVIL CUTS THROUGH THE HEART OF EVERY HU-

MAN BEING. AND WHO IS WILLING TO DESTROY A
PIECE OF HIS OWN HEART?

During the life of any heart this line keeps changing
place; sometimes it is squeezed one way by exuberant evil
and sometimes it shifts to allow enough space for good to
flourish. . . . At times he is close to being a devil, at times to
sainthood. But his name doesn't change, and to that name
we ascribe the whole lot, good and evil. Socrates taught us:
KNOW THYSELF![6]

Do you really know yourself and your capacity for good or evil,
Right or Wrong, and where you are spiritually? This is the question
God put to Adam and Eve after they had made the first choice of
humankind regarding Right versus Wrong and good versus evil in
Genesis 3:9: "Where are you?" Adam and Eve both engaged in a
coverup and evasion of the question. They sought to deny and rationalize away their Wrongs. Adam even sought to shift the blame to God
by reminding God that He had given Adam this woman, who had
caused good ole Adam to sin.

May this be your question in this book! Where am I?

CHAPTER TWO

Is This "The Land of the Free and the Home of the Brave"?

One of the lessons of history is that no civilization can be taken for granted. Its permanency can never be assured. There is always a dark age waiting for you around the corner, if you play your cards badly and you make sufficient mistakes.

Christian Historian Paul Johnson[1]

What is Right and what is Wrong in America today? Today in "the land of the free and the home of the brave" this question is up for grabs because we are playing our value cards badly and making too many value mistakes. There was a time when Right was Right and Wrong was Wrong in America. Today what one person perceives to be Right may be 100 percent Wrong in the eyes of another and *vice versa.*

The two prime colors of Black and White continue to fade into the gray areas of life in the United States of America. Too many people believe there are no moral absolutes today. Moral absolutes are truths that are constant and immutable and do not vacillate with the whims and whinings of human beings. They are eternal truths that come from supernatural God. They form the backbone of our Judeo-Christian tradition in America. They constitute the heart and soul of the Christian faith and can be found throughout the Holy Bible.

In 1991, public opinion polls by secular and Christian pollsters revealed that more than two-thirds of Americans do not believe there are any moral absolutes. Even worse, 72 percent of young people, ages eighteen to twenty-five, disagree strongly or somewhat with the idea of moral absolutes. We are in deep trouble in America![2]

Under man's law, when a person does not have the capacity to distinguish right from wrong he is considered legally insane. America is awash in the swamp of legal insanity today because so many people have lost sight of the reality of Right versus Wrong. This is why we are building so many new prisons across America.

As the late U.S. Senator Sam Ervin of North Carolina proclaimed many times on the floor of the United States Senate in the 1960s, "Everything that was nailed down is done comin' loose!"

In the past few decades we Americans have drifted in a drugged stupor toward crass self-indulgence where life is devoted primarily to the pursuit of personal comfort, personal pleasure, personal convenience, and personal security. This attitude commands: Me First! My Way! My Will! Rugged individualism. Each man for himself. What's in it for me? I can handle it! It won't happen to me!

This same self-styled credo says it's okay to do what I want to do as long as it doesn't hurt anyone. Some say if it doesn't hurt me. This is similar to the old Epicurean credo of the ancient Greeks, if it feels good do it! This is known today as hedonism—the right to pursue feeling good by whatever means. This adds up to the avoidance of pain and the pursuit of pleasure. Eat, drink, and be merry, for tomorrow we die. Thus we have the drug and alcohol culture, all the free sex, all the abortions, all the suicides, all the crime and scandals, all the broken homes and broken lives, all of this moral, emotional, and physical devastation "in the land of the free and the home of the brave."

In January 1992, a new human rights organization named the North American Man-Boy Love Association surfaced in the news media. This activist organization declares that their members, adult men (pedophiles), have the right to have sexual relationships with little boys. A member, Bill Andriette of San Francisco, has publicly advocated their position on national television.

We are getting closer to the end times!

With the increase in this kind of crazy and convoluted thinking, that American God we have been saluting along with the Stars and Stripes has slipped from "God and Country" to "Country and God." We love America and the American way more than God and God's way. God is now a little lower than the angels and the flag. He is down the list of our priorities now because of the lack of time for Him and also because of the priority of the three Ps—pride, peer pressure, and the price. The price means the fear that we may have to give up some of our idols in our American way of life if we fool around with God. Pride boasts that there is nothing wrong with me and so I can handle life without God. Peer pressure means going along with the crowd in order to be accepted.

Why and How Have We Come to This Point?

Two 1991 books provide the answer. One is a secular book; the other is a Christian book. Both books sampled public opinion to get the answers to questions that go to the heart of what Americans believe is Right and Wrong.

The secular book is entitled *The Day America Told the Truth: What People Really Believe About Everything That Really Matters.* Authors James Patterson and Peter Kim maintain that they took the largest survey of private morals ever undertaken in any country to unearth and quantify the personal ethics, values, and beliefs of our time in America.

Interviewing was conducted during one week all across America. Fifty locations were chosen where privacy and anonymity could be guaranteed. The questioners permitted people to unburden themselves with exactly what they really believed in answering the questions put before them. They operated on the belief that most people want to tell someone what they really believe and what they really stand for. So, supposedly, the respondents answered even the most intimate questions of life with truthful responses.

If these authors are Right in their research project, we in America are very Wrong in our personal beliefs as to Right versus Wrong. We are in much deeper difficulty with regard to our moral values than anyone had suspected or predicted.

What their statistical research shows is that "Americans are making up their own rules, their own laws." Here is what the authors conclude on this vital point:

> In effect, we're all making up our own moral codes. Only 13 percent of us believe in all of the Ten Commandments. Forty percent of us believe in five of the Ten Commandments. We choose which laws of God we believe in. There is absolutely no moral consensus in this country as there was in the 1950s, when all our institutions commanded more respect. Today, there is very little respect for the law—for any kind of law.
>
> It's the wild, wild West all over again in America, but

it's wilder and woolier this time. *You* are the law in this
country. Who says so? *You* do, pardner. In the 1950s and
even in the early 1960s, there was something closer to a moral
consensus in America. There is absolutely no moral consensus at all in the 1990s. Everyone is making up their own personal moral codes—their own Ten Commandments.

A letdown in moral values is now considered the
number-one problem facing our country. Eighty percent of
us believe that morals and ethics should be taught in our
schools again.[3]

The authors then list "ten extraordinary commandments for the
1990s."

1. I don't see the point in observing the Sabbath. (77%)
2. I will steal from those who won't really miss it. (74%)
3. I will lie when it suits me, as long as it doesn't cause any real
   damage. (64%)
4. I will drink and drive if I feel that I can handle it. I know my
   limit. (56%)
5. I will cheat on my spouse—after all, given the chance, he or
   she will do the same. (53%)
6. I will procrastinate at work and do absolutely nothing about
   one full day in every five. (50%)
7. I will use recreational drugs. (41%)
8. I will cheat on my taxes—to a point. (30%)
9. I will put my lover at risk of disease. I sleep around a bit, but
   who doesn't. (31%)
10. Technically, I may have committed date rape, but I know that
    she wanted it. (20%)[4]

There is another book with 1991 polling data. This is a Christian
book entitled *What Americans Believe: An Annual Survey of Values and
Religious Views in the United States.* The author is George Barna, and
his work is applauded by the most pre-eminent public opinion expert
and strong Christian witness, Dr. George Gallup, Jr.

The overall thrust of this book is to provide an overview of the
America of the 1990s—an examination of the mind-set, lifestyle, and
heart of the nation at the close of this century. Barna sees the 1990s as
"a make-it-or-break-it era for the Christian Church in America."[5] His
findings parallel the statistics of Patterson and Kim, particularly with
regard to the rise of self-ism in America.

More than before we are witnessing the entrenchment of what some refer to as "secular humanist" attitudes. This means more people now believe that people are responsible only to themselves; that they determine their own destiny on the basis of their decisions and capabilities; and that simple acknowledgment of the existence of a universal spiritual force is sufficient to appease that force.

Americans currently assert that people are, overall, good creatures and are capable of managing their world without assistance from any external force. In fact, there is a prevailing perspective that much of what the Christian faith holds to be so critical toward understanding the world is either false or simply a non-essential part of understanding the fabric of life.

Among the attitudes and beliefs that people are likely to doubt are the existence of Satan; the existence of absolute truth . . . and the distinction between the God who created the universe and rules it today and the gods of other non-Christian religions.[6]

The many other findings in the book about the condition of the church of Jesus Christ is just as gloomy. The answers to the questions of this survey by many church members add to the potential for failure by the church. Even many members who describe themselves as "born-again Christians" are caught up in the trend toward the secularization of America. Why? Spiritual immaturity and addiction to "the things of the world" and thus to the ways of the world. They would not understand what I am writing on this page. Nor would I have been able to comprehend this page as a church leader B.C., before Christ truly entered my life. I was not learned in Right versus Wrong according to God's view of Right versus Wrong, and I was a lawyer and Sunday school teacher. All lawyers, and especially Sunday school teachers, must be well-schooled in Right versus Wrong.

What Is Right?

The word *right* is used in many forms, including *righteous* and *righteousness*. It is one of the biggest words in the whole of the Bible. Why? Because righteousness describes the very nature and character of God the Father and Jesus the Christ and the ultimate end that God intends for our lives: that we be stewards of and witnesses for the *righteousness of Jesus Christ*. Right and Wrong stand for objective characteristics which attach directly and inalienably to acts and their consequences.

We are basically subject to an unconditional standard of value. Some see Right as being judged by the standard of being conducive to the maximum good. While the Bible does not disagree with the ideal of the ultimate good, the Bible holds Right to be doing God's will—being and doing the way God would have us to be and do. And being is more important than doing because if we are Righteous in character, we will do what is Right.

The word *wrong* has an entirely different meaning. It is diametrically opposed to Right, thus meaning not morally right or just, sinful, wicked, not in accordance with an established standard. So Wrong equals disobedience to God and His laws and constitutes sin and sinfulness.

The Bible is the Creator's Handbook on Right versus Wrong. The Ten Commandments constitute the basic law of God, and the teachings in the Bible extrapolate the meaning of the commandments into all the avenues and areas of day-to-day life on earth. It is vital that people know Right from Wrong. We need to understand the difference in the eyes and laws of man and in the eyes and laws of God.

Yes, there is a higher law. It is this transcendent law that is the concern of this book. My dictionary defines *transcendent* as "surpassing, excelling, in theology to mean that which exists apart from the material universe, said to be of God, divine spirit, etc."

This is the overriding law that was in the minds of our founding fathers when they dared to write that bold Declaration of Independence and later that unique and most risky form of government established by the United States Constitution. Here is how these revolutionaries introduced the Declaration of Independence:

> We hold these truths to be self-evident, that all men are created equal, that they are endowed by their Creator with certain inalienable Rights, that among these are Life, Liberty and the pursuit of Happiness. That to secure these rights, Governments are instituted among Men, deriving their just powers from the consent of the governed.

These early patriots recognized beyond question that human rights are provided by God, not by governments. This is why these rights cannot be severed or surrendered. They are, as with all of God's laws, absolute, positive, inviolable, and sacrosanct. That is, they are

Right and thus righteous because they are endowed by a God that is righteous in His character and all of His nature.

The Preamble to the United States Constitution spells out in beautiful brevity and eloquence exactly why the founding fathers determined to establish this unusual but perilous form of government:

> We the People of the United States, in Order to form a more perfect Union, establish Justice, insure domestic Tranquility, provide for the common defence, promote the general Welfare, and to secure the blessings of liberty to ourselves and our posterity, do ordain and establish this Constitution for the United States of America.

All Americans have the solemn duty to protect, preserve, and pass on to our posterity these very "blessings of liberty." Under our American system of government, liberty means the right to enjoy the benefits of personal freedom with a full realization that with every personal liberty there is a concomitant responsibility or duty to exercise that right, not toward only selfish ends, but for what the founders called the common or public good.

Jesus Emphasized Our Responsibilities

When we examine the teachings of Jesus we find that He is constantly giving more emphasis to our responsibilities than our Rights. Christianity and the Cross reflect a giving, serving, and suffering type of faith. They exemplify the very opposite of the material prosperity type of theology where Christians are in the taking rather than the giving business. The recent wave of so-called prosperity or—in my definition, greed—theology is an abomination to our Lord and His mission and message.

The humanists regard human rights as ends in themselves divorced from any reference to God. But *Baker's Dictionary of Christian Ethics* reveals two special meanings of human rights:

> The Christian recognizes that God is the source and sanction of human rights, that human rights are a means to the end of aiding men in meeting their duties to God, and that government exists for the primary purpose of protecting the basic human rights. Man's rights are subordinate to the duties he owes God.[7]

The Bible and the founders point to private virtue producing public virtue. The founding fathers realized that the principal danger to this new form of government would be self-ism, with each person making up his own rules by exercising his personal freedoms against the best interest of society as a whole. Our founders were influenced by the eternal truths of Scripture. They envisioned that religion in America would serve as the glue that would hold a diverse people together as givers rather than as takers.

This is what the distinguished Frenchman, Alexis de Toqueville, observed and then recorded in his classic and oft-quoted volume, *Democracy in America*, in the 1830s. He noted the influence of religion on individual character in America and ultimately on the operation of government. He sensed that religion served as a check on self-ism. With religion flourishing in individual hearts, Right should triumph over Wrong and the common good over rank individualism.[8]

Self-ism Has Taken Over

Self-ism is one of many "isms" being examined in this book. All of the other "isms" eventually lead to destructive self-ism. What the current public opinion research by secular and Christian pollsters is presenting to us today is the unfortunate reality of our present degeneration into a nation of self-ists. As James Patterson and Peter Kim demonstrate with their secular data, "today there is little respect for the law—for any kind of law." We the people constitute our own law. This is expressly what the founding fathers most feared would happen at some time in the future "in the land of the free and the home of the brave."

In today's America we face not only our greatest moral crisis but also our biggest monetary crisis. At the bottom of both of these cesspools is the core of our problems: self-ism. This is the same disease that afflicted Adam and Eve in the Garden of Eden.

Self-ism Is Seen in Finances

Nowhere is self-ism in America best illustrated than in the financial condition of the United States government, our financial institutions, our business community, and our individual indebtedness. There is a best-selling 1991 book on this subject. It is entitled *The Coming Economic Earthquake*. The author is a Christian economist and teacher, Dr. Larry Burkett.

Larry Burkett sees what I have been witnessing with awe and concern ever since I landed in Washington, D.C., in 1954. It is the implementation of the maxim by Karl Marx:

> A democracy is not a form of government to survive. For it will only succeed until its citizens discover they can vote themselves money from the treasury, then they will bankrupt it.[9]

As a twenty-four-year-old newsman, I was appalled at the profligate spending bills coursing their way through the halls of Congress. When at age twenty-five I became a staffer in the United States Senate with the privilege of walking in and out of the Senate floor and the cloakrooms behind it, I became frightened one day listening to the concerns being expressed in the Democratic cloakroom about the mounting national debt.

The two most conservative members of the Senate were discussing within my hearing how soon the United States government would go bankrupt. The two were the late Harry Byrd, Sr., and the late Willis Robertson (the father of TV evangelist Pat Robertson), both of Virginia. At that time the national debt was miniscule in comparison to our current almost four trillion dollar debt.

How big is $1 trillion? If we were to stack one thousand dollar bills on top of one another we would have to stack them up to sixty-three miles high into the stratosphere to add up to $1 trillion.

From the days of the Great Depression forward, the American people have been lobbying their elected officials to provide more and more financial largess in the form of subsidies, entitlement programs, and local projects for their own welfare and enrichment. It was in the Franklin D. Roosevelt New Deal days that laws were passed making transfer payments possible from the government back to the taxpayers.

As usual, politicians are more than happy to acquiesce in the selfish demands of their constituents because all of this leads to more and more votes and longer and longer times of service in public office. So self-ism at the bottom of the political ladder leads to increased self-ism at the top. Karl Marx understood the selfish nature of humans more than we realized. He was wrong about his political brain-child called communism, but he was right about the self-ism endemic in all of us humans. He may have believed this more than some Christians.

Ever since my experiences in Washington as a newsman, a Sen-

ate and White House staffer, and later as a part-time Washington lob-
byist, I have been wondering when all of this fiscal insanity would
explode in our faces. Burkett says this should happen at the close of
this decade, century, and millennium. I believe his projection because
it makes sense and adds up to a long overdue "economic earthquake"
in "the land of the free and the home of the brave."

Here are key points he provides to buttress his prediction:

> The federal government now owes nearly $4 trillion,
> with virtually no way to repay the debt. By the year 2000,
> when the debt will be $20 trillion, just the interest alone will
> consume all the taxes paid by all Americans.
>
> By 1999 the interest on the national debt will exceed the
> government's income. Will our government repeat the mis-
> takes of earlier economies?
>
> What makes our government's debt so dangerous is
> that we are in debt beyond our total asset value. In other
> words, we are actuarially broke.
>
> (Economic) Cycle advocates generally agree that major
> economic downturns occur every sixty years or so. This
> would place the next depression around the turn of the cen-
> tury.
>
> When the interest on the national debt exceeds the total
> income of our government, it would be prudent to assume
> the system is about to "roll over."
>
> Our political leaders are digging an ever-widening fi-
> nancial pit that may one day swallow them and us.
>
> Does anyone realistically believe that politicians are go-
> ing to make the kinds of choices necessary to balance the
> budget?
>
> Every time the taxpayers give the Congress $1.00 extra,
> they spend $1.68.
>
> The government has an income of approximately $1.4
> trillion a year. It is spending approximately $1.8 trillion a
> year.
>
> All realistic estimates now place the potential debt at
> $13 to $20 trillion by the year 2000.[10]

Larry Burkett is but one of many voices of alarm about America's fiscal greed and insanity. The chief economic adviser to President
George Bush, Dr. Michael Boskin, declared on February 5, 1992, that
"the federal government would continue to suffer massive deficits of

nearly $200 billion a year through 1997."[11] This is the most distant year for which the administration estimates federal spending. No president has been this candid about the deficit problem into the future.[12] U.S. Senator Warren Rudman of New Hampshire announced in March 1992 that he would not seek a third term in the United States Senate because of his despair over inaction on the huge budget deficits by the White House and the Congress. His forecast for future financial problems for the U.S.A. was similar to that of Larry Burkett. He called this "our single most pressing problem." Senator Rudman was an author of the Gramm-Rudman Act designed to control budget deficits, ultimately to little or no avail.

Even Congress Is Concerned

The Budget Committee of the U.S. House of Representatives is also very dour on spending deficits. In a 1991 report the committee stated:

> The nation's economy is . . . suffering not only from problems associated with the recent recession but also from serious long-term dislocations which threaten the economic well-being of this and future generations. . . . The nation faces serious challenges in many facets of our society, including education, health care, housing, infrastructure, crime and drugs. THEY RAISE SERIOUS QUESTIONS ABOUT THE QUALITY OF LIFE OUR CHILDREN CAN EXPECT NOW AND IN THE NEXT CENTURY.
>
> Without consistent economic growth, there is a real risk that spiraling deficits will continue to spawn spiraling interest obligations—sending the NATIONAL DEBT OUT OF CONTROL.[13]

The problem is not just with the national government. State and local governments are caught up in financial straits. It even comes down to you and me. Consumer debt is approximately $1 trillion. The credit card binge is destroying personal finances. Personal bankruptcies have multiplied from approximately one hundred thousand in the early 1970s to nine times that in the early 1990s. When we put "easy" money and credit side by side with personal self-ism, we are throwing gasoline into our roaring fireplaces.

This self-ism is also seen in business and corporate debt. This has multiplied in twenty years from $62 billion to more than $700 billion. Bankruptcies also are proliferating.

The savings and loan disaster is now spreading to more and more banks. They have all been insured by "good ole Uncle Sam" through our government guarantee programs for up to $100,000 per bank account with no limits on how many different accounts we can have at various financial institutions. Even our insurance companies are feeling the beginnings of financial insecurity, especially since they have purchased so many of Wall Street's now infamous junk bonds.

Self-ism Shows in Elections

The ultimate public opinion barometer, the public voting record in elections, seemed to reveal the message of self-ism most vividly in the November 1991 elections. Here is an interpretation of the outcomes of various election contests at the national, state, and local levels:

> The voices of the voters said: Stay home. Pay attention to middle-class anxieties, especially jobs and health care. Don't ask Americans to tax themselves to help the poor and minorities.
> Self-interest—understandable if not admirable—is driving the electorate this fall as economic distress spreads and foreign perils disappear.[14]

So, What Are the Answers to the Self-ism Engulfing America?

1. The first corrective action is to re-establish the biblical view that human beings are not innately good. "As it is written: 'There is none righteous, no, not one;' . . . for all have sinned and fall short of the glory of God" (Rom. 3:10, 23).

There is no more clear-cut teaching in all of the Bible about it, but most Americans, including many "born-againers," believe the statement, "People are basically good." Eighty-three percent of the American people agree strongly or agree somewhat with this statement. Seventy-seven percent of born-again Christians agree with this statement strongly or somewhat strongly.[15]

The church must get across the prime teaching of the sin nature of all humankind. It begins in Genesis 3 and continues throughout the Bible. The purpose of God's plan of redemption, salvation, and reconciliation is to change people from habitual sin to habitual obedience of God's law. God's law proclaims that disobedience to God is wrong. Obedience to God's law is Right. It is almost everything!

2. The second answer is to study God's Word so we will better know and understand what is Right in God's sight and what is Wrong in God's sight. The reason so many born-again Christians think people are basically good is that they do not understand even the most rudimentary teachings in the Bible. Why do they think they were born-again—if they were? Dr. George Gallup, Jr., has repeatedly maintained that most church members have a superficial knowledge of the Bible and thus a superficial faith and commitment.

3. If people do not understand about the lostness of humanity and thus the need for salvation, then the whole plan of salvation needs to be studied and mastered by members of the church. I did not understand it as a Sunday school teacher and church leader.

4. Do not assume that people understand even the most major teachings in the Bible. Many people believe that the Sermon on the Mount is about a man on horseback.

5. To understand God's view of Right and Wrong, begin with the Ten Commandments.

6. Study in depth the teachings in the Epistles. The purpose of these letters is to explain not only the plan of salvation but also Right versus Wrong in God's sight.

7. Study Jesus' Sermon on the Mount in Matthew 5, 6, and 7. This message is considered by many to be the foremost lesson in all of the Bible and is all about how we are to discern and live the righteous life as members of the Kingdom of God. As our first priority, we are to seek first the Kingdom of God and His righteousness. Note the importance of righteousness! Included is the Golden Rule. We are to do unto others as we would have them to do unto us.

8. Study Jesus' Olivet Discourse in Matthew 24 and 25. Here Jesus stresses the importance of helping "the least of these." This is righteousness in action. He warns that when we do not help "the least of these" then we are not helping Him, and this is therefore Wrong. What we do or do not do counts on the final exam awaiting us.

9. Study Jesus' Upper Room or Farewell Address in John, books 13 through 17. Note the emphasis Jesus puts on His kind of agape love, known also as unconditional love. He also commands this in the Great Commandment in Matthew 22:34-40. Here is the supreme teaching in the Bible. God loves all of His creation unconditionally. We are commanded to love likewise.

10. Notice also the command in John 13 that we are to be servants, as in Jesus' example of washing the feet of His disciples. We have been called to be servants and not lords. Trying to lord our authority over others is Wrong; projecting an attitude of servanthood in leading others is Right in God's sight and actually works in man's arena.

11. Notice also in John 15 in the farewell address the command that we are to "bear fruit" and that this is impossible without the spirit of Jesus Christ abiding in us. It is Wrong as a Christian not to be involved in bringing lost people out of darkness and into the marvelous light of salvation. This is what it means to "be fruitful."

12. Check the end of each of the Gospels. There you will see that it is Right to be a part of evangelizing the world for Christ. You will find four versions of the Great Commission. Then check the beginning of the Book of Acts at Acts 1:8, and you will find another version. This is the purpose of our Christian faith: Not just for us to be saved but for us to then become a party to the salvation of others. So it is Wrong to neglect our duty for the salvation of the lost.

The Great Commandment and the Great Commission are two paramount commands of Jesus and thus of Scripture. Miss these two central teachings, and we miss God's purpose for humankind, which is to make all of us lovers and servants unconditionally for the glory of God and the good of all of mankind.

13. Study the Psalms. They are all about worship and our relationship with the Lord God Almighty. The first priority in Christianity is worship of God. It is Right to worship God; it is Wrong to neglect or ignore worship of God. Indeed, it is an abomination to the Lord to worship the idols and gods of this world in the place of God.

14. In the Book of Proverbs and the Book of Ecclesiastes you will discover godly wisdom compared to the foolishness of man's wisdom. Psalms 1 and 2 and Proverbs 1 and 2 instruct us as to the difference in a man who walks in the Right way and the man who walks in the Wrong way. Proverbs 3 is loaded with most practical teachings, especially on trusting in the Lord with all your heart and not leaning on your own understanding. Here young people, in particular, can find how to live a righteous life with God's help. Ecclesiastes is especially helpful for men to understand how to live out life on earth the Right way instead of the futile and Wrong way. Again, the key is to fear the Lord and keep His commandments.

15. It is not enough for church members to know the Bible so that we can better discern Right from Wrong in God's sight and apply

the teachings to our conduct in life. If we are going to change the current trend away from Satan's way to God's way, then we must become a part of the solution to the problem and not just a continuing part of the problem.

There are enough Christians in America to make a vital difference in turning America to God's Ways!

16. Stewardship is one of the most powerful teachings in all of the Bible. We are to be good stewards of all that God has put before us. It begins in Genesis 1 and 2 and pops up throughout the Bible. We are responsible for the blessings God has provided and also for our role in His Master Plan as the highest form of God's creation. But stewardship will never be properly exercised until we first understand the selfish, sinful nature of man. It is a problem that is endemic to all of us and is of epidemic proportions today, especially in this country.

Stewardship Equals Responsibility and Accountability

One day we will all answer for what we did or did not do with all the talents, provisions, and blessings entrusted to our use and care. Our posterity will scream at us for throwing away their future!

The question for you is: *Where are you?* This is the first question God put to Adam and Eve when they fell for the temptation from the evil one. This is the one persistent question that runs across the pages of the Bible and the pages of world history.

Do you know Jesus Christ as Lord and Savior? Are you willing to be trained so you can be a part of the solution to the problem? The answer to these critical questions will determine whether you are on the Right side or the Wrong side. Jesus' recipe for changing our country and ultimately the world is heavy doses of "salt" and "light" sprinkled all over society and emanating from the lives of those who really do know Jesus Christ as Lord and Savior.

Our rugged individualism will not clean up the mess in America. Man is limited, fallible, and selfish. What we need is to be connected to supernatural help. This requires a supernatural change to overcome the sinful, selfish nature that has brought America to the brink of destruction as a nation—the most blessed nation the world has ever known.

Our duty as a nation is to take this great blessing God has bestowed on us as a privileged people and to be a blessing to the rest of the world. This was the challenge the Lord God Jehovah put before the nation of Israel. They meant well, but did not know well and did not do well. They too could not handle freedom and prosperity as righteous stewards because of that same sinful, selfish human nature that kept taking them out of right relationship with their Lord and leader.

The prophet Samuel summarized the problem for us in the Book of Judges: "Everyone did what was right in his own eyes" (Judg. 17:6, 21:25).

The prophet Hosea added to these teachings with this admonition: "From their silver and gold / They made idols for themselves. . . . They sow the wind, / And reap the whirlwind. . . . My people are destroyed for lack of knowledge" (Hos. 8:4b, 7a, 4:6a).

Best of all, Moses captured the problem among the Israelites and thus our problem today with these passages in Deuteronomy 8:1, 10–20:

> Every commandment which I command you today you must be careful to observe, that you may live and multiply, and go in and possess the land of which the LORD swore to your fathers. . . . When you have eaten and are full, then you shall bless the LORD your God for the good land which He has given you. Beware that you do not forget the LORD your God by not keeping His commandments, His judgments, and His statutes which I command you today, lest—when you have eaten and are full, and have built beautiful houses and dwell in them; and when your herds and your flocks multiply, and your silver and gold are multiplied, and all that you have is multiplied; when your heart is lifted up, and you forget the LORD your God who brought you out of the land of Egypt, from the house of bondage; who led you through that great and terrible wilderness, in which were fiery serpents and scorpions and thirsty land where there was no water; who brought water for you out of the rock of flint; who fed you in the wilderness with manna, which your fathers did not know, that He might humble you and that He might test you, to do you good in the end—then you say in your heart, "My power and the might of my hand have gained me this wealth." And you shall remember the LORD your God, for it is He who gives you power to get wealth, that He may establish His covenant which He swore to your fathers, as it is this day. Then it shall be, if you by any means forget the LORD your God, and follow other gods, and serve them and wor-

ship them, I testify against you this day that you shall surely perish.

As the nations which the LORD destroys before you, so you shall perish, because you would not be obedient to the voice of the LORD your God.

We Must Face the Truth

Moses and the Lord put the raw truth to Israel three millennia ago. That same raw truth is what we Americans must face today. I do not maintain that America is God's chosen nation as was Israel in the Old Testament. But God has blessed America as He has blessed no other nation in the history of the world, even Israel.

We have been recognized around the world as a Christian nation and as a religious people. But we too, just as Israel, have fallen for the idols of this world. We have permitted all of this great freedom and prosperity to rot the core of our hearts, just as did the Israelites in the Old Testament days.

The vast majority of Americans say they believe in a God. But in actual fact most believe more in the idols of this world than in the God of the Bible. We profess God, but we do not possess God. We see Right and Wrong in our own eyes and not through the eyes of God. We are starved for righteousness because we do not have the requisite knowledge to discern and thus to live for the Right over the Wrong as witnesses for righteousness.

We in America Are Missing the Mark for God!

President Abraham Lincoln warned us about forgetting God and turning our backs on Him in a Presidential Proclamation on April 30, 1863:

> We have been the recipients of the choicest bounties of heaven. We have been preserved, these many years, in peace and prosperity. We have grown in numbers, wealth and power, as no other nation has ever grown. But we have forgotten God. We have forgotten the gracious hand which preserved us in peace, and multiplied and enriched and strengthened us; and we have vainly imagined, in the deceitfulness of our hearts, that all these blessings were produced by some superior wisdom and virtue of our own. Intoxicated

with unbroken success, we have become too self-sufficient to feel the necessity of redeeming and preserving grace, too proud to pray to the God that made us! It behooves us, then to humble ourselves before the offended Power, to confess our national sins, and to pray for clemency and forgiveness.

That is our duty for the gigantic debt we owe to our God and Creator. Lincoln was writing about the great blessings about 160 years ago. Those blessings were minimal as compared to the blessings God has poured out upon us as a people since that time.

No nation has ever set foot on our soil in war nor dropped one bomb on the continental United States. The only time we have experienced war in our nation was in Lincoln's time when we drew swords and fired cannons against one another. We killed more Americans than have ever been killed in all of the wars in which we have participated since that time, including World Wars I and II.

The responsibility for jogging the memory of America is not that of the president of the United States. The responsibility rests on the church of Jesus Christ in the United States of America—all of the various Protestant denominations and the Catholic and Orthodox churches.

We do not lack for troops. We lack for knowledge, for understanding, for real faith and commitment, for discipleship training, for true self-examination, and the kind of genuine repentance required by John the Baptist. Nothing less than the lordship of Jesus Christ reigning and ruling in all Christians will accomplish this mission, for we have lost so much ground in recent decades. We have so much ground to re-take and so many millions of people who have never been touched for the righteousness of Jesus Christ.

Now let us begin to look at Right versus Wrong in the various avenues of life on planet Earth. As we do this, let us, one by one, search our own hearts for the measure of our faith and commitment to the lordship of Jesus Christ in these various areas of our lives.

Let our prayer be that of King David in his beautiful psalm of repentance:

> Create in me a clean heart, O God,
> And renew a steadfast spirit within me.
> Do not cast me away from Your presence
> And do not take Your Holy Spirit from me.

Restore to me the joy of Your salvation,
And uphold me with Your generous Spirit.
Then I will teach transgressors Your ways,
And sinners shall be converted to You. (Ps. 51:10–13)

CHAPTER THREE

The First Church: The Home and Family

The problems of America are the family problems multiplied a million-fold.

Dwight D. Eisenhower[1]

There is a holocaust erupting in homes and families all over the United States of America, the nation the rest of the world emulates. This holocaust is best illustrated in a story by Russell Chandler, the religion editor of *The Los Angeles Times:*

> Arriving home from work, the harried husband, hand on his forehead, has just realized his ghastly goof. His wife—I'm assuming they're married, although that's a bit risky these days—opens the front door to let him in. "Great!" she says. "You remembered to pick up dinner, but where are the kids?"[2]

The home was intended by God to be the prime place of nurture and training for human beings. Yet in recent years the average American home has evolved into the Achilles' heel of American life. There is an old American saying that prophesies: "As the home goes, so goes the nation." Unfortunately, today this is the truth!

But there is hope! God actually has a most practical plan for the home. The bad news is that most people do not realize that there *is* such a divine plan for the home. Indeed, God created the home before He created the first channel of redemption, Israel, and also the second channel of redemption, the church of Jesus Christ. I call the home "the first church" because our time in the church is miniscule compared to our time in the home.

The purpose of this chapter is to assess the Wrongs in the home and then consider how the Wrongs may be eliminated and the home transformed into a training ground of righteousness, unity, harmony, and love. The only way America will be saved from disintegration will be through corrections in the basic unit God designed to steer the nations. God has a plan for the nations, but first He has a plan for the home. The key to what happens in the nations is in the home.

Why Is the Home So Vital?

After a baby is conceived and then born into the world, his or her place of abode becomes the family unit. For the next eighteen to twenty-one years the child will be most affected by the genes inherited from Mom and Pop and also the nurture or lack thereof provided by Mom and Pop.

The kinds of Moms and Pops leading the homes are the products of the kinds of Moms and Pops that led their homes. The sins and shortcomings or the righteousness and strengths of the parents do have a way of rubbing off on the children for Right or Wrong, good or evil. We call this nature and nurture.

Betty and I were born into and reared in what is tabbed by psychologists and sociologists as dysfunctional families. Dysfunctional families are families that were broken in various ways to the point that the family does not function in a normal and healthy way. Betty's father walked out on her family when she was six years old. So Betty grew up in a broken family that lived close to the poverty level.

I was reared in a family that was devastated by World War II and alcohol. My father had a problem handling alcohol, and he had more of a problem after two sons were killed in the war. Unfortunately, a good man became enslaved to alcoholism. It was his only enemy.

My mother had to work full-time and more in order to get five boys through college. The biggest things in her life were the Dent boys. Thus the World War II tragedies had a further adverse impact on her life and that of our family.

Every family has its share of problems. The dysfunctional families have more problems. By and large, the products of dysfunctional homes do not learn how to put together the ideal family when they get to the marrying and parenting stage of life because they have not experienced the Real Thing in marriage and family. The first questions a counselor will ask a client today are about the family background. The blessings and curses substantially flow from "the first church."

An additional adverse factor is that the vast majority of couples getting married receive little or no counseling on how to be a mate or parent for life. In most cases we are trained for our profession or job.

For example, I earned three university degrees in order to prepare myself for a life of success and abundance. But I was not prepared to be a mate or parent for life. Neither was Betty.

In my ignorance as a well-intentioned parent, I did not understand that Right or Wrong relationships are established in the home environment. Nor did I realize the importance of love. God's kind of unconditional love was alien to me. Now I understand that God's love is to be the standard of love in the home. Why? Not just because God commands it, but because it is the only kind of love that really works.

Betty had the same problem. Tragically, we were not alone. Most Moms and Pops are just as unlearned in the art of love and the grave responsibilities in rearing a family as were Harry and Betty Dent. Oh, if we could just start all over again with what we know now and with all the changes for the Right that have occurred in our life together.

Even as a lawyer and leader in national politics I did not comprehend the importance of having and living by such a worldview, a system of beliefs by which we make the choices and decisions in life. All of our responses to the questions of life are fed through this lens or grid.

This worldview is substantially formed and hardened in our home environment for good or evil. Our basic orientation in determining Right from Wrong and our reaction to the choices we face in life will be determined by our system of beliefs. At the bottom of the worldview is this question: By whose standard of Right and Wrong are we going to make the decisions that determine the course of our life here on earth and into eternity? Mighty big question, Mom and Pop!

The law of physics tells us that for every action there is a reaction. The Bible says much the same thing—what we sow we will reap. The Old Testament prophet Hosea warned the chosen people of Israel: "They sow the wind, / And reap the whirlwind" (Hos. 8:7a). Paul also made the point succinctly: "Do not be deceived, God is not mocked; for whatever a man sows, that he will also reap" (Gal. 6:7). We will all stand before the bar of justice here and there in eternity. The big question will be what you did with your home.

While this basic orientation toward Right versus Wrong is determined in the home, it is supplemented in school, religion, and society. As we will see later in this book, when the kids get outside of the home the temptations and pressures regarding Wrong magnify more. They had better be trained up in righteousness in God's sight to survive outside the home in what Charles Colson calls "the new dark age" in our society.

My Experience

I began to deal with the reality of the crucial role of the family when I was practicing law after my service in the White House. I realize now that God was directing broken people, especially young people, in my direction for legal help for my sake as well as theirs.

Instead of criminal courtroom work, I was pulled into helping people who were already serving time in prison. My role was to get my clients relief inside prison or to get them outside of prison by way of parole or post-conviction relief hearings, which are similar to appeal processes. My heart opened up so much more for broken and hurting people, so I was very successful in this kind of law practice.

Fortunately I realized that God was teaching me about brokenness in human lives and the origin of that brokenness. In most cases I would have my client examined by a Christian psychiatrist. In every report the same message kept coming back: "This young man has never experienced real love in his family or loving discipline; he is geared to crime through deep personal anger and instant gratification."

While I was dealing with young inmates in difficulty I was also receiving law cases from others in the hurting grapevine—in mental institutions, divorce courts, and child abuse cases. At the same time I was watching the unfolding drama and trauma of the Watergate political scandal in the Nixon White House from a distance.

It seemed that everywhere I turned I saw more and more human brokenness—more people up against the wall for so many varied reasons. My background had prepared me to empathize with hurting people because the Special Watergate Prosecution Force had even put me up against their wall for a time.

As hard as those Watergate tribulations were in 1973 and 1974, I do not regret those tough times. The experience gave me a warmer heart for people, preparing me for my ministry of recent years. We all need to be up against that wall of adversity in order to really experience the ups and downs of life and thus sympathize with others in the dock. Humility comes to be a foe of personal pride.

A few years later I was beginning to study the Bible in depth and progressively from Genesis to the Revelation of Jesus Christ. One of the first major teachings I encountered was the sin nature of man, beginning in Genesis 3 and running through the rest of the Bible, as one of those big overarching doctrines in the Bible. God was showing me the origin of all human brokenness.

In the beginning of my study I sought to dismiss the idea of an original sin nature in humans, especially in *this* human. Yet I could see it in my clients and all around me. Through the Bible this teaching loomed larger and larger as my life was being opened up more and more to receive the truth of God's Word. Then I began to sense the sin nature in Harry. What a discovery! It changed my life!

I had experienced brokenness in the dysfunctional home in which I had been reared during the depression days and World War II. I had watched my friends in the Nixon White House going to jail. Now I was reflecting on brokenness in life from my old family life, in the prisons, the mental institutions, the divorce courts, the White House, homes, and in my own life. But I had still overlooked the sin nature in Harry. The Bible explained to me that we all are sinners by nature and need to be changed by a supernatural work of the Spirit of God. In this study of the Bible I began to see everything differently, including the role of the family.

The Family Is Our Biggest Crisis

Today we all see the family in America as being in the biggest crisis in American history. Why? For one thing, there are too many "old Harry Dents" without the understanding, time, or expertise to be all that God ordained that fathers be as the spiritual leaders of our families.

The man that Dr. Billy Graham rates as one of the top experts on family life and the home is Dr. Armand Nicoli of the Harvard University faculty. Dr. Nicoli is a Christian psychiatrist and a contributing editor to *Christianity Today* magazine. His experience and studies have led him to conclude that the following are the prime factors for what I refer to as the holocaust in the home:

- Divorced Parents (700% increase in the twentieth century)
- Both Parents Working
- Absent or Busy Fathers
- Frequent Moves
- Too Much Television and of the Wrong Variety
- Idea That the Role of the Parents Is Passé
- The Famous Father (Living Legend) Syndrome
- "Affluenza" and Instant Gratification[3]

Dr. Nicoli is quick to point out that no one wants to hear his message!

The most sensitive point is the second one—both parents working. He rates this problem to be on a par with the number one problem—divorce. In effect, both indicate a divorce; the first is from the other mate, the second is parents from their children, especially by the bonding agent, Mom.

Both parents working full-time is rated as the number one problem in the home by Dr. Ken Magid and Carole McKelvey, authors of *High Risk Children Without a Conscience*.

> Who are these children without a conscience? They are children who cannot trust, children who cannot love, children who will not be loved. They grow up to be con-artists, amoral entrepreneurs, thieves, drug users, pathological liars, and worst of all: psychotic killers . . . and they are often the product of even the best-intentioned families.[4]

The above quote is taken from the back cover of this powerful book put together by secular psychiatrists, psychologists, sociologists, and experts on the family. The authors and contributing authors list several potential causes for serious breaks in the all-important bonding process for kids, especially with Mom. Discussed in the book are day care, parental leave, adoption, foster care, teenage pregnancy, child abuse, and divorce.

High Risk Children is about America's future. It is about babies, parenting, genetics, and crime and how they are vitally connected. The authors tell us:

> A demographic revolution is occurring which may result in future generations that have huge numbers of detached children. Factors responsible include: the increasing number of mothers working outside the home, the child-care crisis, the teen-pregnancy epidemic, a high divorce rate, increasing child abuse and neglect, the shambles of the foster-care system, and too-late adoptions.[5]

This paperback book caught my attention when it was given to me by Sara Southern, a retired schoolteacher. She told me, "Mr. Dent, here is the problem in our schools right here in this book! My thirty years in the classroom attest to the truth of this message."

While practicing law in the prisons I encountered people with personality disorders, particularly those afflicted with psychopathy or, the nice name, sociopathy. The sociological term is Antisocial Personal Disorder (APD). The Bible refers to this type of personality as the "seared conscience." To them Wrong is Right, for they seek only instant self-gratification and feel justified in doing so. What *High Risk Children* is saying is that we are turning loose on the world more and more psychopaths. From where? Our homes!

I studied a number of books looking for the causes for psychopathy and any remedies. Twenty years ago there were no easy answers. What the authors of *High Risk Children* have done is to pull together the major studies and bring the subject up to date. The results point to the family as the origin.

The most critical time is in the first two years of the child's life. A complex set of events must occur in infancy to assure a future of trust and love. If the proper bonding and subsequent attachment do not occur between children and parents, especially the mother, mistrust and deep-seated rage will develop in the child. The authors say the child can become someone without a conscience.

This is a prime reason for the construction of so many new prisons for our young people and also our adults—boys and girls and men and women! As a part of my ministry, I teach in prisons for Charles Colson and his Prison Fellowship Ministries. Thus I get to see firsthand the number of new facilities constantly under construction.

In South Carolina the budgets of the Department of Corrections and the Department of Youth Services are placing our state budget in jeopardy. Because of overcrowding, federal courts are forcing the early release of some inmates.

God Has a Plan

God's plan for the family is diametrically opposed to the way most families are operating today, even families in the church. God created us to need and want to be loved unconditionally—the way God loves—and also to need and want to love *back* unconditionally. God also established in us the need to be nurtured and to nurture, to live in right relationships, to be disciplined and corrected in love, to serve and help one another, to trust one another, and to have a sense of responsibility and accountability. God's plan is that we live in harmony with Him, with ourselves, with one another, and with our environment.

When children are denied this kind of experience in the home they innately feel cheated. In so many cases kids ultimately turn to the things and ways of the world to get their kicks, joys, and fulfillment. This is why alcohol, illegal drugs, free sex, teenage pregnancy, teenage suicide, and teenage crime have become top problems in our nation. Too many youngsters are being robbed of their humanity, and they resent it to the point of anger, rage, and then adverse actions.

Dr. Nicoli warns parents, "We need a radical change in our thinking about the family. If we choose to have children, then, those children must be given the highest priority."[6]

Our daughter, Dolly Montgomery, believes that Dr. Nicoli is correct. She and her husband, Don, are committed Christians, mates, and parents. Dolly resigned as personnel manager of a hospital when the first of three children was born. She was being promoted and was scheduled to receive the employee-of-the-year award. These two Presbyterian parents decided to shuck it all—the pay, promotion, and award—in favor of the well-being of Blake, Clay, and, finally, William Graham Montgomery. For several years now they have been living less well on one salary and rejoicing all the way. First things first!

Three items on the Nicoli list deserve some explanation. "Affluenza" is that dreaded American disease which I define as spending money we don't have on things we don't need to impress people we can't stand. Affluenza is close kin to prosperity theology. In both cases there is an addiction to the things of the world and thus the ways of the world.

The other Nicoli item requiring explanation is "instant gratification." This spells immaturity—the father of much crime, addiction, and human brokenness. It means: "I just can't wait; I have to become gratified right now." Instant gratification also spells addiction to the things of the world and thus the ways of the world. We live in the age of instant gratification and instant everything!

The "famous father" syndrome involves competition with the successful Pop or Mom. How can we ever live up to the achievements of this living legend? I never was that famous, but my children did inform me that they would rather have me in "Our House" than the White House. In most cases, this will be a problem.

What Is Happening to Our Kids Today?

Surveys show that our kids' heroes are the rock stars. Even in Australia, a pagan country, public TV runs programs warning of the terrible damage wrought by the rock star performers. Of special concern is the heavy metal music and the lurid lyrics that foster a sense of futility and hopelessness. They are tied directly to the rising number of teenage suicides.

In America our cable TV systems provide many such programs. Then there are the evil sexual videos.

Two courageous Christian ladies—Tipper Gore, wife of Democratic U.S. Senator Albert Gore, Jr., and Susan Baker, wife of U.S. Secretary of State James A. Baker, III—have waged campaigns against the heavy metal music and the rock videos. Tipper Gore made a presentation on this subject for the University of South Carolina in January of 1988. Her video presentations shocked the audience and further awakened me as to the need for the counteractions that Tipper and Susan have been advocating across America in a bipartisan duet.[7]

Free sex and date rape are rampant, fueling the demands for the so-called right to abort unwanted babies. Advocates for abortion-on-demand are stretching the United States Constitution to try to include the right to murder. How? By permitting constitutional rights to include the right of women to privacy for purposes of legalizing the murder of their own flesh and blood. They want to get abortion, like homosexuality today, out into the open as the norm. These are key signs of the end times of a civilization. I rank the disease of AIDs side by side with the disease of abortion. Both kill! Sin is the deadly cause.

Our teenagers are overwhelmed with the adult example of the use of alcohol and drugs. Our culture reeks with pleasure, treasure, drugs, alcohol, sex, instant gratification, relativism (make up your own rules as you go because there are no more moral absolutes), apathy, boredom, and crime. At the bottom is immaturity.

Our world today is the age of superficiality and junk, the age of the me-generation, the age of materialism, the age of cynicism and apathy (I don't know and I don't care), and the age of the freedom to do-as-I-please. It is an age that needs changing! And changing NOW!

Walt Schreibman, a noted psychologist, makes this poignant observation about the important role of the parents in the home: "The frightening thing about heredity and environment is that parents provide both."[8]

We cannot do much about our genes, but we can change and improve the environment for our children. There is no more compelling duty for parents today than this. And there is no other program that is designed—and divinely so—to bring about these compelling changes than God's Master Plan and its key component, God's Plan for the family.

The essence of the problem in the home is simply that we have too many takers as parents and not enough parents as givers. The selfishness of parents has virtually destroyed the nuclear family concept that was first installed by God. For the past few hundred years the nuclear family has been seen as being composed of the emotional intimacy of a heterosexual couple, their sexual life together, and the nurture and socialization of their children.

Some maintain that we are now in "the postnuclear family trend" whereby we are shifting from a child-centered family to an adult-centered family. In other words, it is every family member for him- or herself. Mom and Pop are too busy pursuing their own agendas of enjoyment and fulfillment.[9]

What Are Some Answers for the Home?

As with the problems of life there is the bad news and the good news. We have sampled the bad news. Now for the good news!

GOD HAS A MASTER PLAN, AND TUCKED INTO THE VERY HEART OF THAT MASTER PLAN IS GOD'S PLAN FOR THE HOME.

FOR THE ANSWERS TO THE HOLOCAUST IN THE HOME PLEASE REFER TO THE MANUFACTURER'S HANDBOOK, THE BIBLE, WITH REGULARITY.

Right and Righteous Relationships

The Bible has many key themes and teachings for life on planet Earth and on into eternity. One of the major themes of the Bible that is embodied in the heart of the cross is right relationships. Indeed, things of the world do not satisfy, but relationships do! The home is divinely designed to be the training ground for right relationships.

Two Equals One

When God breathed life into the nostrils of Adam and Eve, He commanded that the two were to be joined together so that they would become one flesh. Their nakedness would be without shame. Adam and Eve were created to live in right relationship with the Creator and with each other.

As with Adam and Eve marriage partners are to become "one flesh" in a strong bond. We are to cleave together for life, not for as long as we like, which seems to be the order of this day. The problem is that there is too much *leaving* and not enough *cleaving*. Statistics for this century show a 700 percent increase in leaving. One in every two marriages is falling apart today.

Mom and Pop Get Saved First

Genesis 3 teaches that disobedience to God breaks our relationship with God. John, the apostle of love and right relationships, instructs us in 1 John that God has a plan for restoring broken relationships. With God's supernatural help we are to convert the habit of sinning into a habit of obedience. We will always have a sin problem, but one of the purposes of Christian growth is to break the habit of sin.

John reveals the catalyst for spiritual conversion in relating the story of Jesus and Nicodemus on the subject of salvation. Jesus explained to the inquiring Jewish leader that there is only one way to salvation—a person's will must be changed from man's way to God's way, from an orientation to Wrong to a new orientation to Right and righteous living.

Jesus called it a "born-again" experience. It is not enough to be born out of Mom's womb. There must be a second birth—this time by the Spirit of God.

Good intentions, good works, and being born below the Mason-Dixon line in the middle of the Bible Belt will not suffice. I taught this "born-again" teaching in Sunday school, but I did not relate it to my life. Two ex-White House figures, President Jimmy Carter and Charles Colson of Nixon Watergate fame, confronted the world with this most critical teaching by unashamedly proclaiming their "born-again" experiences. Billy Graham attests to their impact around the world.

Then the Kids Get Saved

Parents must be saved if they expect to have a real Christian environment in their homes. So Mom and Pop are to let the Lord work first in their lives. Then Mom and Pop are to help prepare the children for the Lord to work in their lives. How? Feeding them the Word of God. Loving them unconditionally. Getting them into Christian schools where possible.

Most people who will ever come to the Lord do so before age

eighteen. After leaving home for higher education and/or a work career, the individual is subjected to the ever-increasing impact of the "isms" of life. Once the big decisions are made the individual becomes more and more set in a certain rut in life. The older we get the less likely we are to surrender to change even if the rut becomes very uncomfortable because it becomes our security blanket.

The key answer lies in the teaching of Proverbs 22:6. "Train up a child in the way he should go, / And when he is old he will not depart from it."

Young people are more open, idealistic, and willing to be changed. In particular, they tell me that they want to "help people." We are missing the mark with our young people! They are more ready for the Lord than we are!

There is no substitute for getting youngsters into churches with vibrant youth ministries. There are also many student ministries within church life or in para-church organizations. Our daughter Ginny was born again in Young Life. Do not overlook the Boy Scouts and Girl Scouts. Here there is less specificity about God, as with Alcoholics Anonymous, but the door is opened in these organizations for one to find Jesus Christ. Why not get the Scout troops and AA meetings into churches so they can directly get Jesus Christ?

I missed being in the eye of the Watergate storm because of the work in my life regarding Right versus Wrong by a scoutmaster and my fellow troopers. I needed the kind of discipleship and fellowship provided by Troop 62.

What the Home Needs More Than Ever
Is Unconditional Love

Right and righteous relationships do not develop properly on earth until we first get our relationship right with our Creator. The reason is that the key to right relationships is L-O-V-E, God's special kind of love. It is called "agape" love, but I prefer the term "unconditional" love. Reverend Dick Woodward coined the term "anyway" love. Dick says that God loves us "anyway" despite the fact that our sins put His Son on the cross.

The late Southern Baptist Professor W. Oscar Thompson, Jr., best coupled God's love to right relationships in this beautiful way:

> Love is
> NOT a word of emotion,
> NOT a word of feeling.

Rather, love is
A word of reason,
A word of volition or will,
A word of action,
Love is doing!

Love builds relationships;
Love maintains relationships;
Love fulfills relationships;
Love initiates relationships.[10]

Love Is Meeting Needs!

The key to developing and maintaining right relationships is to infuse God's love into man's kind of loves. This allows God's love to transform man's loves from being limited, fallible, and selfish to being unconditional and everlasting.

Our Creator set up the home to be a place of right relationships for peace and harmony in the home and also as a model for the world. God created humans with the inherent desire to be loved unconditionally. Do you know anyone who does *not* want to be loved with no ifs, ands, or buts? I don't.

To lead us toward being a whole person, God also wired us to need to love back unconditionally. It is when we get the unconditional love-cycle moving round and round in the home that the children then move out into the world with the same habit. They become ministers of right relationships for the glory of God and the good of all of mankind.

What a plan! Yet so many, even in the church—and especially in the home—have missed out on this great blessing in life. I did for forty-eight years. So many of the kids in homes are missing their greatest and deepest need: To know they are loved. Indeed, denial of love in childhood results in disabilities in a sense of well-being, the ability to love, and the ability to trust. Too often the reaction is to seek gratification in sin and crime.

Loving Discipline

Christian authors Gary Smalley and John Trent have published a book that explains the two sides to God's kind of love. The hard side consists of loving discipline. It is designed to be protective of the child. The soft side of love is full of compassion and patience. The authors write that it is this balance that "strengthens affection, closeness and lasting commitment."[11]

Discipline is about doing the Right Thing rather than doing the Wrong Thing. It is the ability to defer gratification, and where necessary, to douse it altogether. This is so difficult to do in our age of instant everything. Where discipline is missing, instant gratification will quickly steal its place.

An undisciplined, spoiled child will become a selfish, me-first teenager or adult who can too easily succumb to the temptation to get his or her sexual desires satisfied right now. Or to get the cash needed for fulfilling immaturish desires some youngsters become a party to robbery.

This is what is happening with too many young people and adults today. I dealt with instant-gratification clients in the practice of law. Some of these clients are still serving time in prison. They did not realize that in man's law "the hand of one is the hand of all." It only takes one seared conscience or one teenager influenced by the violence on TV to pull the trigger.

There is one passage of Scripture that I would hang on the wall of my little ones today if I could start over again. It is Proverbs 3. I would use verses 1–8, 11–12:

> My son, do not forget my law,
> But let your heart keep my commands;
> For length of days and long life
> And peace they will add to you.
>
> Let not mercy and truth forsake you;
> Bind them around your neck,
> Write them on the tablet of your heart,
> And so find favor and high esteem
> In the sight of God and man.
>
> Trust in the LORD with all your heart,
> And lean not on your own understanding;
> In all your ways acknowledge Him,
> And He shall direct your paths.
>
> Do not be wise in your own eyes;
> Fear the LORD and depart from evil.
> It will be health to your flesh,
> And strength to your bones. . . .
>
> My son, do not despise the chastening
>   of the LORD,

Nor detest His correction;
For whom the LORD loves He corrects,
Just as a father the son in whom he delights.

Lack of discipline leads to immaturity. Immaturity says "Go ahead and do it! You can control it! You won't get caught!" That is basically what the serpent said to Adam and Eve in the Garden of Eden. He tricked them into believing they could have control over their own lives, that they could be "as God." Even our first family was immature, and they passed that immaturity along as an integral part of the sin nature of humankind.

Immaturity leads to addiction. Addiction leads to compulsive actions. Compulsivity leads to tobacco, alcohol, drugs, promiscuity, crime, and much more. Addictive habits destroy people who could be productive, righteous witnesses. Worst of all, lack of discipline opens wide the doors of hell on earth and on into eternity through what Christian writer J. Keith Miller, still in recovery from alcoholism, calls the Sin-Disease—habitual sin and habitual brokenness.[12]

Bonding and Attachment in the Early Years

Most books on the problems in the family point to the abandonment of the home by so many Moms—65 percent of them. This is a prime question of priorities. *High Risk Children* will scare the extra paycheck out of any Mom or Pop on this subject.

The basic bonding and attachment is made in the first two years of the child. Most of the knowledge the child will ever acquire comes in the first two years. Breaks in the bonding that occur in these critical years may never be repaired. They can affect the child's ability to trust and love in life.

Some parents have to work outside the home. If so, then the working parent or parents should do their best to find a way to minimize the damage.

Absolutely No Child Abuse!

In America today we see more and more child abusers being hauled into court and/or prison. The teaching in any book that reports on child abuse stresses that, in addition to the damage to the abused child, it is the abused child who is most likely to become the child abuser in the future. It is amazing how horrible the habits we carry out of our homes and into the world can be.

No Tobacco, Alcohol, or Drugs

Babies that ingest poisons in Mom's womb may never be right in their life. We are now reading about the adverse results of this disaster in our school systems as more and more disabled cocaine babies and alcohol fetal-syndrome children are moving into schools. This piles more problems on top of our already troubled educational system.

In my state of South Carolina a 1991 research program by the South Carolina Commission on Alcohol and Drug Abuse revealed that "almost 26 percent of infants—or 15,398—had been exposed to drugs." They had drug traces in their stool, or their mother's urine tested positive for alcohol or other drugs.[13]

It is not enough to abstain from drug use during pregnancy. Mom and Pop should not be modeling destructive drugs in the home, or anywhere else for that matter! Children of alcoholics are four times as likely to become alcoholics. There is a genetic link that has not been fully explained. However, as deadly as the genetic defect may be, the impact of watching Mom and/or Pop cover their pains of life with drugs is equally disabling.

Pop as Spiritual Leader

If fathers ever had any question about their role as spiritual leaders in the home it can be settled by a trip through the Bible, beginning in Deuteronomy 6. God through Moses tells all fathers that they are to know God's Law and love, to obey God's Laws and then grill the Law and love into their kids and grandkids.

> Hear, O Israel: The LORD our God, the LORD is One! You shall love the LORD your God with all your heart, with all your soul, and with all your might. And these words which I command you today shall be in your heart; you shall teach them diligently to your children, and shall talk of them when you sit in your house, when you walk by the way, when you lie down, and when you rise up. You shall bind them as a sign on your hand, and they shall be as frontlets between your eyes. You shall write them on the doorposts of your house and on your gates (Deut. 6:4–9).

The message here is to apply these teachings to our hearts, our homes, and our habits.

The duty of unconditional love is to be shared between Mom and Pop, to each other and especially to the kids. (Of course, we will love our grandkids unconditionally because they are the ones who are really perfect!) The children get a strong sense of stability when they perceive God's kind of love dancing back and forth between Mom and Pop. Their lives are fulfilled when they experience this kind of love coming to them.

One could say "If Mom and Pop are for us, then who can be against us!" Here is where kids get their stability and security.

Parents are witnesses for good or evil to the greatest trust we have—the lives of our children and thus our posterity. We will answer one day, not for the nature we bequeathed to our posterity, but rather the nurture we provided for Wrong.

Too many Pops rely on their so-called Ephesians 5 rights to be the head of the home. However, with every right there is a responsibility. The big duty here is to be the spiritual leader and key lover in the home but not a dictator. Oh how this chapter has been twisted for Wrong instead of Right! No one did it more than the "old" Harry.

The father is to be the key role model and also to lead in devotionals and Bible study. It is his duty to get the family to church. He is to love his wife as much as Christ loves His church.

The most important point for Pop to understand and implement is this axiom: Children will never get a clear picture of their "Father Who Art in Heaven" until they see something of God in their earthly father who is in the home.

The key to changing the world goes all the way back to Pop. When Pop gets changed spiritually—born-again, as Jesus commanded—the family of man will begin to be changed. Then when the family of man is changed, the family of God will begin to become all Jesus commissioned it to be. And then, and only then, will the church begin to change the world instead of continuing to permit the world to change the church to the ways of the world.

Dr. Steve Farrar published a book in 1990 that will challenge and convict derelict or lackadaisical Pops to get with God's program for the father's leadership role in the home. The book is appropriately entitled *Point Man: How a Man Can Lead a Family.*[14]

Steve compares the role of leading a family through the moral chaos of the '90s to leading a small patrol through enemy territory in a war—snipers around the bend, booby traps to your right, land mines everywhere. Steve's point is that if a family is to make it through the jungle of this world intact, it needs a trained, God-appointed leader as the point man. As an old Korean War infantryman and father and grandfather since then, I can relate wholeheartedly to the point of the point man. The question Steve raises for his readers is who's leading your family through enemy territory?

Mutual Submission

The ladies have their duties also. First and foremost they get to bear the kids with bulges, pains, and all the tribulations and blessings of pregnancy. Much of the nurture comes from Mom. She too is to love unconditionally and to be a witness to her husband and children.

The husband and wife have a great duty to be in mutual submission to one another and especially to God and His Plan for the two who have become one. Mutual submission means that you each consider the other person over yourself. This is a duty that affects every Christian.

Dr. Bill Bright and his wife, Vonette, wrote out their marital vows and signed them when they were married some years ago. Then the two became one and petitioned the Lord for His plan not for Bill or Vonette, but His plan for the two who had now become one. This is known as mutual submission to the Lord. Within a year God answered their prayers by giving them one of the world's greatest and most vital ministries, Campus Crusade for Christ. Today there are approximately seventeen thousand young Christians witnessing to college and university students around the world through Campus Crusade.

Build on the Rock

In closing out His greatest message, the Sermon on the Mount, Jesus' final admonition was to build your home on the rock and not the sand (Matt. 7:24–27). There is a great Christian hymn, "How Firm a Foundation," that defines the word *rock* so well.

Joshua underscored the spiritual strength and vitality of the home in his farewell address: "But as for me and my house, we will serve the LORD" (Josh. 24:15b). This is one verse worthy of hanging over the doorpost of every home, as Moses admonished fathers to do in Deuteronomy 6:4–9. It now hangs over our doorpost. The kids are gone, but at least our grandkids see it now when they visit. Better late than never!

King Solomon articulated the teaching most beautifully in Proverbs 24:3–4: "Through wisdom a house is built, / And by understanding it is established; / By knowledge the rooms are filled / With all precious and pleasant riches."

Obey Your Parents

Paul also admonished the children that they too have a role to play in the home.

Children, obey your parents in the Lord, for this is right. "Honor your father and mother," which is the first commandment with promise: "that it may be well with you and you may live long on the earth" (Eph. 6:1–3).

Paul concludes his teaching on the home in Ephesians 5 and 6 with the strong admonition, "And you, fathers, do not provoke your children to wrath, but bring them up in the training and admonition of the Lord" (Eph. 6:4).

This follows Solomon's advice in Psalm 127 that "unless the Lord builds the house, they labor in vain who build it." Why? Because "children are a heritage from the Lord." There is no higher trust and thus responsibility than this!

For the Moms, here is a good recipe for child-raising.

Recipe for Child-Raising

1 cup of Proverbs 22
2 tablespoons of Proverbs 19:13
1 dash of Proverbs 23:13
1 teaspoon of Proverbs 3:5
½ cup of Titus 2:3–7

Mix all the ingredients, add a pound of persistence, one cup of love, and whip until right consistency. This recipe is recommended by the Creator of Mankind. Please add a pinch of Ephesians 6:4.[15]

We All Need the Blessing and Affirmation

My mother, Sallie, died as I finished college and was heading to the Korean War. She worked and worried herself to death for her family. I do not remember her ever telling me that she loved me. However, I will never forget the great blessing she laid on my life over and over again. She was my chief cheerleader.

Sallie Dent probably did not realize the importance of a child's need for affirmation. But she kept telling people in and out of my presence that I was the greatest and that one day I would be somebody and accomplish many good works in life. She believed in Harry Dent and everyone around her knew this.

I did not understand my mother's great contribution to my sense of self-esteem and well-being until I read Gary Smalley's best-selling book: *The Blessing*.[16] Esau missed his blessing, and he went through life as a grouch. We all need affirmation, and we all must pass on the blessing to our kids and to others. Self-esteem is described by Charles Swindoll as "a sense of self-respect, a feeling of self-worth." He sees conceit as "whitewash to cover low self-esteem."[17]

In his book, *Frog in the Kettle*, George Barna writes that America is besieged by a low sense of self-esteem. People need to know that we are created "in the image of God" and "in His likeness." This is the basic source of our self-worth. Unfortunately, too few people realize this source. We must make certain that our children are not among that number.[18]

So the greatest and gravest duty we have on planet Earth is to make certain that we have a plan for our families. We have a plan for most everything else, except the most important purpose, to raise up our children in the fear and admonition of the Lord. In a sense my kids impacted me more than I impacted them for good.

The Family Must Come Under God

It has been aptly stated by Ann Graham Lotz, the daughter of Billy and Ruth Graham, that "We will never be one nation under God until the family comes under God."[19] This is why signing up to be part of a family, especially the head of a family, carries such a high degree of accountability and responsibility. The ramifications resonate throughout America.

The family will not come under God until the family comes together again. There is no substitute for a father and a mother spending good quality time with their children, especially in prayer and in study of the Bible.

My Democrat friend in Columbia, Det Bowers, and his wife, Polly, begin every day with their three boys in prayer and Bible study before the boys go to school and Det goes to work. What better way to prepare them for all the adverse peer pressures they will encounter at school and out in the world each day.

The Greatest of These Is Love

Nothing tops love, the key to communications and relationships. God's kind of love is the catalytic converter for blowing out all of the soot of worldliness that devastates too many homes. This will even open a man's heart to talk and tell whatever is in his heart.

Why is a dog known as man's best friend? Because the dog loves his master, anyway. Dogs love unconditionally, but people are not so smart.

Infusing God's love into the relationship between Mom and Pop so that their limited and exclusive love becomes truly unconditional and everlasting is important for the family. Not only will Pop be talking to Mom, but perhaps he will even engage in some pillow talk for a change—all to his benefit. Then he will begin asking, "Honey, what can I do for you?" instead of "What have you done for me lately?"

Most wives I know would reciprocate immediately. This is the way God divinely designed His love to work in us and in our homes.

Once this new unconditional love relationship gets moving between Mom and Pop, it will flow down to the kids, then out to friends and, as Jesus admonished us, even to their enemies. It will no longer be "You scratch my back and I'll scratch yours." Even in politics and the business world, love can be made unconditional. There is no better way to turn enemies into friends.

How God's Love Can Destroy Divorce Courts

God's love can not only destroy bad relationships, it can demolish divorce courts. My state of South Carolina was the last state in the Union to give in to enacting a divorce law. When Betty and I were married forty years ago we could not have gotten a divorce if we wanted one. Betty says that once or twice she considered murder, but never divorce! It was not an option. Today it is an almost instant option—instant divorces in the Age of Instant Everything.

As a consequence, we see more divorce courts in existence in this conservative state in the middle of the Bible Belt than all the rest of the courts in South Carolina added together.

Today there is only one practical antidote to divorce and that is Christian counseling. Mike and Linda Bledsoe of Lexington, South Carolina, have made a side ministry out of bringing broken Moms and Pops back together B.C.—before court. Mike offers ten one-hour sessions to the broken Pop, and Linda offers ten one-hour sessions to the broken Mom. They have mended each challenge because they have been using "The Manufacturer's Handbook for Marriage and Family Unity," better known as the Holy Bible.

Betty and I have found a whole new love life since we began loving unconditionally with supernatural help. We tell people that if they want to do away with divorce courts and put lawyers in the soup line—and most do—then apply for a heavy infusion of God's kind of love into man's kind of limited, selfish, and fallible loves. The prescription is a good dose of the Holy Ghost and the Holy Bible. This is how God works best to lead us to major in Right over Wrong.

When we get God's love moving in all kinds of relationships in America, beginning in the home, then we will begin to experience harmony and peace in the home and even in our culture. For it is true that as the home goes, so goes the culture. The answer to the problems in all relationships and especially to those in the first church, the home, is "I love you, anyway!"

Our dear Christian pastor-friend, Dick Woodward, has so simply and eloquently expressed this kind of love this way:

Anyway Love

People are unreasonable, illogical and self-centered . . .
   Love them ANYWAY!
If you do good, people will accuse you of selfish ulterior
   motives . . . Do good ANYWAY!
If you are successful, you will win false friends and true
   enemies . . . Succeed ANYWAY!
The good you do today will be forgotten tomorrow . . .
   Do good ANYWAY!
Honesty and frankness make you vulnerable . . . Be
   honest and frank ANYWAY!
The biggest people with the biggest ideas can be shot
   down by the smallest people with the smallest
   minds . . . Think big ANYWAY!
People favor underdogs but follow only top dogs . . . Fight
   for some underdog ANYWAY!
What you spend years building may be destroyed
   overnight . . . Build ANYWAY!
People really need help but may attack you if you help
   them . . . Help people ANYWAY!
Give the world the best you've got and you'll get kicked in
   the teeth . . . Give the world the best you've got
   ANYWAY![20]

There it is! My pastor-friend has focused us on the answer: "I love you, anyway!" What was Jesus doing on that cross but sacrificing His life for our sins, *anyway!* The answer Jesus bequeathed to us from that cross was the implementation of the Greatest Commandment ever given—to love unconditionally—and the Greatest Commission ever given—to serve unconditionally. Why? For the glory of God, for the good of all of mankind, and especially for the foremost institution of all, the home!

In closing this chapter, we recommend a 1992 secular book for your study. It is entitled *Today's Children: Creating a Future for a Generation in Crisis,* by the president of the Carnegie Corporation, Dr. David A. Hamburg. This foundation is a leader in child development research. In this book Dr. Hamburg boldly asserts that we have lost a substantial portion of the generation of kids under sixteen "to drug abuse, crime and teen pregnancy, but also to more subtle corrosives like malnutrition, illiteracy and poor self-esteem." He goes on to charge our nation with "social selfishness." Yes, he calls for sacrifice by us older folks to help our posterity survive and lead the way to a brighter and better future for America and humanity. As in this book, he sets forth the problems and also the answers, directing them to Mom and Pop and to the Congress and the president of the U.S.A. We must reallocate our time and resources toward this most critical end.[21]

The Church: The Second Channel of Redemption

The church does the most for the world when the church is least like the world.

Warren Wiersbe[1]

The problems afflicting "the land of the free and the home of the brave" in society and in the home are basically the same problems afflicting the church of Jesus Christ: Immaturity and addiction to the things of the world.

Isn't the church supposed to have THE ANSWERS?

Yes, the church does have THE ANSWERS! They are securely locked within the four walls of the church. But the church has its own problems that stem out of the same source as the problems of the society and the homes. Society and the homes are composed of people, as is the church. Remember the problem of the human condition? It is known as self-ism. It is a problem that is endemic to all people everywhere, and it is of epidemic proportions whether in society, the home, or the church.

But isn't the church supposed to make the difference in society and the home? Isn't that Christianity?

Again, yes—but—so many of the people in the churches just cannot get around to it. For one thing, it is all we can do to put out the fires in the church. And there are so many other priorities in this busy and fast-changing world today.

The weekends are so busy and crowded today. There are sports events all day Saturday and Sunday. And Sunday is a great day for shopping now that the Blue Laws are gone. And there are so many vacation spots to visit. Besides, remember that more than half of the Moms are working all week on a job outside of the home. So there is no time for church activities during the week. Then it gets back to the weekend again, but that really is the *only* time Mom and Pop have together—to clean house, relax, and catch up on the financial books.

This is the problem of the church. It is akin to dancing on the deck of the Titantic while the good ship is slowly sinking. The new priorities of the world have been moved up to the front-burner. Get all the gusto you can! And don't worry, it won't happen to us!

Jesus was sent into the world by God the Father about two thousand years ago for a number of very special reasons. In this chapter, we are particularly examining Jesus' mission to establish His church to provide the answers to the human condition. The church would function as the second channel of redemption by saving and discipling ordinary people. The answers come out of God's Master Plan, the implementation of which is vested in all the members of the church—pastors and pews.

God the Father was the role model for Jesus, and Jesus was sent to earth as the God-man to be our role model. In turn, the world is supposed to be able to see the righteous character of Jesus Christ in our lives as Christ-i-ans. We Christians constitute the body of Christ.

So the purpose of the church is to give to the world a unified and loving group of people for the world to experience the Real Thing and the Right Thing in the members of the body of Christ.

As God the Father sent Jesus to do His work, so Jesus sent the Holy Spirit, the third person in the Godhead, to live in us and thus to convict, teach, and guide us in implementing God's Master Plan. We have the great privilege of finishing the work that Jesus began on earth when He established the second channel of redemption, the church of Jesus Christ, through His disciples.

The First Church

The real first church is the one we study in "The Book of the Acts of the Holy Spirit in the Apostles and All of God's People." This is my title for the Book of Acts. This book tells the story of the establishment of the second channel of redemption. The essence of the story is "The Son went up, the Spirit came down, and the Church went out!"

Dr. Luke continues his narrative from his Gospel as he records for us the beginning of the church and its implementation of the Great Commission. Churches were planted all over the then-known world. Letters were subsequently written to the churches for purposes of correction, reproof, and instruction in righteousness. These letters explain to us what Christianity is all about, including salvation and the mission of the church.

The essence of what the model church was about is set forth for us in Acts: 2:42–47. To sum it up:

1. They loved one another unconditionally and praised and worshiped God.
2. They broke bread together in real fellowship and harmony, sharing with one another, especially those in need.
3. They prayed together and for one another with fervor. (As in Romania, Korea, and the old USSR.)
4. They studied the Word of God together in light of Jesus' life and interpretation of the Scriptures.
5. The apostles preached with power the message of Jesus Christ and worked signs and wonders—all through the indwelling of the Holy Spirit.
6. They brought others into a living relationship with Jesus Christ—again, through the power and working of the Holy Spirit.

These apostles were mere fishermen, zealots, tax collectors, and doubting Thomases who executed a shameful coverup in the shadow of the cross for fear that they might be next. They were changed by the coming of the Holy Spirit at the Festival of Pentecost. They were emboldened and affirmed in their mission by their witness of the resurrected Jesus Christ. Paul could never forget his Damascus Road experience when he also, at a later time, became another eyewitness to the presence of the resurrected Christ, whose followers he had persecuted.

The church was born out of the cross, the empty tomb, and the coming of the Holy Spirit. For us this means dying to self, being raised to new life in Christ, and being empowered with the indwelling and the leadership of the Spirit of Jesus Christ to guide us in our walk, witness, and mission as members of the second channel of redemption.

The Mission of the Church

The letter to the church at Ephesus and to other nearby churches is another fertile source for getting a firm grasp on the mission and purpose of the second channel of redemption. It is recognized both as the "Queen of the Epistles" and also as the "Magna Carta of the Church." This was the Apostle Paul at his best, overflowing with his time of training in the desert and with the power of the Holy Spirit.

This letter was prepared for believers who did not comprehend the spiritual riches they had available to them in Christ. They were living as spiritual paupers ignorant of their real spiritual net worth and great purpose in God's Master Plan. That setting is so similar to the problem of church members today. This is why we need to put Ephesians on our priority study list.

Chapters 1-3 provided understanding for these early Christians and for us today as to the spiritual endowments that Christ has provided for all who trust in Him—adoption, acceptance, redemption, forgiveness, wisdom, inheritance, the seal of the Holy Spirit, eternal life, grace, and citizenship in the heavenly Kingdom.

In the opening of Ephesians we get a glimpse of the rich spiritual food to follow:

> Grace to you and peace from God our Father and the Lord Jesus Christ. Blessed be the God and Father of our Lord Jesus Christ, who has blessed us with every spiritual blessing in the heavenly places in Christ (Eph. 1:2-3).

Dr. Jerry Kirk has memorized chapter 1 as his favorite chapter in all of the Bible. In particular, Presbyterians are predestined to be very strong on Ephesians, but all members of the church should attempt to follow Jerry Kirk's example so we can better understand and assimilate who we are and what we have in Christ. In chapter 3, Paul then unveils the mystery of the church. The two major purposes are to edify and equip the saints to be used of God to change the world to Jesus Christ—His ways, means, love, and service. In essence, this is edification and evangelism.

Chapters 4-6 then instruct us as to how to live as members of the body of Christ. As with most epistles, the first part explains the doctrine or what we are to believe and the second half shows us how to translate our beliefs into the practice of righteous behavior. The aim is that we become spiritually transformed so that we imitate and reflect for the world to see and experience the righteous character and love of our role model, Jesus Christ, the head of the church.

These teachings tie into all that Jesus presented in word and deed during His time on earth, in His death on the cross, through His resurrection from the empty tomb, His ascension to be our mediator with the Father and the sending of the Holy Spirit to empower the saints to implement and complete Jesus' mission for the world. Jesus' farewell address at the Last Supper planted the seed for many of the teachings in Ephesians and the other epistles.

The World Needs the Example of the Church

In His high priestly prayer (John 17:20–26) Jesus explained that the world will know and accept Jesus as the Lord and Savior of the world when it sees the church unified and in love with one another—unconditionally.

The world has not yet experienced the Real Thing or the Right Thing. The world has not seen the church in unity and in love with one another unconditionally. The world still does not fully comprehend Right versus Wrong!

Just as God put eternity in the heart of every person (Eccl. 3:11), so He has put in each of us the desire and need to be loved unconditionally. Our number one need as humans is to live in right relationships with our Creator and with our fellowman.

God also put in us the desire and need to be whole persons. The way we become whole persons is to love back unconditionally just as we are loved unconditionally. So God has done His part of the work. The question is this: When are we going to do ours? It has been approximately two thousand years since Jesus turned the church over to the Holy Spirit and all the people of God. Yet today the world's ways are winning over God's ways. And the world is prevailing with the kind of loves that accentuate the perversion of the sex drive and self-ism as against God's charity, giving unconditionally and expecting nothing in return. This is the kind of love the world needs, but the church is failing to show and tell the world about the Real Thing.

I've often heard Charles Colson, who was also Special Counsel to President Nixon, sum up the situation this way: "There is too much of the world in the Church and not enough of the Church in the world."

Betty and I have been on a great learning experience in our little lay ministry that has taken us into more than seven hundred churches of various sizes and descriptions on five continents. The problem in the church is similar to the favorite saying of Pogo, the satirist opossum in the cartoon: WE HAVE MET THE ENEMY, AND HE IS US!

Why Are We Our Enemy?

The essence of the problem is that the church of Jesus Christ has become too institutionalized, too caught up in itself and thus guilty of its own style of self-ism. We have substituted program performance for a living, powerful relationship to God and thus to one another. Structures have been erected with good intentions, but they can bring Wrong results, similar to government bureaucracies. Instead of permitting the spiritual body of Christ to function biblically so that the people worship God, there is too much worship of the institutionalism and its insistence on bodies, buildings, and budgets that has been created. Performance and results are pursued to the point that the supernatural power of God becomes elusive.

Bible Calls for Lay Ministry

In all of my years as a pew member and church leader I never heard one word about the fact that the Bible message commands every member of the body of Christ to find, develop, and implement his or her own ministry.

There is no way that God's Master Plan will ever be implemented by just the 1 percent in the pulpits—as capable and dedicated as they may be. I wonder how in the world God is ever going to get His work done with 1 percent power on the part of His people.

The Scriptures and practicality convince me that God is looking for the work of the 1 percent in the pulpits plus the 99 percent in the pews. Added up, this totals one hundred! By and large, God may be getting about 20 percent efficiency. In church lay renewal groups this is known as the 80/20 principle: 80 percent of the people in the church come to sit and soak while 20 percent do the work. Every time I mention the 80/20 principle in teaching, the real workers signify the veracity of the principle by nodding their heads in the affirmative.

In the main, laypersons are asked to keep the programs functioning and are not prepared for the ministry of evangelism and discipleship that the Lord has assigned to all of the people of God. The principal function of most of the folks in the pews is to attend, listen, and contribute. Yet the people in the pews are the ones living in all of those homes (the first churches), working in all those marketplaces, recreating in all of the rest and relaxation spots, attending all of those athletic contests, and passing all of the laws of man.

Lay people have the most and greatest pulpits—in numbers, practicality, and proximity—that the world has ever known. They have the best opportunities to be the "salt" and the "light" and to pass on "the blessing" in the world. The most effective witness for Jesus Christ is not a pastor but a trained and spiritually turned-on layperson. At this time and for most of history, lay folks have been substantially missing the mark in ministry. Why? Because most do not know they are called, have not been trained to witness or minister, and have not been challenged to meet their moments of opportunity for witness and ministry.

George Barna's 1991 research statistics reveal the weak views that abound about the subject of evangelism.

> Just over one-fourth of all adults (28%) strongly believe that they have a responsibility to share their religious beliefs with others who they feel have a different set of beliefs. An equivalent proportion of adults (25%) feel equally strongly that they do not have any such responsibility. The rest of the population is caught somewhere in the middle on this issue.[2]

Even one-fourth of people who classify themselves as born-again Christians feel they have no duty toward evangelism. Members of evangelical-type churches are more favorable to evangelism than those in mainline or Catholic churches.[3]

Previously I would have rebelled at the thought of bothering others with my hazy view of Christian witness. Not understanding the Bible too well, I did not understand evangelism and was not a believer in evangelism. But the Bible is filled with the subject of evangelism. It is impossible to study the Bible and miss the importance of the subject. People who really know the Bible and do not practice, preach, or pursue evangelism must not believe the Bible's teachings.

Thus, one reason so many people in the pews do not realize that they are in the church for the purpose of evangelizing their world is their ignorance of God's Word. There are pastors and church leaders who may be afraid of an unleashed laity. These are likely to be the authoritarian types who believe they can better control their pews if the members just come and listen to the preaching and support the ministry. Some actually believe that there is only one ministry in their church—the pastor's. In too many cases, the aim seems to be to get the work done through organizational and institutional forms of Christianity and the preaching of the pastor.

The Life of the Church

There is no life in an organization or institution. There can only be life in a human being. The kind of life I am addressing is spiritual, relational, and supernatural. It cannot be reduced to writing or programmed. It comes through the Word of God, the Spirit of God, and that of a human heart yielded to the leadership and lordship of Jesus Christ.

What is sorely missing is spiritual life, the life of Jesus Christ alive and serving in the hearts and minds of all the people of God as they are dispersed to their duty stations in their workaday worlds. Jesus defined this as "salt" and "light" (Matt. 5:13-16). Paul called this "ambassadors for Christ," "ministers of reconciliation," and "living epistles" (2 Cor. 5:20, 18; 3:2-3). Peter used the terms "living stones," and "His own special people" (1 Peter 2:3, 9). Generally, the biblical term is *the laos,* meaning "all the people of God."

The premier interpreter of Southern Baptist traditions is Dr. Herschel Hobbs. It is his view that all the people of God (*the laos*) is composed of all who have believed in Jesus as Savior. He adds this pertinent comment:

> The devil won a great victory when he led Christians to distinguish between clergy and laity. This infers that the clergy should do the Lord's work, leaving the laity in the role of spectators.[4]

Even if Herschel Hobbs and Harry Dent should be wrong in this view, why would anyone want to continue under the present system?

Not only are most "saints" not equipped to do "the work of ministry," as set forth in Ephesians 4:12, but many do not really understand the Bible and major doctrines of the faith. I certainly did not as a church leader and teacher. Dr. George Gallup, Jr., accuses the church membership of today of being "superficial" in understanding and "superficial" in commitment. How can one be committed to something that is not understood?

Our travels in and out of so many churches have convinced us that Dr. Gallup is a most credible pollster of the reality in the church and in the world. Other findings by Gallup are equally true and disconcerting:

1. Americans are religious but not committed.
2. Americans revere the Bible but do not know it.[5]

The most discouraging finding by Dr. Gallup on church members was published in 1985. It reports:

> There is not much difference between church members and world members in understanding of the Bible or in behavior. What is needed in the church is not religious involvement, but DEEP SPIRITUAL COMMITMENT.[6]

Betty and I have concluded that the biggest problem in America is that many people have become numbed to real Christianity. They have been inoculated by the things of the world and the freedom to do as we please. What a difference it makes to get hold of the Real Thing!

God Helps Those Who Help Themselves, Doesn't He?

Most people in America believe in a heaven and a hell. And most all of them believe they are going to heaven instead of hell. Why? Because most people in the church believe that salvation is by good intentions and good works, just as I once believed and taught in Sunday school. They sent the right teaching from headquarters in Nashville—which is heaven to Southern Baptists, United Methodists, and a few other denominations—but I didn't believe it. I believed that I could bootstrap myself to heaven as I had to the White House.

George Barna's 1991 research is very revealing on this subject also. As to man's ability to determine his own destiny in life, even 79 percent of born-again Christians agree strongly or somewhat that they can bootstrap themselves to their destiny. In answer to the question of whether "God helps those who help themselves"—another of my former strong convictions—more "born-again" Christians vote yes than no. It was Benjamin Franklin, not God, who coined this saying.[7]

A special problem in the church is the stubborn belief that we are in control, not God, despite the Bible's clear teaching on grace and the sovereignty of God. More than half of the people in church are hooked on works salvation, the idea that we are saved, not by God's grace, but our works. We Americans tend to believe we can do anything through our freedom, prosperity, and power.

Bits and Pieces

We are convicted that people must grasp the big picture of whatever teaching subject is before them to fully comprehend the subject matter. One of the worst problems in the church is that people are being fed bits and pieces and Bible stories from here and there in Scripture without ever getting a presentation of the big picture of the whole Bible. One pastor calls these bits and pieces "snippets from the pulpit."

No one ever presented me with an overview of the whole Bible in any church. Betty gave me the opportunity to participate in *Walk Thru the Old Testament, Walk Thru the New Testament,* and *Walk Thru the Prophets* seminars under the teaching of Dr. Bruce Wilkinson. That is when I finally realized I did not really know the Bible.

Today Betty and I show and tell people the big picture of the whole Bible with approximately two thousand color overhead transparencies that have been conceived by us and crafted by a lay minister named Milton Powell. Walk Thru the Bible Ministries shows their students the times, dates, places, and people. We also put up the meat of the teachings of the Bible from Genesis to the Book of Revelation of Jesus Christ. The people in the pews need the times, dates, places, and people in the Bible and the essence of the major teachings as they unfold in the Bible.

The people in the pews need all the help they can get to better be able to receive the preaching, the teaching, and the discipleship training materials! Then people could be better prepared to study and interpret the Bible by reducing the tendency to take passages of Scripture out of the context of the Bible.

Importance of Study Bibles and Books

Every time Betty and I come across a new study Bible we rejoice that the folks in the pews have more explanations available to them in seeking to understand God's Word. I strongly recommend two study Bibles: *The New Open Bible* and *The Disciple's Study Bible*. Dr. Larry Richards, the author of more than one hundred Christian books, has *Richards' Complete Bible Handbook,* an *International Children's Bible Handbook,* a *Teacher's Commentary,* and *The Bible Reader's Companion.*[8] The more study tools that are made available to the people in the pews the better!

The Bible is not easily understood, and most people prefer light to heavy reading. We cannot absorb the teachings of the Bible by osmosis. The Holy Spirit is certainly our best helper and teacher, but we also need all the study guides because we learn the most when we see and the least by just listening. The problem with the listening system is that the minds of people wander, even in the brief time of a sermon. I remember my wanderings. I am so concerned for the need of biblical understanding that I use my color overhead transparencies to preach-teach revivals. The most frequent response is, "Thanks! For the first time in a revival I learned something because I saw the message as well as heard it."

After going through the *Walk Thru the Bible* series of courses, I visited the Baptist Bookstore in my city of Columbia, South Carolina. That began a study of the Bible that has never abated. I bought a whole set of Bible commentaries and other Bible study materials. For a quick study of the whole Bible, I also purchased the classic book by the late Dr. Henrietta Mears entitled *What the Bible Is All About*. I recommend books such as these because they open up explanations of the whole Bible to lay folks, as well as to pastors.

I have asked a number of pastors why they have never taken their people through the whole Bible. The most frequent response was "I couldn't do that." I realize the shortage of time, but what a difference this would make for the people in the pews who have never been to seminary. What a difference it would make in the pastor's preaching! Every time I write a book or take people through the Bible I am enriched in my understanding and in my teaching of the Bible.

"Pet Rock" Religion

One of the reasons why we have so many divisions in various churches and denominations is that people have a tendency to take "pet-rock" Scripture passages out of context and preach them or seek to live by them. This was at the heart of the disaster of Jim Bakker and his PTL scandal. He picked out various prosperity theology passages, especially from the Old Testament, and convinced his followers that Christianity was about materialism and the things of the world.

Jim Bakker is only one of a number of TV and church preachers who have twisted the Bible to their own end, with or without bad intentions. Some feed their listeners on a steady diet of American materialism, adding to the problem of worldliness in the church. Prosperity-type pastors are still preaching this message all over the air waves and around the world. And the news media are exposing them. It is incredible that *The Charlotte Observer* in Charlotte, North Carolina, brought Jim Bakker to justice instead of his own denomination. Church discipline appears to be a lost teaching of the Bible. As a consequence, many people may hear more perverted preaching than the

Real Thing if they are getting much of their preaching from the television screen. One exception to this rule is Dr. Charles Stanley of First Baptist Church in Atlanta, Georgia. More church members ask me about Dr. Stanley than any other preacher. He is all over America on TV and radio proclaiming the gospel without dilution or perversion.

In our study and interpretation of the Bible we are to focus on Jesus as the center of the big picture of the whole Bible. Jesus exemplified sacrifice, suffering, and servanthood. Teachings that promote the idea of prosperity theology foster increased addiction to the things of the world. Such preaching and teaching constitute an abomination to the life and teachings of Jesus Christ.

Non-Christians in America have been provided with too many excuses for passing up church attendance and/or membership because of the actions and/or the lack thereof by church members, leaders, pastors, and church hierarchy, whether in churches or in TV or radio broadcasting. Some do it with substantial understanding and unlimited gall and guile. Even worse, many people with good intentions are led to become a part of scams or charades, as happened with some of the followers of the Bakkers and some of the other prosperity theology hawkers.

Educate the Educators

B. P. Brooks, for many years the editor of the Southern Baptist Sunday school lessons, has been especially concerned about the uninformed Sunday school teachers. In his book, he says that they can do more damage to the understanding of Christianity than atheists.

> Twenty years of work with Sunday School teachers has driven me to conclude with James D. Smart that "the church school, after a century and a half of almost exclusive concentration on Bible study, cannot and does not claim to have produced a church that is capable of understanding and using the Bible."

He continues:

> Nothing is more difficult to find in a congregation than people who have an intelligent grasp of the Scriptures as a whole and a knowledge of how to get at their meaning, either for themselves or for anyone else. It is true that modern

church members have considerable knowledge of the Bible, but most of it is in bits and pieces. They do not know whole books of the Bible.[9]

Betty and Harry Dent sell only our books that show people the big picture of the whole Bible and the big picture of salvation. This constitutes our follow-up in church appearances. We keep the price low so more church members might become enticed to read a Christian book, in many cases, for the first time in their lives. Surveys show that fewer than 10 percent of church members ever go into a Christian bookstore. I did not do so until I was forty-eight. Now I am one of their best customers.

I once had a gentleman come up to me in a church and inform me that he only reads one book, the Holy Bible. I commended him for being an avid Bible student. Then I told him that I had discovered that God has anointed many good Christian writers to fully explain the key teachings of the Bible and that this had much better prepared me to teach the Bible.

It was through the study of the Bible and good books about the Bible that I made an all-out commitment to Jesus Christ as my Lord and Savior. Then I began teaching the Bible from cover-to-cover in nine months. The more I taught, the more I studied and the more my library of Christian books grew. Today my secular books are in the garage, and my Christian library consists of a few thousand volumes. I thank God every day for the post-graduate education He has provided for me in the Bible and Christian books, periodicals, and travels.

I advise people that a secular education, no matter how many degrees are earned, is limited without an education in God's perspective. My advice to young people preparing for any career is that they get at least one year of structured, in-depth study in the Holy Bible, as Charles Colson advised me in 1981.

I also recommend a continuing study through the use of many Christian books and publications. The ultimate aim is to be able to overlay man's perspective with God's perspective because I have found that giving God the right-of-way is in my own best interest. We all need supernatural wisdom and help!

Our ministry today is directed toward the "old Harry Dents" in the pews. I have discovered that they basically appear to be as weak and confused as I was with regard to the principal teachings of the Bible—the sin nature of humanity, repentance, salvation, righteousness, unconditional love, the ministry of all God's people, spiritual gifts, stewardship, the Holy Spirit, discipleship, how to witness, family life, holiness, the theology of suffering, prayer life, the Great Commandment, and Great Commission.

The Role of the Holy Spirit

Another weakness in the church is that many church members have never understood the operation and work of the Holy Spirit. That was also my problem for years as a church leader. Dr. Bill Bright of Campus Crusade for Christ says that more than 90 percent of the people in the church do not understand the operation and work of the Holy Spirit. He could be high but not very high!

In one church where I taught with my color overhead transparencies for several sessions I was confronted with this problem. When we had feedback time at the end, one of the older gentlemen arose to tell me that the group had never understood how one man could live in another man—"all this business about 'in Christ.'" They had missed the spiritual perspective. Ever since the time of the Enlightenment man has been trying to pull God down from supernatural to natural. The tendency is to see everything around us in terms of the natural rather than the supernatural. It took me many years to recognize that weakness in my understanding and experience or lack thereof.

The problem is not so much that God is so unseen. The larger difficulty is that the world has so many seen substitutes for the Real Thing that we have a marred sense of Right versus Wrong because of our enslavement to ourselves. As a consequence, we are taking too many of the ways of the world into the church, and we are spreading the virus of self-ism all over the church. Self-ism is akin to the disease of arteriosclerosis or hardening of the arteries. Our vulnerability is in the heart and mind of man. This was the same problem that shackled the first chosen people who were God's first channel of redemption. The Bible called this the "hardening of their hearts."

Good News and Bad News

For Christianity in America there is good news and bad news, according to George Barna. Christianity still has a relatively good name with the American public. For the local churches, however, there is bad news. Only about one-quarter of the American people strongly agree that Christian churches in their area are relevant to their needs. The further bad news is the churches get poor ratings for teaching, especially for our youngsters. The news gets even worse. Less than one-half of most committed church folks say their church performs primary duties with excellence. And, what's more, the preaching could stand some improving![10]

Barna's most important statistics highlight these concerns for the church:

- More than half of church members say they have not been "born again" as commanded by Jesus in John 3. Only 35 percent in America say they have been "born again."
- Millions of people who need to be reached for Christ are living in the U.S.A. So many want a deep relationship with God but not necessarily the church.
- People need to understand themselves as well as God.
- The missing link in America today is belief in real TRUTH. "To most Americans today nothing is a simple, black-and-white issue: everything is a shade of gray." Relativism reigns.
- America is too pragmatic, so pragmatism reigns also.
- Too few people believe in a sin nature of man or a real Satan. Thus, too many people do not know the enemy—even in churches.
- Too many people accept a "generic God," as universalism, which says that all are saved automatically, gains more credibility in America.
- Enjoyment of life is number one today.
- Distortion, misunderstanding, and lack of understanding about the Bible prevail.
- Too much time is spent searching for limited relationships rather than in-depth relationships.
- Superficiality also reigns.
- The more money and education we have the less we feel the need of God.[11]

But, hold onto your pews, there are some good tidings! There is a hungering for a deep relationship with God. The more brokenness in humanity, the more people will reach out for God. Fortunately and unfortunately, there appears to be much more brokenness on the way. *The Day America Told the Truth* reports that people are concerned for the future of America and many are willing to volunteer to help America recover her sea legs.

Inside the churches the fields are also "white unto harvest" as 52 percent of the people in the churches say they have never been born again.

What Are the Answers for the Church?

READ AND STUDY THE BIBLE AND GOOD CHRISTIAN BOOKS; BE PREPARED TO CHANGE METHODS BUT NOT THE GOSPEL.

Read and study the Bible and books about the Bible and Christianity and the church. For example, read George Barna's book, *User-Friendly Churches: What Christians Need to Know About the Churches People Love to Go To.* User-friendly churches are described as being churches that are in touch with the needs of those they want to serve. Each of these churches affirms the gospel of Christ boldly and without apology. But they are equally firm in their intent to listen to the audiences they target and to meet contemporary needs as the gospel directs.

Another good book on this subject is *10 of Today's Most Innovative Churches: What They're Doing, How They're Doing It & How You Can Apply Their Ideas in Your Church.*

The vast majority of Christian churches in the U.S.A. are holding where they are or slipping to where they do not want to be. This is true even in the Bible Belt. Relatively few of the three-hundred-thousand-plus Protestant churches are increasing their worshipers by 10 percent per year. But the real measure of a church is not so much growth in numbers as in spiritual maturity of the numbers on the church rolls. It is important to get people into the churches so that they may come to Christ, grow in Christ, and then begin to go for Christ.

Generally speaking, the church plays a numbers game of how many baptisms, how big and beautiful are the buildings, and how big is the budget. When the people who are baptized into membership in the body of Christ really get to know the Bible, are discipled, and then sold on their duty for personal ministry, the numbers really begin to work. There will be many baptisms, more space will be required—or preferably, more churches will be planted—and more funds will be available for missions to the spiritually lost, to "the least of these," and to properly educate and train the troops for their personal ministries.

The logo of every church should read Saved to Serve or The Purpose of Life Is to Serve God. Too many people have been led to believe that the purpose of the church is just to get church members to a front-row seat in heaven and to bind up their own wounds. These are on the list of goals of the church, but there are other vital purposes of the church. Most succinctly the mission is to be found in the composite picture of the five versions of the Great Commission coupled with the Great Commandment.

"Brother Ralph" Neighbour, as he is affectionately known, has written several books on what's Wrong in the church and how it can be made Right in the church. One particularly helpful book is *Future Church*. Neighbour compiled the book, and it has several noted Christian authors such as Ray Stedman, Larry Richards, Os Guinness, Jack Taylor, Roy Edgemon, and John Newport. (Another helpful one is *The Shepherd's Guidebook.*)

Future Church is my kind of book because the various authors espouse and advance Christian actions and ideas that best fit the Master Plan of the Bible. The average church is pictured in this book as having no spiritual power; the future church is described as being Spirit-filled. Step one in the future church is to make the Holy Spirit the president of the church, rather than the pastor, lay leaders, or founding families. Step two is to make certain that the pastors are real servants and that the people understand that they too are to be servants and not lords.

Communicate with Relevance and Reality

The church is in need of more effective methods of communicating its purpose and message. George Barna's books are very helpful here. So are two books by James Engel, *What's Gone Wrong with the Harvest* (with Wilbert Norton) and *Contemporary Christian Communications: Its Theory and Practice.* Dr. Engel sees the cutting edge of the church as having become duller in recent years. He believes that Christians must apply basic principles of communication to their evangelism. He is the one who coined the now popular phrase "meeting their felt needs." He advocates that we find out where people are itching and scratch it for them. Above all, he says, avoid abstract principles and make use of concrete felt-need communications. By all means, do not ignore human needs!

Dr. Engel is a very realistic Christian leader. Here is how he sees the prevailing belief systems in the world today.

- God, if He exists at all, is just an impersonal moral force.
- Man basically has the capacity within himself to improve morally and make the right choices.
- Happiness consists of unlimited material acquisition.
- There really is no objective basis for Right and Wrong.
- The supernatural is just a figment of someone's imagination.
- If a person lives a "good life," then eternal destiny is assured.
- The Bible is nothing other than a book written by man.[12]

These concerns of Dr. Engel are basically affirmed by the research found in other books I have cited in this book.

Teach 'Em and Train 'Em: Application and Discipleship

Follow-up, follow-through, and application are big missing links in the implementation of God's Master Plan on earth. Crusades must do more to ensure real follow-up with their converts. Immediately after any revival or renewal, there must be a plan implemented to get the people into small groups and begin discipleship programs. The whole purpose of discipleship is to bring people to a point of spiritual maturity through the development of the fruit of the Holy Spirit. This adds up to holiness and righteousness in character, like that of God the Father and as exemplified in the life of Jesus the Christ. This means growing up spiritually in Christ.

Spiritual growth dictates change for individual Christians working together with the Holy Spirit and in fellowship with one another in the church. One of the best books on this subject is by Dr. J. Oswald Sanders. It is entitled *Spiritual Maturity*. Dr. Sanders maintains that God puts us down to lift us up and that where there is no cross there is no crown. Today I believe the truth of these statements. It is difficult for the world to understand that losing can mean winning, but this is required to bring stubborn man into the presence of God. If man can do it on his own, man will do it on his own.[13]

Dr. Sanders says that God's three purposes for His disciplines are to cultivate the soul with Christ-like character, to provide spiritual food for others, and to prepare for living in eternity with God. The key to God's Master Plan is the holiness, righteousness, and spiritual maturity of God's called saints.

The aim is not merely to become "holy" and think "holy thoughts." Spiritual growth or sanctification is the route to knowing and enjoying a deep personal relationship with God. Public opinion polls reveal this to be a top concern for many Americans, in and outside of the church. Spiritual growth blows out the soot in our hearts and lives, thrashing away the weeds and thickets that Satan plants to block our personal relationship with God.

The Apostle Paul placed sanctification at the top of the list regarding God's will.

> Finally, then, brethren, we urge and exhort in the Lord Jesus that you should abound more and more, just as you received from us how you ought to walk and to please God; for you know what commandments we gave you through the Lord Jesus. For this is the will of God, your sanctification (1 Thess. 4:1-3).

In the remainder of the first 12 verses of 1 Thessalonians 4, Paul calls us to three paramount commitments: (1) holiness, sanctified; (2) loving spiritual fellowship; and (3) honor, ethics, or moral integrity so that willful and habitual sin is broken in our lives.

There will be no growth toward spiritual maturity without follow-up and discipleship. And there will be no real Christian witness, ministry, and evangelism without the requisite changes. Spiritual transformation is an absolute necessity in the Christian life.

Verse 1 of Romans 12 calls for total commitment to Jesus Christ as a "living sacrifice." Verse 2 demands that the church member not be transformed by the ways of the world but rather that the member should become a part of the solution of the problem in the world. The remainder of Romans 12 commands us to discover and develop and deploy our gifts for ministry and to convert our beliefs to behavior. How do we do this? By loving God and our fellowman unconditionally.

Ephesians 4 is one of the most vital chapters in all of the Bible. It drives home the ultimate end of Scripture and God's Master Plan, the ministry of all 100 percent of God's people. In verses 11-16 of Chapter 4, Paul summarizes the overall message of the Bible and thus the mission of the church:

And He Himself gave some to be apostles, some prophets, some evangelists, and some pastors and teachers, for the equipping of the saints for the work of ministry, for the edifying of the body of Christ, till we all come to the unity of the faith and the knowledge of the Son of God, to a perfect man, to the measure of the stature of the fullness of Christ; that we should no longer be children, tossed to and fro and carried about with every wind of doctrine, by the trickery of men, in the cunning craftiness by which they lie in wait to deceive, but, speaking the truth in love, may grow up in all things into Him who is the head—Christ—from whom the whole body, joined and knit together by what every joint supplies, according to the effective working by which every part does its share, causes growth of the body for the edifying of itself in love.

God has provided many spiritual blessings to various churches and denominations. One of the best was the call of Dr. Avery Willis, Jr., to return from the mission field in Indonesia to become involved with Dr. Roy Edgemon and Dr. Howard Foshee of the Southern Baptist Sunday School Board in Nashville. In a dozen years they have turned out more than a dozen discipleship courses. The first and most-used is *MasterLife*. This six-month small group discipleship program has now been planted around the world and translated into thirty-five languages. Wherever Betty and I minister and find that *MasterLife* has been used we see a vital difference in the spiritual life and maturity of the discipled saints.[14]

There are many other good discipleship programs, such as the Navigators' *Colossians 2:7* course. It covers two years of intensive discipleship.

Pastor James Goforth of First Baptist Church in Rusk, Texas, had Betty and me help him launch *MasterBuilder*[15] as a follow-up after almost every member in the church completed the *MasterLife* course. He had most of the membership present for this course also. Why? Because Goforth was saved in going through the *MasterLife* course after he was a pastor.

While *Masterlife, Colossians 2:7,* and other discipleship courses are having good impact where they are being utilized, the Twelve Steps is the most effective and widely used discipleship program. This is the key to the success of Alcoholics Anonymous and now for many other fellowships patterned on the AA mode. The Twelve Steps come right out of the Holy Bible on motion of the late Dr. Sam M. Shoe-maker, one of the most noted and effective parish priests in the history of the Episcopal church.

Back in 1935 one reformed drunk took another drunk friend of his to Sam's church, Calvary Episcopal Church in Manhattan, New York. Ebby Thatcher had found sanity and sobriety in visiting with the Oxford Group at Sam's church, and Bill Wilson found sobriety through the witness of Ebby Thatcher, who told him the formula he had found in Shoemaker's Oxford Group: "Realize you are licked, admit it, and get willing to turn your life over to the care of God."[16]

The Oxford Movement was initiated by an American Lutheran clergyman, Frank Buchman. This movement had a strong evangelical identity in those days. Bill Wilson developed a fellowship of alcoholics dedicated to helping one another stay sober through a spiritual program. He drew on the teachings of the Oxford Group but set AA's goal as sobriety, not necessarily Jesus Christ. The idea was to reach beyond Christianity to people of all kinds of persuasions.

Christian author and psychiatrist, Dr. M. Scott Peck, calls the founding of AA "the greatest event of the twentieth century." In the fifty-six years since, AA membership has grown from two individuals to nearly two million. AA's Twelve Steps, which owe nothing to modern psychology or medicine, are embraced by courts, hospitals and a large number of addictive disorders, from sexual addiction to overeating.[17]

AA now reaches into most of the countries of the world. AA leaders indicate that when persons complete the Twelve-Step program the vast majority remain sober. Those who drop out along the way are very likely to fall back into alcoholism. This discipleship type of program actually works! And it works out there in the world, outside of churches, as well as in churches. Thousands and thousands of people are sober today because of an Episcopal parish priest named Sam Shoemaker and a Lutheran pastor named Frank Buchman. And most of these sober alcoholics are committed Christians, probably more highly committed than most church members.

An AA member will, by and large, be much more responsive to the hurts and needs of fellow alcoholics and anyone else than most deacons, stewards, or elders in churches. The AA member will travel a long distance to keep a buddy from sinking into the bottle again. God bless Alcoholics Anonymous! May we in the church of Jesus Christ rise to their standard of discipleship, fellowship, love, and service to hurting mankind!

One of Christianity's most popular writers and video teachers, J. Keith Miller, is now a principal advocate of AA and the Twelve Steps. He has written three books on the subject of alcoholism, the Twelve Steps, and recovery from addiction to sin, alcohol, and other ways of the world. His latest book is entitled *A Hunger for Healing: The Twelve Steps as a Classic Model for Christian Spiritual Growth.*

Miller fell to alcohol and found in his recovery program an extra dimension to his faith. The first post-alcohol book he wrote is entitled *Sin: Overcoming the Ultimate Deadly Addiction.* This *Sin* book is one of the best books on the subject of the sin nature of man. (His publishers have since changed the name of the book because of the unpopularity of the title. I still prefer the old title, but I do want to see this book sell. The new title is: *Hope in the Fast Lane.*)

In this book Miller points up the two characteristics of what he calls the sin disease. They are deniai and delusion. Denial leads to delusion, and delusion results in unreality and thus irresponsibility. Miller sees sin as being the matrix or seedbed out of which all addictive behaviors arise. Previously Miller had not been emphasizing the original sin nature of man in his very popular Christian writings and videos.[18]

The "new" Miller is now establishing the Twelve-Step program in churches, not for alcoholics but for the people in the pews.

> My experience in Twelve-Step groups has convinced me that God has provided a way of spiritual healing and growth that may well be the most important spiritual model of any age for contemporary Christians. I wrote this book because I have found more self-worth in God, more serenity than I have ever known, and a way to deal specifically with the personal problems that have kept me anxious and afraid all my life. I sense that there are many other Christians who know their lives and relationships are in trouble but don't know how to change. . . .
>
> I believe the Twelve Steps offer a discipline that is thoroughly of and for today. Millions of people find that working these steps frees them from compulsion and creates serenity, peace, joy, and healthier relationships with God and others. And, significantly, the program produces people who reach out to others in pain.[19]

Keith Miller has my highest admiration. Since reading his books and also AA's "Big Book," *Alcoholics Anonymous,* and the Twelve

Steps, I am telling people in churches that all church members should become involved in the Twelve Steps for healing and growth. I recommend *MasterLife* as the first study so that the commitment is truly to Jesus Christ.

So what is the teaching? Get with Jesus' program of discipleship! Jesus did not spend His time wowing big crowds by pounding pulpits. In fact they ran Him out of His hometown and beat Him when He first tried that approach. Jesus called people to follow Him, and He poured His life into the lives of twelve men for the entirety of His ministry. The Master Himself proved the value of "each one teach one." It works, when we get with Jesus' program!

Preach, Teach, and Deploy All the People of God in Ministry

Dr. Hans Kung, maverick Catholic theologian, is a strong proponent of the ministry of all of God's people. In one of his most respected works, *The Church,* Kung makes this point:

> All the faithful belong to the people of God; there must be no *clericalization* of the Church. . . . Everyone belongs to the chosen race, the royal priesthood, the holy nation. All members of the people of God have been called by God, justified by Christ, sanctified by the Holy Spirit. All members are equal in this.[20]

The teaching here is the ministry of all of God's people, the whole of the church of Jesus Christ. That is the way it was in the Jerusalem church. Deacons were selected in Acts 6 to help the apostles to devote their full time to preaching the Good News. Then in Acts 8:4 we read, "Therefore those who were scattered went everywhere preaching the word."

The message all the way through the Bible is keyed to the use of all of God's people in ministry wherever they have their being—in their homes, churches, workplaces, athletic contests, wherever! It is not so much that people are to stop other people on the streets and talk to them about Jesus Christ. For some this may be the way to do it. But for most, witnessing for Jesus is more like showing people the Christian character and life and answering questions or praying with or for people.

Ministry and witness are much the same because they both mean working for Jesus and helping people. Ministry usually means touching, helping, serving, loving people. How? By using the gifts and strengths that God has provided for our lives. There is one fruit of the Spirit: love, God's kind of love. There are several facets of that basic fruit called love. Here is how the character grows in the life of Christians:

Love produces Joy;
Joy produces Peace;
Peace produces Patience;
Patience produces Kindness;
Kindness produces Goodness;
Goodness produces Faithfulness;
Faithfulness produces Gentleness;
Gentleness produces Self-Control.[21]

Self-control means we can now begin to get our behavior and conduct under proper control so that we no longer sin habitually but obey habitually. This is what Christian growth is about.

The Bible lists about twenty spiritual gifts. But these can be extrapolated into the thousands of strengths that can be discovered, developed, and deployed in ministry and witness. For instance, one is the gift of love, the key gift and key fruit. There is no higher calling than to love people unconditionally. This is what people need and want more than anything life has to offer. And out of love can flow so many other services we can render to people.

As we use our spiritual gifts to help others, we can also tell them why we minister. Everyone should have a testimony! The spiritual book I recommend is *Mirror, Mirror on the Wall* by Dr. Ken Hemphill.

Love is the apex of the Christian life. The people must experience God's kind of love in the life of the pastor and staff, the lay leadership, and the world should see and experience God's love in all the people who call themselves "Christ-i-ans." Nothing should precede "the greatest of these." A church will not work Right without this wonderful contagion being a reality in the lives of God's people. Gimmicks and games may get people inside, but gimmicks and games will not change people from the inside out.

Give People the Big Picture of the Bible

The churches are going to have to quit confusing people by adding to all the mixed-up gumbo of Bible preaching and teaching. Satan rejoices as long as the people in the pews are continually fed bits and pieces and jots and tittles. Let 'em fight over the jots and tittles, but for the sake of Satan, please never let them ever get a glimpse of the warp and woof of the whole of God's Word. In particular, do not let the "cat of lay ministry" out of the bag! This way the churches will continue to go around and around in circles like a dog chasing its tail.

Remember What Jesus Called "The Least of These"

Jesus set us up for the final exam when He admonished us, "But what have you done for the least of these?"

> Then He will also say to those on the left hand, "Depart from Me, you cursed, into the everlasting fire prepared for the devil and his angels: for I was hungry and you gave Me no food; I was thirsty and you gave Me no drink; I was a stranger and you did not take Me in, naked and you did not clothe Me, sick and in prison and you did not visit Me" (Matt. 25:41–43).

It is amazing how God works. I did not fully comprehend this until I listened to a friend who I helped to get speaking in Christian ministry. Bob McAlister, the chief of staff to the governor of South Carolina, has a special ministry to "the least of these." He works death row in Columbia, South Carolina. He is particularly noted for being used to bring the late Rusty Woomer to salvation several years ago. Rusty was one of the most-hated men on death row in South Carolina. But Bob discipled him, and when Rusty went to the chair he was clutching a big Bible and expressing joy at going to be with Jesus and Momma. Rusty had killed four people while on a drug rampage.

Bob's boss, the governor, did not grant clemency, but Bob's other Boss pardoned Rusty one evening when Bob reached through the bars of Rusty's death-row cell to lead him to Jesus Christ. This was the most publicized execution in the history of South Carolina, and Jesus Christ was honored in the ministry of Bob McAlister, the governor's right-hand man. Governor Carroll A. Campbell, Jr., commended his aide for standing by his man.

One of the strongest lay witnesses in America is Governor John Ashcroft of Missouri. He proves that a politician can be a real man of God and win as a bold speaker and witness for Jesus Christ.

The Texas Baptist Men, led by Bob Dixon, are among the best lay ministers in America. When emergencies arise, here or overseas,

Bob rounds up the necessary men to provide emergency assistance. They are equipped with cooking and feeding vans and all of the necessary gear to assist in times of hurricanes, floods, or whatever the tragedy is. In addition they are much involved in lay renewals in addition to their ministry evangelism chores.

Lay or personal ministry can be accomplished anywhere—in politics, the marketplace, the home, and wherever people are hurting.

CHAPTER FIVE

The Church's Player-Coach: The Pastor-Teacher

I would have far more fear of being mistaken, and of finding that the Christian religion is true, than of not being mistaken and believing it true.

Blaise Pascal[1]

There is no higher calling in this world than the role of being a shepherd of a flock of God's people in the universal church of Jesus Christ. Being a bishop, an associational director, or superintendent, a seminary professor, or any other full-time Christian position is not the same. Pastors hold that hallowed responsibility to feed the flock. It is the most vital work in the church in implementing God's Master Plan.

This is also becoming the most difficult job, based on what Betty and I have experienced in our ministry. Today the average pastor-teacher seems to have less authority, respect, joy, or job security than ever before. Dr. James Dobson's *Focus on the Family* ministry documents the modern-day perils of pastoring. Dobson's assistant, Rev. H. B. London, Jr., reported in a 1992 study that a majority of American pastors are suffering spiritual burnout. He says that a large percentage have considered quitting the ministry.

London's findings show that pastors are living an unbalanced life and often have no one with whom to share personal struggles. Handling problems with their own teenage children becomes a major tribulation.[2]

One of the foremost pastors to pastors, Dr. Lyle E. Schaller, caught the attention of the pastor world with his 1987 book *It's a Different World!: The Challenge for Today's Pastor*.[3] He affirmed what most pastors had already concluded: that being in that pulpit requires much more patience, prayer, and persistence than ever before. Indeed, there continues to be a decline in interest by college students in church-related vocations (even in Christian institutions), especially for the pastoral vocation.

The average pastor once had more support from the families in his church. He also had an increased awareness of God prevalent in the schools and communities. There are several key changes that so adversely affect the work of the pastor and the church. Most of these are conclusions which Betty and I have drawn. Some are derived from our interpretation of Dr. Schaller's points in chapter one of his insightful book.

1. The dissolution of the family.
2. The elimination of God from the schools.
3. The increase in diversity and in pluralism.
4. Higher standards for the pastor, especially with the advent of the charismatic personality and preaching of the TV preachers.
5. The increase in counseling necessitated by the rise in the brokenness of people in the church and community. Pastors could spend all their time here.
6. Working pastor-wives and member-wives.
7. Increased pulpit-jumping and pulpit-ejecting.
8. Competition among churches for membership and the emphasis on numbers.
9. The mobility of members.
10. Decline in membership in major denominations.
11. Divisions in the church over the truth, authority, and interpretation of the Bible.
12. The shift in percentage of church membership to women and senior citizens, and the decline in youth and men.
13. The pull and tug of the ways of the world on the families in the pews and the families in the pulpits.
14. The emphasis on the study of theology and theologians over in-depth teaching and study of the Bible in too many seminaries.
15. Limited attention to spiritual formation in the life of too many seminary students.
16. The overemphasis on pastor performance in so many areas that the average pastor must be the jack-of-all-trades.
17. The notion that the church is to serve the people in the pews rather than the people serving in the mission of the church.

18. The low level of biblical knowledge and spiritual strength, thus the limited commitment of so many people in the pews.
19. The large diversity of views on subjects and behaviors in the pews which compels the pastor to feel he has to preach his way through a mine field on every ascent to the pulpit.
20. The construction of so many church edifices on credit and the consequential expectation of the pastor to be the minister of finance.

People Don't Know Right from Wrong

The principal problem for the pastor-teacher today consists of the vast changes in American thinking about Right versus Wrong and the escalating dash to enjoyment of materialism (which in turn leads to commitment to the ways of the world as the main aim in life). This is the foremost danger facing America and the church. People are racing through life and seeing everything in the fuzzy, gray perspective, not black and white or Right and Wrong. For them, the meaning of life is personal enjoyment and success.

Even pastor-teachers and lay people who say they are "born-again" Christians are falling for some of the lures of the "isms" of the world. This is why people in the pulpits are also falling into sin-traps, especially regarding sexual immorality and destruction of their vocations and families. The distance between moral failures in pulpits and the pews is narrowing too much. All church members, especially pastors and born-again Christians, must remember we are always being watched as witnesses for Right or Wrong. We are to be stepping-stones rather than stumbling blocks.

Doubt and Division

Doubt and division plague the church as much as any other problem. Why? Because of relative beliefs about the Bible and divisive views about belief in the Bible. There are clearly two basic views of the Scriptures: those who place much stock in the veracity of God's Word, whether line by line or as a whole, and those who have less confidence in the truth of Scripture on some teachings. Some people refer to this as a difference in personal interpretation of Scriptures.

There have been many battles over this subject with much local and national publicity. Many people inside the church are not certain where they stand on questions raised in these arguments because they do not know enough theology to have a position. There are even more people in the world who only know that Christians are fighting, and they have a vague notion that Christians are supposed to be ministering instead of fighting.

Sometimes the fighting appears to be so un-Christian that the battles become witnesses *against* Christianity. In some instances, where the very liberal view prevails, there is a diminution in the strength and influence of the church, as in Western Europe. Church participation and spiritual impact have dropped markedly in this century in Western Europe. The spiritual emphasis has been clouded or lost in the great institutions of higher learning originally established in the name of Christianity to foster that particular faith. Examples are Harvard University and the University of Chicago, among others. Such institutions are now paragons of relativism.

The more conservative churches and pastors must be concerned about the possibility of authoritarianism and legalism. "Legalism" is holding people to live by the jots and tittles of Scripture as interpreted by humans rather than the law of love. Jesus was especially concerned about the pharisaic legalists of His day.

Good-bye to God in Holland

Betty and I participated in Billy Graham's Amsterdam '86 training conference for several thousand itinerant evangelists. This was one of the best works for which our Lord has used Dr. Graham and his team. In attendance were so-called barefoot itinerant evangelists from the jungles and other far corners of the world, as well as "well-shod" itinerant evangelists.

During our time there, we toured the countryside of Holland with Billy Graham's first cousin, Rev. Ed Graham, a Presbyterian pastor in Asheville, North Carolina, and his wife, Gail. As we approached towns and villages the tour guide pointed out the high-rising steeples and commented that the buildings were no longer being used as churches. Some had been converted into museums, community centers, or tourist attractions.

In Amsterdam we found that there was no one place known as the "red light" district; the whole city seemed to constitute the "red light" district. Amsterdam is the pornography capital of the world today. It also ranks among the busiest drug capitals in the world. Unfortunately, America has made big strides to surpass that achievement in these past six years.

My thoughts reflected on my grammar school studies of the

clean little Dutch towns and villages. I could remember pictures of boys and girls wearing their wooden shoes and walking among the beautiful tulips and quaint windmills. God used to have a good influence in that area of the world. Now it appears that the Spirit of God may have departed from this once-vibrant bastion of Christianity.

The dilution of spiritual faith and fervor that has occurred in Western Europe is a direct consequence of the advent of German theology, where biblical criticism has been carried to excess. Former theology students have had their hearts and minds ravaged by theological debate. They then stepped into their pulpits with little faith, limited messages, and a plague of doubts. Yet the dear saints who have suffered from religious persecution behind the old Iron Curtain are ablaze with their faith and fervor for Jesus Christ. What a contrast!

The Bible Answers the Big Questions of Life

There are people teaching and/or preaching out of the Bible, but they do not accept the first eleven chapters of the Book of Genesis. If their students or parishioners do not come to understand the first three chapters of Genesis they will never comprehend the message in the remainder of the Bible. In the first two chapters God explains how and why He created us as humans. In the third chapter He shows us what is wrong with us. The rest of the Bible progressively reveals to us God's rescue plan (salvation) to bring us back to God's plan for us to be lovers, servants, and stewards of righteousness over all the rest of God's creation. The three most important questions in life are these:

What is the meaning and purpose of life?
What is wrong with me?
And how can I be made whole so I can live
in right relationships here and in eternity?

We don't just *believe* the Bible has the answers to these most critical questions. We *know* the Bible has the only answers to life on earth and in eternity. If I had doubts, I would return to the practice of man's law and politics and build a retirement program for us. The idea that the Bible contains truth but is not truth reduces it to the reliability and worth of any other book. Most books contain some snippets of truth. The Bible and Creation are our most tangible evidences of the reality of God, and the Bible is our number one book of moral absolutes.

We must and do have one standard book chock full of moral absolutes to which we can repair in this new age of moral ambivalence and uncertainty. Today is the time to exalt and not fault the Holy Book that God has bequeathed to us for our final understanding of what is Right and what is Wrong.

The essence of the problem of the dilution of biblical teaching was best set forth by an Australian news columnist in April 1989 while we were ministering there.

Within each leading denomination there are now, for all intents and purposes, two "Churches" in the sense that there are two sets of people, claiming to belong to the same denomination, who have nevertheless distinct and different belief systems. One Church may usefully be described as the Church of doctrine. The other sees itself as the Church of compassion.

The Church of doctrine . . . believes that the Christian faith is about the personal acceptance of Christ as God and of the truths He revealed as of divine origin.

The second Church . . . is composed of those who believe that the essential purpose of the Christian faith is not so much to proclaim the doctrines of Christ as to manifest, and be seen to manifest, His compassion towards other human beings. Its devotees rarely deny the basic doctrines of the faith. They simply refrain from asserting them, especially those that they find unpalatable.

Christianity succeeded in the first centuries because those converted to it were prepared to die for it. What they were prepared to die for was not a reformist political program—these are a dime a dozen—that treated the world as if it was the only reality, but for a set of absolute truths, belief in which might bring little with it in this world, but would one day open the gates of paradise.[4]

Dr. Denton Lotz, secretary general of the Baptist World Alliance, addressed this subject most eloquently in the H. I. Hester Lectures of 1987 before the annual meeting of the Association of Southern Baptist Colleges and Schools in Kansas City, Missouri. He spent fifteen years serving as a Baptist missionary in Eastern Europe in the days of religious persecution.

In the twentieth century we (Western Christianity) have lost the intellectuals and have the peasants. The consequences of this spell a dreary future for the Christian faith, if we cannot reverse it! Basically America's intelligentsia have rejected the Christian faith.

Now the Christian educator and Christian college, living in this culture, must rediscover and reassert the purpose of Christian higher education. . . . We are in fact, living in a neo-pagan society. . . . It is the task of Christian higher education to prepare the groundwork for the conversion of this neo-pagan society. . . .

The question remains. Can the West be converted? The answer is yes if Christian colleges regain the vision of the unity of all things in Jesus Christ as the universal center around whom and in whom all truth confides.

Conversion is the call of Christ to every generation of men and women. It is a call to the Christian college to teach young people the mystery of God's grace beyond the truth of science, beyond cause and effect, to show that mystery revealed in Jesus Christ in whom the final purpose of history shall be revealed.[5]

I have come to understand this controversy causing so many problems within the bounds of the Christian faith. The best way to eliminate this controversy is for both "churches" to come together in united belief in Jesus Christ as Lord and Savior and to make certain that His compassion is the key mark of this unified faith.

When I began my search for "the Real Thing" fifteen years ago, I was most impressed with the message in a book by a liberal Methodist minister in a liberal organization, the National Council of Churches. The book is entitled *Why Conservative Churches Are Growing*, by Dean Kelley. I was in a very liberal church that was not working well. This book explained "the why" to me.

Kelley said that the conservative churches tend to provide answers to the first concern of church members: "the purpose, promise, and possibility" in "the human predicament." He called this religion's "distinctive and indispensable service: making sense of life." If a church is focused solely on social programs, then even as worthy and necessary as the work of compassion is, the church will still be missing the first concern of the people sitting in the pews.[6]

Dr. George Gallup, Jr., has consistently stated what people want to know and need to know: God, why did you create me? What is the meaning and purpose of life?[7]

Both questions are vital to the work of the church: belief in the teachings of the Bible and compassionate work among hurting and disadvantaged people. Jesus was very specific about His concern for what He called "the least of these." Jesus pictured our concern for and ministry to them as being equal to our concern for and ministry to Him. Some call this passage of Scripture in Matthew 25 the final exam before we check out of planet Earth.

This is how Jesus expressed His concern:

> "Then He will also say to those on the left hand, 'Depart from Me, you cursed, into the everlasting fire prepared for the devil and his angels: for I was hungry and you gave Me no food; I was thirsty and you gave Me no drink; I was a stranger and you did not take Me in, naked and you did not clothe Me, sick and in prison and you did not visit Me'" (Matt. 25:41–43).

Needed: Real Faith and Real Compassion

What is needed is real faith and real compassion, both demonstrated in word and deed. What a shame it is that we Christians cannot present a unified presence to the lost world! This was the final plea of Jesus Christ before He went to the cross. He prayed to His Father in heaven that the church would be unified and in love with one another. Unity and love is what Jesus saw as being the key to the world coming to the church in full faith.

All the people in the church bear the responsibility to bring about this kind of harmony and unity, but none more than God's shepherds of His flocks.

I had the opportunity to become ordained and to take on the role of pastor-teacher. It would have provided income, some form of a retirement program, and a big church near our home. However, it did not take five minutes for me to say no. Why? Because my call to ride the circuits has been so compelling. Besides, I hit and run; the pastors have to hit and stay and then face the music.

After I turned down the opportunity to be a pastor, Betty and I mused over the question of what we would do if I should become a pastor-teacher. We decided that we would make what the U.S. Army calls "an estimate of the situation." This means riding around the walls of the church body, the people of God, and making a realistic estimate of the state of the spiritual health of the church body: what appears to be Right and what appears to be Wrong; what needs to be fixed and what needs to be left alone. This was the first order of business for Governor Nehemiah when he returned to Judah to rebuild the walls of the city of Jerusalem. He checked the broken walls before seeking to rebuild them.

What Would We Do in Their Place?

If I were called to be a pastor-teacher, the first thing I would do would be to visit every family in the church at their home (with the whole family present) as soon as possible. We would let the family know that we are convinced that God had called us—Betty and I—to this vital role in His Master Plan. We would not take the call unless it were from God.

- We would set forth the role and duties of the pastor-teacher and his mate.
- We would pledge unconditional love for this family and every family in the church and in reasonable access to us. When the church would begin to get too large for them to access us, we would lead the church in planting another church as a prime ministry of this church.
- We would pledge to resist ego trips on our part and request prompting on such a problem whenever this would become evident. Thus we would not give significance to the three Bs: body counts, budgets, and buildings. Our concern would be the development of the spiritual life of each church member and the ultimate ministry of all church members. This would be our stated and real goal. Thus, we would either be interested in planting a church or getting a new and smaller church.
- We would make our visit when the entire family could be present, so that each of them would realize that our concern and ministry would be for the benefit of each one of them. We would explain that we could not permit one person or family to dominate our time. In regard to counseling, we would explain that we are not the experts, but that we would do limited counseling and make recommendations on expert counseling. Above all, there would be no man-to-woman or woman-to-man private counseling. Betty would be better than I in counseling.
- We would set forth the plan of salvation and God's mission

for the church in God's Master Plan. We would ask if any member of the family had any question about their salvation or their willingness to be active in the implementation of God's plan for this church. We would answer the questions and deal with the need for salvation, or whatever, at that time. We would provide a book on this subject for every family.

• We would have a questionnaire for all to answer to see how they could help in the implementation of the role of the church according to their time, gifts, and desires. Their suggestions would be welcomed on the form.

• Finally, they would be asked to consider any broken relationships that existed between any of them and anyone else in the church and to pledge to seek to resolve the problems in prayer and love.

Our Guidelines

Betty and I also formulated the list of guidelines that we would seek to follow in leading the church body.

• First and foremost: The people must know that the pastor-teacher and his wife love the Lord unconditionally and every church member and family member the same way. This would be our first requisite, and we would hold each other accountable to this commitment. If I got off the mark (and I would be the problem one here) Betty would prompt me, as she is always willing to do. I would not have to worry about Betty—this is her strong suit. However, I would also serve as her prompter. We are very straightforward with each other these days and are the closest we've ever been.

• The people must be able to discern Jesus Christ alive in the life of their pastor-teacher and his mate. The two must be "one in Christ." Thus, both must be open and vulnerable before God and His people. We know this would not be easy, but it would be our aim. If we have concerns about problems, we should seek to face and resolve them in the right way without permitting them to fester and erupt. Again, Betty is an expert in this area of ministry.

• The pastor-teacher and his mate must know that they have been called by God, not by Mom or anyone else, to be a pastor-teacher and help-mate.

- The pastor-teacher must be a teacher as well as a preacher of God's Word and God's will. He must realize that preaching is not everything and that, indeed, it can turn the pulpit into an ego pit. Beware of the addiction to preaching for the unwitting purpose of building up the ego of the pastor-teacher at the expense of edifying and equipping the saints to do the work of ministry in their homes, churches, and workplaces. Indeed, Ephesians 4:11–16 would be on the church bulletin week after week to remind the pastor and pews of the purpose of the church. Above the name and title of the pastor-teacher would be the title of the people. Ministers: All the People of this Church.

- The pastor-teacher must be a prayer-warrior and known as such. People need to know their pastor-teacher is praying for them. That is the right thing to do.

- The pastor-teacher must never forget where he was spiritually before he was saved and how little he understood the Bible, the mission of the church, and the work of the Holy Spirit. I reflect on this vast gulf every day. When pastors do this it will be so easy to remember that the "kiss" (Keep it simple, stupid!) principle is vital, especially in preaching and teaching.

- The pastor-teacher must be interested in more than just bringing people down the aisle; he must also be interested in bringing them into a follow-up program of discipleship training and Bible study. The pastor-teacher must be the prime equipper of the saints. The ultimate purpose of the people of God is to possess the righteous character of Jesus Christ (the fruit of the Holy Spirit) and to know, develop, and deploy their spiritual gifts in ministry and witness as stewards of righteousness.

- The pastor-teacher must make certain that the people have a strategic grasp of the big picture of the whole *Bible* so they can relate the pieces to the whole and the whole back to the pieces, then they can make appropriate applications to their own lives. His people must be able to keep everything within the context of Jesus: His death, resurrection, ministry, and unconditional and everlasting love. Jesus as the pre-eminent lover and servant for the glory of God and the good of all of *humankind.* They are to center on Jesus and not the building, the church, doctrine, or the pastor-teacher. The people should understand that our faith has

the name of "Christianity" because it is about the life and
teachings of Jesus the Christ.

• The pastor-teacher should have periodic clinics on how to
study, understand, and apply the Bible. Very few churches
do anything like this. Lay people do not have the background or understanding of the Bible that the pastor should
have. They need to be acquainted with study Bibles, commentaries, concordances, and other study aids as well as
know how to systematically study the Bible and make applications of its teachings to their lives.

• The pastor-teacher must be well read in the Scriptures and
in current events. He should be steeped in his understanding of and belief in the Bible. His major study should be the
Bible. Being able to preach to current events and moral
conditions enables the people to better assimilate and apply
the teachings in the preaching message.

• The pastor-teacher must be the true spiritual leader and
role model in his own family. This does not mean that his
family will be perfect. In fact, preachers' kids have more
pressure on them than other kids because they live in glass
houses. Every father in the church must know the real
meaning of Ephesians 5: mutual submission, the father's
love for his mate above all else on earth, the father's role as
the real spiritual leader and not as the dictator of the family.
How will the lay fathers know except to watch the pastor-
teacher?

• The pastor-teacher must ensure that his help-mate is also
available to the people of God as well as her own family.
Thus, Betty would not work at a job outside of our home
and church. She would be an integral part of the ministry of
the pastor-teacher. The church should assure that the pastor is paid enough to provide for the family and have no
need for the wife to work outside of the home and church.
Someone is going to have to model the nuclear-family operation for the families in the church. Who else but the pastor
and his wife and kids?

• Preaching certainly has its place in the church, but it is not
to consume the pastor-teacher. Unfortunately, pastors and
pews put too much emphasis on that pulpit. Baptist pastors
have to come to bat in that pulpit three times a week—
Sunday morning, Sunday evening, and Wednesday evening. Then there are the funerals, weddings, etc. I would

use the pulpit more for teaching than preaching—at the least, the expository preaching-teaching method. It would also be my policy to make the pulpit more available to others, including church members, for teaching and/or preaching. Personal testimonies are powerful sermons.

Church Size Is Important

Any pastor reading this list of priorities for his position in the church and his own family may conclude that this is impossible. This is why we are concerned about the size of individual churches. In the big churches the pastor is virtually inaccessible. His staff is made available to the people according to the group with which the staff member is to relate as a first priority, such as youth or senior citizens. However, the people want and expect a personal relationship with their pastor.

The big church does have its place in larger cities because there is a need for specialty-type ministries, such as singles or singles-again. There should be special ministries available in a large city for people with special needs. In smaller cities, towns, and rural areas the pastors should be able to get their different churches to work together in special ministries. What a waste to see individual churches having all of their facilities to themselves when they are used so little except on the weekends. Why can't we come together even across church and denominational lines? We do it in a Billy Graham Crusade.

The church was set up to be a fellowship with people knowing one another, loving one another, helping one another, and praying for one another. Fellowship is a vital part of the community of God's people. Fellowship among people coming out of broken marriages is particularly important. There are other groups with special common interests that promote good fellowship. In a crusade, the cohesion of the people of God from different churches and denominations is almost as important as the commitments of those who come down the aisles. In reference to Billy Graham Crusades I stress the coming-together aspect as filling a vital need for Christian people.

The "Ego Pit"

Pastor-teacher-equipper Lewis Abbott is one of a small percentage of real equippers of the saints. He warned me years ago that the pulpit can become an "ego pit." At 11:00 A.M. each Sunday the pastor-teacher moves into the pulpit. This is the most important hour of the week for him and (he may think) for the people of the church. This is the time when he stands before the people as God's messenger to preach and teach them what is Right and what is Wrong. I came to see that this can be an even bigger ego trip than when the president of the United States stands up to address the people and the world. The difference is that the president is not seen as being God's messenger on Right versus Wrong.

I have been in many pulpits in recent years, and I try to remember this word of wisdom from Pastor Abbott, lest I fall for Satan's trick that I too can be as God.

Another pastor friend, Dick Woodward, has a reminder each week of what his people are looking for in the pulpit. They placed on the front of the pulpit a petition saying, "We would see Jesus!"

There is no greater purpose for the pastor-teacher than this admonition by the people of the Williamsburg (Virginia) Community Chapel. The most effective and eloquent sermon that the pastor-teacher can present to his people and the world is a life that resembles that of Jesus Christ. They need to see and know "the Real Thing" so they can better understand how to do "the Right Thing."

In the pulpit a pastor-teacher should speak with authority, conviction, boldness, and enthusiasm. Most of all, the people must sense the character and love of Jesus Christ in the message and the messenger. His message is much better received when his words fall on friendly ears and open hearts who love their pastor because he loves them and is available to them.

Pastors Are Visual Aids of God's Love

Two pastors in particular have impressed me with their relationships with the people of their churches: W. L. Collins and Joe Novenson. W. L. Collins was formerly a pastor near my home city, but is now at Calvary Baptist Church in Florence, South Carolina. When I began teaching in the church, I realized why the people were so favorable to his preaching. He was first and foremost preaching the message of Jesus' love through his life and his concern for them and their needs. People want to be assured that the pastor loves them *unconditionally*.

The second pastor I mentioned is Joe Novenson of Lexington, South Carolina. As soon as we began ministering in Joe's Presbyterian church we could sense the love bouncing back and forth between the pastor and the people. No sermon is more effective than the sermon of love and service that walks around the church building and the people all week long. No one has ever been able to wipe that loving smile off of that Yankee Polish face of Joe Novenson in the land of Dixie. No one tries. That smile is all about "counting it all joy!"

Joe taught me another lesson, one about knocking on doors. In seeking to get people in the city of Lexington to help him establish a new church, Joe and some of his church members began a campaign to visit people in their homes. At first they used a canned approach of talking to these people. It was confrontational, questioning them about their salvation in the Bible Belt. No fruit came out of the first visits. Then Joe had an *aha!* experience and he and his co-workers changed their game plan. They began saying something like this:

> Hello, we are from Lexington Presbyterian Church. We have come to answer any questions you have about the church, Jesus Christ, and what it means to be a Christian. We are not here to put you on the spot, but to let you put us on the spot.

The doors opened, and many of those contacted joined in helping to build the new church. The church has grown and grown. My advice to Joe was, "Bottle your new approach and peddle it for free to the whole church of Jesus Christ."

With so many pastors failing today because of their own imperfections, because of the immaturity of the people, or a combination thereof, this is a time for reconsideration about how the church should function. The pastor-teacher and his people need to convene and pray over what they are doing right and what they are doing wrong. Then do it right!

Beware of Burnout and Fallout

A major problem in the church is the burnout, fallout, and lack of joy experienced by too many pastors. The highest calling in life can turn into a disaster for the pastor-teacher and his family, as well as the people in the pews. Most pastors are overworked, but some could stand more work.

Lewis Abbott asked the Woman's Missionary Union in a previous church to designate the number of hours he should spend in ten areas of his work assignments. When he added up the hours written down by the ladies he found that they expected him to work 178 hours per week. It is just such expectations that are pushing pastors into despair, frustration, and burnout.

Betty and I addressed a valentine party for pastors and wives one evening. In speaking, Betty had recited how little time I had previously devoted to our family. When the meeting was concluded a number of the pastor's wives rushed up to Betty to complain that they have even more problems with their husbands than she had with me. Too many pastors' families are on shaky grounds while the pastor is trying to minister to families in the church.

If the pastor is to be an equipper of the saints, a leader, a spiritual example for others to emulate, a teacher-preacher of God's Word, a counselor, a visitor of the sick and elderly, a conductor of weddings and funerals, and an evangelist, he has little time to spend with the Master. Many pastors have told us that this is their worst fault and problem!

One pastor broke down in tears in the presence of his deacons when I was speaking to them about the need to be a part of shared ministry in the church. He blurted out that his only time for prayer was on the way to and from his hospital visits. I spoke for him to his deacon board about his time problem and need to have more time with the Master.

Pastors Need Strong Spiritual Lives

Several years ago Lewis Abbott led a number of pastors in a year-and-a-half study of a book entitled *Spiritual Life Studies* by Dr. Harold Burchett.[8] Lewis permitted me to attend a few sessions. The lives of those pastors were being spiritually renewed and revolutionized. The purpose of the study was to focus on their relationship with God through Jesus Christ as Lord and Savior.

One of the shortcomings in many seminaries today is that they don't do enough to help students develop a personal and in-depth relationship with the Lord. Courses in this subject can be helpful, but the actual practice of developing this most vital relationship with what Dr. Os Guinness calls "our audience of One" is most critical.[9]

The Columbia Bible College and Seminary in my hometown emphasizes the formation of the Bible and the Holy Spirit in the lives of their students. Both are required, and application of the biblical teachings in their lives is a requisite, especially in the writing of papers and on some examinations. The student may score 100 on the paper, but if there is not a certification of application of the teachings to the life of the student and repentance where necessary, the score drops from 100 to 0. The alumni divorce rate there is 2 percent. Maybe more institutions should require application.

Here is how the church historian at Union Theological Seminary in New York, Dr. David Lotz, described this spiritual deficit in Christian workers:

> In the Protestant seminaries there is now no spiritual formation. That has evacuated our understanding of God. Today there is a need in seminaries to restore the centrality of spiritual formation, for the sake of those who are to form others into the body of Christ and into the image of Christ.[10]

This statement was made in the presence of a distinguished assemblage of theological scholars at the Rockford Institute headed by Dr. Richard John Neuhaus. There was agreement among the scholars participating in the symposium on the problem of apostasy in the church. In the final session Dr. Carl Braatan of the Lutheran School of Theology at Chicago "summed up the conclusion of many." Dr. Neuhaus quoted Braatan as asserting that "theological education today has abdicated its responsibility to teach theology." In the "academic model" of theological education, said Braatan, "we do not teach theology: we teach about theology, and mainly we teach about theologians." Braaten concluded his remarks by saying: "Probably the major divinity schools are already into the abyss."[11]

Beware of Preaching Different Gospels

The comments were hard on a number of examples of seminarians and pastors teaching and preaching "different gospels."[12]

The noted social scientist, Dr. Peter Berger, likewise expressed his concerns about the perversion of Christianity with conservative or any other brand of politics in our day.

> "Different gospels" lurk all across the spectrum. . . . The vocation of the church is to proclaim the gospel, not to defend the American way of life, not to "build socialism," not even to "build a just society"—because, quite apart from

the fact that we don't really know what this is, all our notions
of justice are fallible and finally marred by sin.[13]

Pastor-teachers must believe the cardinal teachings of the Bible.
They cannot preach "any other gospel," as Paul warned. The people
in the pews cannot handle ivory-tower theology and doubts.

> I marvel that you are turning away so soon from Him
> who called you in the grace of Christ, to a different gospel,
> which is not another; but there are some who trouble you and
> want to pervert the gospel of Christ. But even if we, or an
> angel from heaven, preach any other gospel to you than what
> we have preached to you, let him be accursed (Gal. 1:6–8).

Paul repeats "let him be accursed" again in verse 9, so Paul is
doubly emphatic about false gospels and thus false prophets. We certainly may disagree on our interpretations of Scripture, but there are
some teachers or preachers who are denying the clear teachings regarding Jesus Christ in the Gospels. I am not a legalist or a literalist. I
live with the big picture of the Bible and especially the big picture of
Jesus Christ, the centerpiece of the Bible. I cannot memorize or interpret every jot and tittle, nor do I try.

Betty and I are believers in what the Bible has to say about Jesus
Christ as Lord and Savior. Our Bible tells us to focus on Jesus Christ:
His virgin birth, crucifixion, resurrection, and His life and teachings
of righteousness.

Lift Up the Bible, Don't Let It Down

A pastor-teacher must be knowledgeable about the Holy Bible
and must believe in the truth and authority of the Bible and the deity
of Jesus Christ. Pastors must also know for certain that the Holy Spirit
of the Godhead is living and leading in their lives.

Dr. Marcus J. Borg writes of a historical Jesus who was executed
for seeking to reform Jewish society. He was not sired by the Holy
Spirit. Jesus was just a prophet, as most of the world religions say. Of
particular concern are Borg's statements that most of the mainline
seminaries understand and accept the truth of his discoveries and that
of others who deny the deity of Jesus. I hope not. If so, they have
exorcised the virgin birth out of the Bible and crowned Jesus as a man

with a mission of change and compassion, but not as the God-man. He would only be a "historical Jesus."[14]

Beware of Destroying Fragile Faith

Such "different" gospels can easily destroy fragile faiths in seminary training and in church pews. Young idealistic future pastors and most of the people in the pews cannot handle such conclusions by seminary scholars. That same Borg message was taught to me in a church. What especially shocked me was the denial of the veracity of the whole Gospel of John. When I challenged the statements of my teacher, a recent seminary graduate, I was asked to prove the truth of the Gospel of John and the deity of Christ. I could do neither because at best I was one of those superficial Christians. I was the only person to question that teaching. It sounded to me as though it were "a different gospel." Now I know that it was! This embarrassment prompted me to search the Scriptures.

Our edification, motivation, and work are all substantially determined by the work of the Holy Bible and the Holy Spirit in our lives. It is this holy combination that strengthens the life and work of God's people, especially those employed in full-time ministry. Deficiencies in this prime requisite are a principal reason for the increasing casualties we are seeing among so many full-time Christian workers.

Pastors Need the Help of Their Denominations

When I was director of The Billy Graham Lay Center and Ben Lippen Summer Conference in the early 1980s, Betty and I saw this problem while going in and out of various churches. We scheduled a pastor-family retreat from a Monday through a Thursday for a total cost of twenty-five dollars per family. Ira and Betty Craft helped us to subsidize the conference. Our conference center was packed. Here we discovered that when the pastors are hurting, the wives are hurting more.

Church denominations need to be doing more to help pastors and their families. Basically, pastor families have little or no tenure and limited, if any, "academic" freedom. One too many sermons on the original sin nature of mankind can be grounds for dismissal at the next or special-called meeting of church leaders and/or dissenters and malcontents. My advice to the church hierarchy in denominations is that more direct help needs to be provided beyond holding seminars for pastors and their families. Circuit-riding counselors should be on the road encouraging and helping pastors and their families. Seminaries can be used as havens of rest and restoration.

Pastors and their families are serving in the frontlines; they need understanding, encouragement, love, and where necessary, counseling.

I made my mistakes as a church leader in not understanding how different the ways of God and the ways of man are. Today I would be very careful to follow God's plan in the administration of a church, especially in working with a pastor and his family.

It Pays to Know Your Flock

A Lutheran pastor, Larry W. Smith, taught us the importance of having good political skills in ministry. This pastor beats any politician I have ever encountered in being able to call the names of his people. After speaking in his pulpit in Gilbert, South Carolina, he stood with Betty and me at the door as the parishioners were leaving the service. More than three hundred men, women, and children came by us. The pastor introduced us to each of his people by name and/or nickname. We were also impressed with his church bulletin. It listed his name as pastor. Below was this title of the other ministers. MINISTERS: ALL 583 MEMBERS.

Later we had lunch with the pastor and some of his people. We discovered that this pastor is relatively free of trials and tribulations. He has met the first-felt need of his people: know me and love me! I asked how he could remember their names so well. He spends much of his time during the week in their homes. He is truly a brother "in Christ." He knows his people and loves them anyway! And they love their pastor anyway, too!

Beware of Gradualism and the Other "Isms"

George Barna has moved to the fore as the unofficial futurist of the church in America. In his book *The Frog in the Kettle* Barna makes many suggestions for changes in style and approaches by churches in looking at future ministry in the 1990s and into the twenty-first century. He pictures the changes as coming subtly and imperceptibly so that, like the proverbial frog, the church could be boiled to death by maintaining the status quo in its slowly boiling environment.

Barna calls this the "danger of gradualism." He cites Great Britain, our mother country, as a case in point.

Once representing the vast majority of that great nation's population, true believers are estimated now to be only about two percent of the population.[15]

America tends to lag a decade or so behind our mother country in moving left politically and spiritually. The "isms" of man began crawling across America and into the churches in the early years of our democracy and then picked up speed on a gradual basis. The explosion occurred in the early 1960s with the advent of the Beatles from England, the "God is dead" theology (also from Europe), post-war prosperity and the attachment to "the things of the world," and more and more television. With all of these distractions people became more superficial in their faith and commitment. Gradually relativism, secularism, humanism, materialism, hedonism, and universalism gained stronger authority and power across our land, homes, and places of worship. Now we have been boiled. How can we tell? Look at the stark statistics supported by the realism of a nation amuck in crime, scandals, riots, hate, disunity, debt, and devastation of our moral character. The changes have been so subtle and unseen that we were unprepared for the confrontation of the earthquake tremors shaking the foundations of America. One such example was the 1992 record-setting riot in Los Angeles.

Now the raw statistics are being made available to us in books, TV, and other secular media. Even they are concerned after being a part of the problem in recent years. Most Americans missed the trends and tremors because of the gradualism of the movements to Wrong over Right. This is what Dr. Barna and Dr. Gallup are saying to us in their talks, books, and statistical data.

Beware of Superficiality

Why did the gradual approach succeed? Because of superficial faith and superficial commitment in the principal place of correction and righteousness: the church of Jesus Christ. Barna and Gallup see religion in American as being skin-deep. It is the duty of the pastors and their trainers to properly shepherd the "saints" in the faith and in their commitment to the righteousness of Jesus Christ. Superficiality means that people profess faith but do not know enough to be aware of the subtle and gradual rise of the "isms" in life that are the enemies of Jesus Christ and the mission He delegated to His church.

Relativism, secular humanism, universalism, and hedonism are four "isms" that are making a difference in America, the world, the church, and among too many people who profess to be "born-again" Christians.

Most Americans believe people are basically good, not sinful. They believe people are capable of managing their world without assistance of any external force. There is the feeling that people are only accountable to themselves. This is enough. To portray people as less than capable of perfection is to commit warranted judgment and unjustifiably limit the potential of other people.[16]

The focus is on the love of God for His creation rather than the pain caused by the enduring disobedience and selfishness that have characterized that creation throughout history.

Religion is seen as important—in a way—but not central. They realize it can be an important and powerful part of a person's life. Too many members want to get by with as little of Jesus as they deem to be required for heaven.

Years of pounding with relativism (there are no moral absolutes) have finally penetrated the American psyche. Many people doubt the existence of Satan, deny the existence of one true God, and question whether or not there is a God who hears and answers prayers. While one-half of Americans believe the Christian faith is relevant to the way we live today, only one-half as many believe the local churches possess such relevance.[17]

The churches have a much lower rating than Christianity. People still see America as a Christian nation—whatever that may be in the fuzzy thinking pervading the mind of America today. However, they do not feel there is much value in being in church. Individual churches have a bad image as being judgmental and closed to outsiders.[18]

Beware of Universalism and Hedonism

Universalism is the belief that all people will be ultimately saved and that we can worship any god or participate in any religion. This means people with this type of belief system feel that when people are praying to Allah or Buddha they are praying to the same god as the Christians are worshiping. Barna's poll shows that two-thirds of Americans accept the concept of universalism.

Hedonism means the extreme enjoyment of the secular and sensualistic pleasures of life. The Greeks also had a name for this "ism": *epicureanism,* meaning "eat, drink, and be merry for tomorrow we die." This is the credo of our day. People want to be entertained; Jim Bakker did not disappoint his fans. He featured entertainment and prosperity religion, which was exactly what his fans and contributors wanted in a God.

Beware of Self-Sufficiency

Over and over again Barna's statistics reveal that the major problem is with the rich and highly educated folks. Regarding belief in God's Word, the ratio of drop-offs from the lowest affluence and lowest education levels to the highest affluence and highest education levels is two-to-one. The message is: when I have money and brains I don't need God; I can handle it myself. This is known as self-sufficiency and immaturity. I can thus be my own God.

What is needed in America today is for more pastor-teachers to preach, teach, and model what real righteousness is all about.

Ministry Evangelism by All God's People

The two pastors who have impressed me most with their ministries are Dr. Jerry Kirk, formerly of College Hill Presbyterian Church in Cincinnati, Ohio, and Dr. Charles Roesel, pastor of First Baptist Church in Leesburg, Florida. Jerry Kirk is now steering the National Coalition Against Pornography from his home in Cincinnati.

During his time of ministry at College Hill, Jerry found himself near the burnout or fallout stage of ministry. He took a six-month sabbatical and visited a dozen of the best-performing churches in America. During this time he had a new spiritual experience—realizing that God's plan for the church is the ministry of all of God's people.

Jerry came back to his pulpit and won the favor of his congregation by proposing a whole new direction for the church. This would mean discipleship and training courses and ministry for all the members of the church. One reason his new approach won the cooperation of the church was because of his great powers of persuasion (one of many spiritual gifts the Lord had provided Jerry).

In 1982 Betty and I visited Jerry's church for a weekend clinic for pastors and lay leaders. The concept was working so well that Jerry and his staff were then teaching other churches how to move the ministry of the church into the hands and hearts of the people in the pews. Even counseling was being handled by trained lay people.

Charles Roesel became pastor of his hometown church after pastoring elsewhere. Like Jerry Kirk, Charles began to see that the key to God's Master Plan lies in arming the people in the pews to becoming involved in ministry. Charles began preaching and teaching in this subject area for twelve years to prepare the people for what he calls "ministry evangelism."

Betty and I visited Charles and his church on January 26, 1990. Earlier I had heard him tell the story of the proliferation of many ministries by his people and others in Leesburg, a city of approximately 20,000 people. Today his church population constitutes almost one-fourth of the population of Leesburg. His church baptizes more than 300 people annually.

Not only has the church membership grown, but the church coffers have grown despite the amount of money expended to "help the least of these." Recently they took the $150,000 from the church building program to use in the many ministries designed to help the poor and hurting people of Leesburg.

First Baptist Church in Leesburg is in effect running a Salvation Army-type operation on both sides of what he calls "Grace Boulevard." Old houses near the church have been purchased, and ministries have been established in these buildings.

Charles gets help for operating the ministries from within his own congregation, but he also gets help from the community. Jews, Catholics, and other Protestant church members are participating in the ministries by providing their time and money.

Charles is convinced that people outside of the church are not interested in the church's regular evangelism program. However, they like and even love to find ways to reach out and help needy people. His name for this is "ministry evangelism." It accomplishes three major purposes of the church: discipleship in order to minister, evangelistic witness, and servanthood ministry.

Jerry and Charles serve as the best evidence that the ultimate end of Scripture, the ministry and witness of all of God's people, can be made to work to not only accomplish witness and ministry but also to fill the pews and coffers. They too realize the value of lay renewals and lay revivals where lay people pour out their testimonies and fellowship with one another. More commitments are made in renewals than in the type of revival where lay folks have no participation.

Missions over Maintenance

The vast majority of churches in America are basically engaged in maintenance work as opposed to missions work. The message of the Bible is clear and consistently proclaiming that the purpose of the church is REDEMPTION, MINISTRY, AND EVANGELISM. Preaching, teaching, training, singing, praying, and loving all have as their ultimate end the production of fruit-bearing witnesses for *righteousness*.

Yet the biggest weakness of the church of Jesus Christ is the Great Ommission: the failure to equip and train the people in the pews to be more than spectators who come and go to church to watch the pastor and staff perform.

I recognize that this is not an easy task and that the pastor's time is limited. However, the reason his task is hard and his time is limited is that he is doing most of the work of the church for the people instead of the people sharing in the ministry of the church. Many pastors are experiencing burnout and fallout because they are basically doing the work of the church either by choice or because of the resistance of the people. Yet Jerry Kirk and Charles Roesel have shown that the people welcome running with the ball themselves. God implanted in all of us the urge to help others. This is why sending lay people on short-term missions here or overseas impacts their spiritual lives the most.

The Visions of a Parish Pastor

There was another outstanding pastor I never knew, the late Samuel M. Shoemaker of Manhattan and Pittsburgh. As an Episcopal priest, Sam exemplified the best ideals in pastoring and nurturing his parishioners. He is the man who put together the famous Twelve Steps for Alcoholics Anonymous right out of the Bible. In addition, Dr. Shoemaker claimed the city of Pittsburgh for Jesus Christ with the vision that "one day Pittsburgh would become as famous for Jesus Christ as it is for steel." Sam's call of others to his vision for Pittsburgh was for all of them to see Pittsburgh as their extended parish. "Get changed, get together, and get going" was one of his creeds. With several businessmen, Sam established in 1955 a city-wide ministry called The Pittsburgh Experiment.

A Young Life ministry layman named Reid Carpenter came to Pittsburgh looking for ministry opportunities. He teamed up with another layman, Don James, and subsequently several others (including a visionary and wealthy lady, the late Dora Hillman, who helped to launch Dr. R. C. Sproul in his Ligonier Ministries).

Another new arrival for the group was a young traveling bard from Oxford named John Guest. Soon John was changed from being a part-time youth minister and bard to director of one of the largest Episcopal churches, St. Stephens Church in the affluent suburb of Pittsburgh, known as Sewickley. Now John is a world evangelist, and we minister with him.

The circle continued to expand, and the vision likewise, so they launched the Pittsburgh Offensive. This operation crossed all denominational lines in the interest of implementing Sam Shoemaker's vision to make Pittsburgh "a city for God." Today there are more than 30 ministries in operation through what is now known as the Pittsburgh Leadership Foundation and related organizations.

Thanks to the Japanese steel industry, the Pittsburgh reputation as the steel city has declined. Due to the vision of Sam Shoemaker and the PLF (Pittsburgh Leadership Foundation) visionaries and workers, Pittsburgh is developing more and more as a potential "city for God." In recent years it has been awarded the honor of being the number-one city in America.[19]

What is the teaching for pastors? Be a man of vision like Sam Shoemaker, and extend that vision beyond the bounds of your own church.

In this chapter we have piled many "to do's" on the desks and—we pray—in the hearts of pastors and their staffs. Sam Shoemaker did much of this. The Bible speaks directly to this matter of vision in Proverbs 29:18 (KJV).

Where there is no vision, the people perish; but he that keepeth the law, happy is he.

Nehemiah was a great visionary, builder and leader. So was the Apostle Paul. From a self-centered ambition Paul became motivated by two ambitions: to win the smile of the Lord and to preach the gospel where it had not been heard (2 Cor. 5:9; Rom. 15:20-21).

The prophet Jeremiah challenged us to look beyond our own designs and desires for life in Jeremiah 45:5.

"And do you seek great things for yourself? Do not seek them; for behold, I will bring adversity on all flesh," says the Lord. "But I will give your life to you as a prize in all places, wherever you go."

Above all others, pastor-teachers must watch their pride, perks, pecuniary interests, materialism, and their witness for righteousness. Your people and others are always watching to see if you really are like Christ. How will lay folks know what is right unless they see the right thing in the man God has sent them to be their shepherd?

President Abraham Lincoln and my old boss, President Richard Nixon, said it this way: "Give your life to a cause bigger than yourself." Pastors, you have given your lives to a Person bigger than yourselves. The teaching is to latch onto that Person and His vision that is far bigger than your church building and your pride. Look upon your parish as extending to the whole of your city, like Sam Shoemaker. When you get a post of duty, try to stay there and grow your flock in God's Word, God's Spirit, and God's will and ways. One-year, two-year, and three-year ministries do not amount to much.

Years ago, when there was only Harvard and Yale divinity schools, there was one place of ministry for the graduating pastor: his first and final place of ministry. If he did not finish his course there he was considered a failure as a pastor.

My friend Bob Fenn has spent 36 years in lay renewal work as a layman. Bob teaches that lay renewal is not an event, it is a process that should be ongoing for a minimum of twelve years. Charles Roesel did not get his people ready for ministry evangelism until he had preached and taught it for twelve years. Pulpit-hopping has got to be stopped. It raises the question of whether pastors can hold their jobs or are more ambitious for position, fame, and monetary gain. Above all, a pastor-teacher is not to be self-serving.

The pastor-teacher is not to be the whole football team, as the only one carrying the ball. His role is that of "the player-coach" as defined by Dr. Elton Trueblood. The folks in the pews should be carrying the ball, blocking, and tackling for the church, as they are doing for Charles Roesel. The pastor plays in the game also, but his job is primarily to coach the team and help them to get across the goal-line: to be ministers and witnesses of righteousness and ultimately illuminators of the path to glory.

Finally, all pastor-teachers should live in Paul's pastoral epistles: 1 Timothy, 2 Timothy, and Titus. They are for all of the people of God, but they were designed in a special way for pastor-teachers. The thrust of these powerful letters from prison is:

TO MAINTAIN PURITY OF DOCTRINE
AND PURITY OF LIFESTYLE

It is here that pastor-teachers are being most fiercely attacked today by the forces of Satan.

What you have experienced in this chapter is "the view from the pew" by Harry and Betty Dent. After many years of missing the meat of the message in the pews we discerned the reasons why we were doing so during the past twelve years while ministering to the pews in more than seven hundred churches.

CHAPTER SIX

Future Generations: Preparing Our Posterity

I am much afraid that schools will prove to be the great gates of hell unless we diligently labor in explaining the Holy Scriptures, engraving them in the hearts of youth.

Martin Luther[1]

More than two thousand years ago, Aristotle posed the question, "What constitutes education and what is the proper way to be educated?"

The richest, and what should be the most literate, nation in the world has a major problem with Aristotle's question today. We recognize the importance of education in our society. So did our founding fathers. It is the prime requisite for maintaining our republican form of government and thus our individual freedoms. Even more, education is so vital for preparing our posterity for life.

Who is our posterity? Our children and our children's children and then their offspring, *et al*. One of the purposes of this book is to burn into the hearts and minds of all Americans the reality of a mortgaged and endangered future for our country and thus for our posterity. As parents of eight children—two boys and two girls and their mates—and seven grandkids, Harry and Betty Dent are dearly concerned about our posterity.

A 1992 book, *Racing Toward 2001*,[2] presents a very scary future for our posterity. Author Russell Chandler writes that they will be living in an entirely different world. He says that Christianity will move from being a religion of the majority to a religion of the minority, TV will be king of the hill, our values will be further eroded, and the home will be more decimated by absenteeism and self-ism. We had better educate our posterity in Right versus Wrong now!

Our Educational System Is Lacking

Although we believe in the priority of education, we are mixed up and divided about what constitutes education. Is it mind alone? Or is it mind and heart together? Will it be educated knaves or educated saints? Or will even the mind itself be neglected?

I thought I was an educated man with three earned degrees until I got an education in the eternal verities of life by studying God's Holy Word from Genesis to the Revelation of Jesus Christ. This powerful combination of tying man's perspective and God's perspective together finally joined my mind and heart together, fusing intellect and integrity. Then I knew what I really believed and why. Finally I had grasped the Who, What, When, Where, Why, and How of life. These were the questions I was forced to answer every time I wrote a news story as editor of my high school and college newspapers and as a young Washington reporter.

> Who am I?
> What am I doing on planet Earth?
> When—why at this particular time?
> Where—why was I destined to do His thing here in the greatest country in the world?
> Why did God create me—what is the meaning and purpose of my life on earth?
> How am I to accomplish my mission in life?

Most of us in America believe that God did create us, but most people have never sought or found the answers to these critical questions of life. I thank God over and over that He led me to find the answers. This was the high point of my life. I was willing to give up my livelihood for which I had trained so long and even life itself, if necessary, to get across to my fellow citizens God's overall meaning and purpose of life.

Now I am convicted as to what constitutes education. It is the combination of intellect and integrity so that the *summum bonum*, the supreme good, can be mined out of the life of every person and refined and developed for the glory of God and the good of all of mankind. There is tremendous untapped potential for good in this world and especially in the United States. Unfortunately, most of this potential is wasting away because the vast majority of people have never sought the answers to the Who, What, When, Where, Why, and How questions.

Presidential candidate, and one of America's most successful and outspoken businessmen, Ross Perot has this to say about what education should not be in America:

> When I was a child, our public school system was the envy of the world. Today we rank at the bottom of the industrialized world in academic achievement.
>
> We have the largest number of functional illiterates in the industrialized world. Every time I say that I have to rephrase it: We've got the dumbest work force in the industrialized world.
>
> We have reverted our schools from places of learning to places of playing. But our international competitors are going for excellence.
>
> Our 11th-graders, in a recent world-wide algebra test, ranked 14th out of 15 nations tested. If it's any comfort to you, we beat Thailand.[3]

One of the foremost public opinion experts in America is Dr. Louis Harris. In a September 1991 assessment of American education, Dr. Harris presented a similar picture of the sad state of education in America.

> The areas employers and educators criticize most about the quality of high school education today are basic and telling. Two-thirds of the employers and higher educators express real worry about the functional literacy of high school graduates. Employers report they have to turn down five of every six young people who apply for a job.
>
> Two-thirds of employers and 65% of higher educators say they often get recent high school graduates who cannot do "arithmetic functions." Sixty-four percent of employers and 58 percent of higher educators report recent graduates are unable "to read and understand written and verbal instructions."[4]

Dr. Harris reports other concerns to be the lack of "real discipline in their work habits" and the lack of "a real sense of dedication to work." Also, very few seem to be able to "solve complex problems."[5]

Americans were surprised to find in February 1992 that our high school students ranked next to the bottom in math and science scores among fifteen nations although we spend more money on education than most of the competing countries.[6]

Social Engineering and Relativism

The book that best explains why we have come to this low point in American education is *The Closing of the American Heart: What's Really Wrong with America's Schools.*[7] The author, Dr. Ronald H. Nash, now of Reformed Theological Seminary in Jackson, Mississippi, has written twenty books in his role as a professor of religion and philosophy.

In essence Nash contends that the secular humanists who deny transcendental values have succeeded in subverting the American educational system during the past fifty years. They have filled our young people to overflowing with philosophies that say there is no God and no moral absolutes—the very core of secularism and relativism. Just be tolerant and have an open mind to anything. You can handle it!

Nash's book followed the 1987 best-selling book by Dr. Allan Bloom called *The Closing of the American Mind: How Higher Education Has Failed Democracy and Impoverished the Souls of Today's Students.* Bloom shows how American democracy has unwittingly played host to vulgarized continental ideas of nihilism and despair, of relativism disguised as tolerance. Relativism is the key "ism" which posits that there are no moral absolutes or truths. Nihilism says there is no hope.

Bloom, not a religious man, avers that when students get to the university level they are already full of relativism. When they get their university degrees they have been fully relativized. Here is what Bloom asserts:

> There is one thing a professor can be absolutely certain of: almost every student entering the university believes, or says he believes, that truth is relative. If this belief is put to the test, one can count on the students' reaction: they will be uncomprehending.
>
> They are unified only in their relativism and in their allegiance to equality. And the two are related in a moral intention. The relativity of truth is not a theoretical insight but a moral postulate, the condition of a free society, or so they

see it. They have all been equipped with this framework early on, and it is the modern replacement for the inalienable natural rights that used to be the traditional American grounds for a free society.

The danger they have been taught to fear from absolutism is not error but intolerance. Relativism is necessary to openness; and this is the virtue, the only virtue, which all primary education for more than fifty years has dedicated itself to inculcating. Openness . . . is the great insight of our times. The true believer is in real danger.

The students, of course, cannot defend their opinion. It is something with which they have been indoctrinated.[8]

Nash commends Bloom for pointing out the problem of relativism in education, but he maintains that Bloom is only half right. The graver problem, he maintains, is that it is not just minds that are being shut down by today's educational system but also American hearts.

He defines the heart much like the Bible uses the term in pointing to the religious and moral center for the lives of human beings. Here is where our ultimate commitments are forged and our value systems determined. So the danger is the loss of our value system in deciding what is Right and what is Wrong in making the choices of life. The Bible tells us:

For as he thinks in his heart, so is he (Prov. 23:7a).

Keep your heart with all diligence,
For out of it spring the issues of life (Prov. 4:23).

Right Versus Wrong

It is this loss of a realistic sense of Right versus Wrong that has crippled the minds and hearts of our society. The United States of America is being weakened not only in education, but in religion, in behavior, in our work ethic, and thus in basic American character and values.

Why have crime rates skyrocketed all across America, even in the Bible Belt? I remember years ago when we in the South pointed our fingers northward to New York City as the cesspool of crime in our country. But we have seen so many public scandals and so much corruption in government at every level, on Wall Street, in the sports arenas, in religious television, in pulpits, in education, in unions, and in the corporate world in recent years.

As a nation, we Americans have been secularized, relativized, universalized, self-ized, and neuterized. We don't know for sure what we believe as a people or why we believe what it is that we believe. Black and white have turned to gray. The authors of *The Day America Told the Truth* expressed it this way:

> Almost all of us have highly individualized moral menus . . . today. We decide what's right and wrong. Most Americans have no respect for what the law says. . . .
> We see most moral issues in shades of gray, not in black and white as our parents did. We've become wishy-washy as a nation. Some would say we've lost our moral backbone.[9]

Situation Ethics and Relativism

Right versus Wrong is fuzzy today. Make up your own rules, known as situation ethics, was made popular by the late Reverend Joseph Fletcher. In his book, *Situation Ethics*, Fletcher presented his definition of situation ethics.

> Every man must decide for himself according to his own estimate of conditions and consequences; and no one can decide for him or impugn the decision to which he comes. Perhaps this is the end of the matter after all. *This is precisely what this book is intended to show.*[10]

What situation ethics postulates is that since there are no moral absolutes, we just need to be tolerant and open to whatever comes along. Be broad-minded.

But God is not neutral. In fact, God is rather dogmatic about most things.

Relativism, a similar idea, became popular in the early 1920s when Dr. Albert Einstein became a world hero for his new theory of relativity, which postulated that all mass has energy encapsulated in the equation $E = mc^2$. His theory postulated that there is no absolute motion. This led to the far-fetched view that there were no longer absolutes of time and space, of good and evil, of knowledge and— above all—values. As historian Paul Johnson has concluded: "Relativity became confused with relativism." John writes further:

No one was more distressed than Einstein by this public misapprehension. . . . Einstein was not a practicing Jew, but he acknowledged a God. He believed passionately in absolute standards of right and wrong. His professional life was devoted to the quest not only for truth but for certitude. . . . He insisted the world could be divided into subjective and objective spheres. . . . He lived to see moral relativism, to him a disease, become a social pandemic, just as he lived to see his fatal equation bring into existence nuclear warfare. . . . It [relativity] formed a knife, inadvertently wielded by its author, to help cut society adrift from its traditional moorings in the faith and morals of Judeo-Christian culture.[11]

The famous British scholar and Christian apologist, C. S. Lewis, wrote *The Abolition of Man: How Education Develops Man's Sense of Morality,* to warn the world about the danger of obscuring and obliterating the traditional values of any society. The key chapter, "Men Without Chests," described how teachers with a bent to changing the world to their way of thinking, their "ism," can bend the chests of children in that direction. The human chest is pictured by Lewis as being the location of the personal will of humans. He contends that the chest—the seat of "magnanimity and sentiment"—connects the cerebral man (the mind) with the visceral man (the heart). It is here that our system of beliefs, sentiments, values—our worldview—as to Right versus Wrong is forged, perhaps for a lifetime.[12]

Lewis writes that debunking society's traditional values and lifting up the "isms" of the teachers are two ways to accomplish this end. What seems to be Right can be made to appear Wrong to the kids in school. Then a new sense of Right can be substituted so that the young new adult will see the old values as being "contrary to reason" and/or "contemptible." Why does Lewis think such brain and heartwashers seek to so influence school kids?

They [Lewis's two fictional characters] write in order to produce certain states of mind in the rising generation, if not because they think those states of mind intrinsically just or good, yet certainly because they think them to be the means to some state of society they deem desirable.[13]

This strong Christian apologist says that even the concept of "value" can be rejected. He concludes that the end of the systematic devaluation of stable sentiments and values can result in the systematic destruction of a society. As a teacher, Lewis should have understood how the system works because he did the same thing himself before his salvation. This can be done with the best of personal motives, believing what is being done is designed to promote what is Right over what is Wrong.

My "A.C."—"After Christ"—experience has made a gigantic difference in how Harry Dent sees Right versus Wrong, and I grew up in the Bible Belt, where being born virtually amounted to being born into the church. This is why Dr. Billy Graham says his crusades bring smaller harvests below the Mason-Dixon line. There is the assumption of salvation down South.

The *Ordo Amoris*

Augustine defined virtue as *ordo amoris,* the ordinate condition of the affections in which every object is accorded that kind and degree of love which is appropriate to it. Aristotle believed that the aim of education is to make the pupil like and dislike what he "ought."[14] The question here is, whose "ought"? Whose sense of duty or desirability? This is why parents, teachers, and peers have such an impact for good or evil, Right or Wrong, with all of us, regardless of age. Everyone has a witness for good or evil. So we must all watch our witness. We must consciously seek to be stepping-stones instead of stumbling blocks.

The move to secularism and relativism has had an impact even in Christian schools. Dr. John P. Newport, of Southwestern Baptist Theological Seminary, has expressed concern about Christian colleges that have "deliberately adopted the academic stance of disinterested relativism which characterizes the contemporary secular campus." He sees these institutions as being "unsure about their message. . . . They have what has been called a 'low cal' theology."[15]

Dr. Newport notes that the 1960s brought vast changes and that even more followed in the 1970s and 1980s. "There developed a moral pluralism," he observes, and it "took its place alongside religious pluralism in America."[16]

My concern is that, by design or miscue, education has produced the "astute rascal"[17] that bothered Aristotle and other ancient Greek philosophers. They realized that excellence is not intellectual alone. The good man or woman is the well-rounded individual, sound of mind, strong in body, and healthy in spirit and heart.

The "astute rascal" that worried Aristotle is the individual who has all the practical knowledge to achieve what he wants but lacks the moral character to seek the Right rather than the Wrong ends. I represented some very "astute rascals" in my practice of law. America is loaded with them.

In June 1990 I had the pleasure of briefly addressing 143 young presidential scholars before they received their prestigious medallions from President George Bush at the White House. Those of us on the White House Commission on Presidential Scholars had picked the youngsters from among a few thousand contestants across America. Some had perfect SAT scores of 1600 and grade-point averages of 4.0. My charge to the young scholars was taken from the key song in the 1955 Broadway musical hit, *Damn Yankees*.

> You have the greatest young minds in America. But it is not enough to have the greatest minds; to be a whole person you must also have *grand hearts*—a value system for which you are willing to live, and if necessary, to die. A Broadway musical before your day put it this way: "But, ya' gotta have heart—miles and miles of heart!"

What pleased me was their reaction. They heartily applauded the reminder that what really counts is a grand heart over even a great mind. This is the cornerstone upon which our republic was established. This is the best way to ensure private virtue and thus public virtue in a land where the people are to be the governors. Youngsters will catch this message if we proclaim it to them because of their great sense of idealism.

MORE THAN ANY GROUP IN AMERICA, OUR YOUNG PEOPLE WANT TO KNOW THE RIGHT THING AND THE REAL THING!

Values, standards, and norms must once again be central in the educational process. We must recover the belief that there is a transcendent moral order. Reason (knowledge) and virtue must be recoupled because development of the intellect and moral character are so intimately related.

The "Ism" Creators

Dr. David Breese has written a book that attributes our current American dilemma to our ignoring of this truth and to "seven bodies that lie cold and dormant in the grave." The book is *Seven Men Who Rule the World from the Grave*. The men are Charles Darwin, Karl Marx, Julius Wellhausen, John Dewey, Sigmund Freud, John Maynard Keynes, and Søren Kierkegaard.[18]

These men were key "ism" creators. Breese says they continue to rule from their graves because they have altered the thinking of society. They generated philosophies that have been ardently embraced by masses of people who do not understand the evil inherent in these seemingly harmless thoughts. Today these ideas pervade our schools, workplaces, homes, and even the church. Nowhere have they had more impact than in education and particularly in higher education.

Darwin put into the minds of humans the idea of evolution. This means that there was no creation by a transcendent God. Everything has come into being in this world, including you and me, by accident and a process he called evolution. This philosophy came to be known as Social Darwinism.

Today evolution has been made into the Real Thing in our schools, and evolution says there is no God. Before evolution could become "king of the hill" in school, God had to be ejected. This was accomplished a few decades ago. So the God-consciousness that pervaded our schools when I was a student more than forty years ago no longer exists. What a difference this has made in devaluing our old system of American values!

The man who installed Social Darwinism in our schools is celebrated as the modern-day father of our public school system, John Dewey. He came along in American education at the turn of the century. His conviction was that nothing is constant, given, or finally true, but rather that all things are pragmatic, adaptable, and subject to whatever interpretation seems appropriate for the time.

In 1904 Dewey was given the chair of education at Columbia University in New York. Soon the Columbia Teachers College became a training center for teachers from around the world, and Dewey's educational philosophy of the various new "isms" of life was spread across America and around the world. Dewey was bent on moving American society from belief in the supernatural to belief in the natural. His concern was for the here and now and not eternity. His key "ism" was the American-made "ism" called pragmatism. This means that truth is what works now—not in any supposed eternity. That is the course set for Americans today and the source of our big problems in American education.

What Kind of Child Are You Trying to Produce?

Dr. R. C. Sproul, the noted Reformed Christian apologist and teacher, illustrates the concern all parents should have about how the hearts and minds of their children are shaped in school. He asked a teacher of one of his children to explain the purpose of the child's curriculum. Seeing that the teacher did not understand the question, Dr. Sproul then clarified the question this way: "What kind of child are you trying to produce?"

The teacher responded, "I don't know. No one has ever asked me that question." The response shocked and concerned Dr. Sproul. This is the big question we all should be asking.[19]

Sproul is convinced that the dominant influence on public school education in the United States today is humanistic philosophy. Humanism says that man is the measure of all things, ruling out the influence of God or any transcendent power. Humanism is another worldview, and it shares the skepticism and agnosticism with respect to God found in secularism. The first humanists in the world were Adam and Eve, made so by the siren song of the serpent that "you shall be as gods."[20]

On June 8, 1978, Aleksandr I. Solzhenitsyn delivered his famous commencement address at Harvard University, the educational center in the U.S.A. for secular humanism. He directly addressed the problem of humanism and its adverse consequences in America and the Western world.

> How did the West decline from its triumphal march to its present debility? . . . This means that the mistake must be at the root, at the very foundation of thought in modern times. I refer to the prevailing Western view of the world which was born in the . . . Age of the Enlightenment. It became the basis for political and social doctrine and could be called rationalistic humanism or humanistic autonomy: the proclaimed and practiced autonomy of man from any higher force above him . . . anthropocentricity, with man seen at the center of all.[21]

Unfortunately, Solzhenitsyn's words fell on ears deadened by many years of unreality and irresponsibility by higher education scholars at Harvard, a school where there once was belief in God, but where today belief in man prevails over belief in God. It is so easy for scholars to become victims of self-pride and fall in love with their knowledge and thus themselves.

Education's Top Seven Problems

CBS News has given us a scary picture of what their research reveals about the kind of child being produced today in our American education system by these "isms" of life. CBS News rated the top seven school problems in the 1940s when I was a student at St. Matthews High School in St. Matthews, South Carolina.

1. Talking out of turn
2. Chewing gum
3. Making noise
4. Running in the halls
5. Cutting in line
6. Dress code infractions
7. Littering

We were real troublemakers back in the ferocious '40s. While I made A's on my subjects, I had difficulty making the All-A honor roll because I kept getting B's and C's on conduct.

Then CBS News took a look at the conduct in the schools forty years later, and here is what they found to be the top seven problems in the schools in the '80s:

1. Drug abuse
2. Alcohol abuse
3. Pregnancy
4. Suicide
5. Rape
6. Robbery
7. Assault[22]

I have used these statistics in color overhead transparency form in many churches, schools, and civic club meetings. Teachers and principals have attested to the truth of these CBS News statistics.

I believe the top two problems have changed places in the 1990s because alcohol is legal. Adults show the youngsters that it must be okay because so many drink it. Yet alcohol creates more devastation among our young people and adults than all of the illegal drugs combined.

Teenage drinking has become epidemic. The United States Surgeon General conducted a survey in April and May 1991 among school students. Surgeon General Antonia Novello called the findings "an alarming trend." The survey found that more than half of the 20.7 million students in grades seven through twelve drink alcoholic beverages. Most began drinking in their early teens.[23] Why? Out of boredom. To get high. To wash away their problems.

The news media in South Carolina have been featuring news stories on teen drinking in 1991. They label alcohol the number-one killer of teenagers in the state. Almost half of the young people between seventeen and twenty-four who died in 1987 in South Carolina died an alcohol-related death.[24]

Sex, the number three problem in the CBS News survey, has gone wild in America, especially among our youngsters. In my Bible Belt state of South Carolina 68 percent of all high school students say they are sexually active. For seniors the statistics report that 71 percent of the girls and 79 percent of the boys are involved in sexual intercourse. No wonder the U.S. leads the world in teenage pregnancies![25]

Teenage Tribulations Mount

Here is a paragraph from our daily newspaper on the behavior of American teens:

Something's wrong with America's youth; they're rude, irresponsible, promiscuous and violent. Some educators think the answer is to teach them the difference between right and wrong.

Here is the adjacent headline:

South Carolina considering "values education"—but carefully.[26]

One more daily news story:

In a disturbing measure of the impact of economic and social change, a new study says the status of children in the United States has declined by almost every measure over the past 30 years.

Adjacent to it:

> The collapse of traditional family structure has played a
> partial role. . . .[27]

My state is also witnessing the escalation of teen crime year by
year. This news story reports the sad story:

> More juveniles are becoming killers, rapists, robbers,
> drug dealers and users because parents are not supervising
> their children, authorities say. The number of serious and
> violent juvenile crimes referred to Family Court increased 44
> percent for the first eight months of the 1989–1990 fiscal
> year, compared to the same period last year, according to the
> report issued by the Department of Youth Services [youth
> prison].[28]

A survey by the *Raleigh News and Observer* in 1990 shows that
the worst problem in North Carolina public schools is apathy. "I
don't know and I don't care." Here again is one of the final signs of
the end of a civilization.[29]

The concern today of Harry and Betty Dent is for our posterity—our children, grandchildren, and great-grandchildren. Unfortunately, change is moving in the direction of the "isms" and their
basic view that there are no absolute truths, there is no eternity, there
is no transcendent and ever-loving God, there is no hope.

With the disintegration of the home as "the first church," parents are depending on the schools and/or the baby-sitting services to
mold and make whatever value systems, if any, their children will
have.

The "Boob Tube"

And what other teaching aid are parents depending on for the
education of the kids? The "Boob Tube"! While our educational system tends to secularize and neuterize our kids, TV soaks up more of
their time and adds violence, sex, and even more secularization. It
steals away time for reading or study.

As with the "isms," TV has gradually increased its hold on
American hearts and minds. In the 1950s and 1960s TV programs
were produced under established moral guidelines. Over a period of

time this was condemned as lacking tolerance. As the fight for audiences has become more competitive, the networks and the cable systems are appealing more and more to the sensuous desires of darkened hearts and minds.

As a consequence we are seeing increased intensity of violence, illicit and perverted sex, and stronger profanity. Subtle changes in TV programming began in the late 1960s. Then widespread changes began to occur in the latter 1970s. Statistical correlations of dramatic changes in sexual mores and diseases, criminal acts, and aberrant behavior affirm the adverse impact of TV on America's mad dash to immorality and lawlessness.

Indeed, TV is discipling more people in the ways of the world than our churches are discipling people in the ways of Jesus Christ. The time we spend in church is miniscule compared to the time we spend before the tube, especially kids. So wherever our children turn in today's world they are being subjected to the predominant view in America that says there are no moral absolutes because there is no God.

The principal problem confronting our young people is spelled I-M-M-A-T-U-R-I-T-Y. "But it won't happen to me!" "I can handle it!" Television promotes immaturity. As one of my friends, Henry Foster, remarked to me one day: "We never grow up; we just grow old."

The "isms" of this life and TV serve to promote immaturity and addiction to the things and the ways of the world because we think we don't have to answer to anybody but ourselves. No wonder we have so much misbehavior, crime, drug addiction, short-term marriages, and irresponsibility. When there is no hope and no truth people tend to be apathetic and fill the boredom with alcohol and sex.

We Set the Example

Immaturity is not just a childhood disease. It is a bane for the so-called brightest and best. The strategy that resulted in the Watergate scandal of 1972 is an example. As the plan to commit the crime of burglary against the offices of the Democratic National Committee was being concocted by Republicans, immaturity was reigning supreme. The idea in taking such a high risk was minimized because the strategists had recruited old experts in the art of doing "black-bag" jobs. They had signed up ex-CIA and ex-FBI agents to do the breaking and entering. False delusion was bathed in immaturity and stupidity. So much for great expertise built on limited maturity and reality!

The companion thought that flows out of such raw immaturity followed: "Even if we do get caught the crime can be covered up at the highest levels of government, like the White House and the Department of Justice." The conspirators had little or no concern about getting caught, however. This is the same basic immature approach youngsters use.

What happened in the Nixon Administration's scandal is that the ex-CIA and ex-FBI agents did get caught and imprisoned. How? A security guard with a sixth-grade education outsmarted the brightest and best. This security man at The Watergate Complex on the Potomac River noticed during a check of locked doors that one door's locks were taped. This door led to the offices of the Democratic National Committee leaders. The first two black-baggers had taped the door so that the other burglars could enter without having to pick the locks again.

When the break-in team realized that the guard had removed the tape the group had to reconsider the burglary plan. G. Gordon Liddy, a lawyer formerly of the FBI, the Treasury Department, and White House staff, decided to proceed with the plan. The rationale was that the security guard wouldn't think to check the door lock again—he's just a security guard. But the guard showed more maturity and responsibility. He checked the door lock again. This time he sounded the alarm that called in the District of Columbia police and initiated the fall of the White House team and president.

While practicing law I found that immaturity put more people in jail than any other human ailment. Had the Watergate break-in crew and their bosses believed that winding up in prison was a reality, only one—Gordon Liddy—would have taken the foolish risk they took. The same could be said of so many others whose lives have been broken by pushing the immaturity button rather than the reality button in making vital choices.

One of the greatest blessings our Creator bestowed on us is the privilege of choice. But God planned for us to choose wisely and not immaturely. This is why He has also provided a program by which we can come to Him and grow spiritually in His ways and in His kind of wisdom, which majors in reality and morality. The Bible tells us that it is the knowledge of the real truth that will set us free.

Our problem in this world today is that we have so many temptations from so many gods and idols that bind us to immaturity, unreality, irresponsibility, and consequently to stupidity and cupidity. As long as we remain limited in our understanding of God's plan and God's ways we, and our children as they imitate us, will continue to major in immaturity and suffer the adverse consequences that flow from our flawed choices.

A Warning About Our Kids from "Code Blue"

In 1990 a commission of educational, political, medical, and business leaders met to examine the problems of American children. They issued a report called "Code Blue." Their most disturbing and unprecedented report concluded:

> Never before has one generation of American teenagers been less healthy, less cared for, or less prepared for life than their parents were at the same age.[30]

The essence of the report made the point that the challenges to the well-being of our youth are not primarily rooted in illness, economics, or deprivation as they were in the past. Rather, the prime cause of suffering is profoundly self-destructive behavior such as drinking, drugs, violence, and promiscuity. U.S. Senator Dan Coats describes the critical finding as "a crisis of behavior and belief, a crisis of character." He said the report pictured "children who seemed drained of conscience."

As the Republican leader on the Senate's Select Committee on Children, Senator Coats warned us:

> Every culture depends, from moment to moment, directly on individuals who will act with integrity. Keeping the law, respecting life and property, loving one's family, fighting for national goals, helping the poor, paying taxes—all these depend on individual virtues like courage, duty, loyalty, charity, compassion and civility. . . .
> The character of our children is the leading indicator of our future as a culture. How did we come to this grim and dangerous state of affairs? We live in a century in which "facts" are glorified while "values" are assigned an inferior status as mere matters of opinion. We have seen the development of a militant relativism that dictates that it is impossible to prefer one value above another, since all conceptions of the good are equally subjective.[31]

Values Determine Our Future

Why are values so essential to our society? They constitute the key to the very salvation and future of our unique American system of government. Values keep us vigilant to the difference between what is Right and what is Wrong. They keep us on the road to balance, to fairness, to human dignity, to human hope, to human restraint, and self-discipline by bridling our instinctive drive toward self-ism. Our whole free market economic system depends on value-directed leaders who know and respect the boundaries of business ethics. Our entire American system, which has made us the envy of the world, depends directly on the private virtue of individual Americans because it is the individual Americans who have the precious power to govern or destroy the system itself.

British statesman Edmund Burke argued:

> Men are qualified for civil liberty in exact proportion to their disposition to put moral chains on their own appetites. . . . It is ordained in the eternal constitution of things that men of intemperate minds cannot be free. Their passions forge their fetters.[32]

If we hope to avert the potential disintegration of our American system, from our house to the White House, we must return to the basics that put us on the road to success. People are going to have to learn all over again how to live by rules, how to value our responsibilities over even our rights, and how to discipline our appetites for all the things of the world. We are going to have to become literate all over again functionally and morally. And, yes, people are going to have to get back to God—and fast!

The change in our public school system, and our children, began when God was ejected from the schools in 1962 and 1963. That marked a turning point in American values—with all indicators pointing down instead of up.

The dramatic restructuring of educational policies was caused by a reinterpretation by the United States Supreme Court of the church/state question. Concerning religion, the First Amendment to the United States Constitution was written, "Congress shall make no law respecting an establishment of religion, or prohibiting the free exercise thereof."

Previously this had been interpreted to mean that Congress

could not establish a national religious denomination. The founders of our republic intended to protect the free exercise of religion so that private virtue might flourish in the hearts of all Americans and so that public virtue might thus be the norm in America. They realized that man could not be trusted with power without a system of checks and balances.

The founders understood that people who believed in a transcendent God would be more likely to behave and to be less selfish. It would take this kind of national character for the new risky form of government to work and survive. So their aim was to foster belief in God while at the same time assuring that no single religion or denomination would control the republic as had been the case in the old country.

The Supreme Court's Influence

In 1962 the Supreme Court removed student prayers from schools. The next year they abolished any Bible readings in schools. Even the word *God* was deleted from school correspondence by the Court in 1976. In 1980 the basic law of the world, the Ten Commandments, was removed from view in schools. The secularist trend continued so that in 1985, 1986, and 1989 all benedictions and invocations were ruled unconstitutional.

In ten years the Supreme Court had repudiated 170 years of precedent in court decisions by removing all religious activities from public schools. From 1962 forward the public schools began a slide from top to bottom not only in ethics and behavior but also in academics and achievement.

While we in America are leaning over so far to protect individual rights from subjection to any religious exercises or materials, it is ironic that in pagan Australia there are chaplains in many public schools. I spoke in sixteen schools while in Perth, Australia, in 1989, and I was amazed at the latitude I was given to talk about God and the Christian value system.

Why the U.S.A. Is at Risk

In 1983 the United States Department of Education commissioned a special task force to study the ills of the national public education system. Its report was appropriately called *A Nation at Risk*. Here are key excerpts:

For the first time in the history of our country, the educational skills of one generation will not surpass, equal or even approach those of their parents.

Nearly 40 percent of 17-year-olds cannot draw inferences from written material, and only a third can solve a math problem requiring several steps.

In many schools, the time spent learning how to cook and drive counts as much toward a high school diploma as the time spent studying mathematics, English, chemistry, American history, and biology.[33]

We Lead the World Wrongly

One concerned citizen is statistically documenting what he perceives to be the adverse consequences to our nation by the Supreme Court decisions against prayers in schools. David Barton's footnoted statistics show a sharp upward trend in bad behavior patterns. He begins with illiteracy, then moves into violent crimes, child abuse, and a number of other problem areas. He sums it all up with six areas in which America leads the world: violent crime, divorce rate, teenage pregnancy in the Western world, voluntary abortions, illegal drug use, and documented cases of AIDS.[34]

What would George Washington, Abraham Lincoln, and Benjamin Franklin think about our current moral predicament, especially in light of their thoughts about right and wrong?

Of all the dispositions and habits which lead to prosperity, religion and morality are indispensable supports. . . . Whatever may be conceded to the influence of refined education . . . reason and experience both forbid us to expect that national morality can prevail in exclusion of religious principle (George Washington).

But for [the Bible] we could not know right from wrong. All things most desirable for man's welfare . . . are to be found portrayed in it (Abraham Lincoln).

He who shall introduce into public affairs the principles of primitive Christianity will change the face of the world (Benjamin Franklin).[35]

They would be as concerned as we should be that we have turned our children over to the new Number One Religion in America: secular humanism.

See what are the answers to these problems that confront our posterity in the most vital areas of our lives, education and the rearing of our kids?

Guard Their Hearts

The Bible warns us to, above all else, guard our hearts. Much stress is placed on the heart throughout the Bible because the Bible pictures the heart as being not only the place of our emotions and feelings, but also as the very center of a person's being. Our physical heart is noted as the pumping station for our physical life and its blood supply system. But biblically speaking the heart is also our moral center, our volitional will center, and the center of our value system and our choices and decisions.

Too many Americans are living with a spiritual disease I call "heart anemia." Spiritually, too many folks have major heart disease insofar as their value system is concerned. Some have minor disease, but none of us is free from our flawed human condition. What Christianity offers is supernatural help so that our major disease—our sinful selfish nature—can be reduced to a minor disease. We will continue to be sinners, but under Christian leadership we no longer sin habitually; we obey and thus habitually behave better through our new value system. We know how to get forgiveness for our sins. As the bumper sticker says, "Christians are not perfect, just forgiven." We get forgiveness through repentance before God.

Become Involved in Their Education

Parents must become much more involved in the education of their children. This requires more than attendance at PTA or PTO meetings. It means studying with the kids as much as possible and keeping your fingers on the good blood (life) flowing in their budding value systems. You have to know your child and what your child is and is not learning. It is imperative to understand what kind of person the child's education is producing through the value system of that child.

This could entail enrolling your child in home studies, Christian schools, or other quality private schools if possible. Dr. Stephen Tchivijian, a Christian psychologist and son-in-law of Dr. Billy Graham, recommends enrolling your children in Christian schools. Going to one of his seminars will cause you to re-think the education of your child. He believes there is all the difference in the world between the value quality education your child will receive in a Christian school than in the public school system. I agree!

The four areas that most affect the life of your child are the home, the school, the church, and the influence of peers and friends. Too many parents are neglecting all four of these vital areas of training for their children. You would be better advised to spend the money on them now rather than leave it to them later after you have checked out and have lost your choices in affecting the values of your children. The time to best prepare our children is NOW—not later or never. We must assure that the education of our children connects virtue with knowledge.

In viewing the riot ruins in Los Angeles on May 7, 1992, President George Bush dispensed the best advice of his presidency when he challenged all Americans to commit themselves to family strength and faith in God and "teaching kids right from wrong," declaring: "Government can't do that." He was speaking with a quavering voice in Mount Zion Missionary Baptist Church in the heart of the worst devastation of a riot in America this century. One key problem in South Los Angeles, where there have been two such riots in recent years, is that most kids are either fatherless or family-less.[36]

Substantially missing in today's system of education is virtue. We have this current crisis in our educational system and the type of conduct by young people as set forth by CBS News because of it. We will answer one day for what we did with our most trusted treasure—the hearts and value systems of our children and grandchildren.

Be Aware and Active About Values and "Isms"

Parents should become involved in civic movements that lobby public officials to put values back into all levels of our educational system. It is imperative that parents be informed on the "isms" of life so they can detect their insidious burrowing into the hearts of our young people. It is these philosophies that teach young hearts that there is only the here and now (secularism), and there are no moral absolutes (relativism), and thus there is no hope (nihilism).

Become Posted on Public Affairs

Parents must be educated on current events and public affairs. They need to read and study more. Their ignorance and inaction can be most detrimental to the future of our posterity. Schoolteachers are good people, who come up to me in my teaching sessions in churches and affirm the problems in education today. However, the ultimate shaping of that schoolteaching curriculum for the purpose of molding the life and worldview of your child needs your attention. What are the predominant "isms" at the core of the curriculum? As R. C. Sproul inquired, "What kind of child are you trying to produce?"

Be Careful of the "Boob Tube"

Young people are watching too much television. They need to develop the habit of reading good books to program their value systems. There is much quality education available to all people in good books. One of the greatest experiences of my life has come since I began systematically reading Christian books and also secular books that further increased my understanding of this world and the meaning and purpose of life. The experiences of life, including traveling all over the world, also helped. But my greatest education came through studying the Holy Bible and hundreds of books about the Bible and its great teachings and value system.

TV can add to the richness of a good education, but values should be established in a young person's life before he or she becomes addicted to television. It is imperative that youngsters be able to distinguish good from evil and Right from Wrong, especially in watching television. This is why a person's value system must be installed as soon as possible. There are some very helpful educational programs on television, but it is the discipline in a person's life that provides the restraints and the sense of responsibility that is so necessary for the proper use of television for Right instead of Wrong.

Parents: Get Involved with Your Kids

Parents must be involved with their children in their home, play, peers, school, church, and especially in their moral and spiritual development. Mom and Pop are going to have to spend much more time with their kids. This means camping out, being present at their athletic events, having question and answer times, and having family devotionals led by Pop. Mom and Pop must know their children's minds and hearts so they'll know when they need special counsel, love, and special correction and discipline. Yes, the *hard side* and the *soft side* of love. Your kids are your posterity and a heritage from God!

Get with the Three Cs

One of the most outspoken experts on education is former Secretary of Education under President Ronald Reagan. William Bennett believes we can make progress in the schools, the families, and the churches. Bennett boldly advocates the use of the Bible in public schools. His point is that the Bible teaches "moral values we all share. . . . And [its stories] shouldn't be thrown out just because they are in the Bible."[37] Here we have the greatest value system in the world, and it is banned from schoolrooms, even as literature.

Bennett proposes what he calls "The Three Cs of Education." These are content, character, and choice. Content is what students learn in school. Character is the basis of our value system for what is good and what is right.[38] Even Russell Kirk states that "the great end of education is ethical."

> In the college, as at all other levels of the educational process, the student comes to apprehend the differences between good and evil. It is this humane tradition and discipline which makes us true human persons and sustains a decent civil order.[39]

Bennett's third "C" is choice. This is the provision of parents with vouchers or payments from the government to permit them to choose the school which is better for their own child. This concept is also being backed by the Secretary of Education under President Bush, Lamar Alexander.

In his 1992 book *The De-Valuing of America* the former professor and education secretary describes the three fundamental flaws of education as a soft curriculum, a general lack of accountability, and a lack of parental choice.[40] Bennett sums up the essence of what he has learned from his decade of Washington experience:

> The American people's sense of things in most instances is RIGHT; the liberal elite's sense of things is in most instances WRONG.[41]

He is correct!

Bennett believes our schools themselves must have an "ethos"—meaning good character. For this to work, teachers and principals must be willing to articulate ideals and convictions to the students through ethical candor, not just indoctrination. He further suggests that "we must have teachers and principals who not only state the difference between right and wrong, but make an effort to live that difference in front of students."[42]

The former secretary is talking about moral example. This principle is true not only in the field of education but also in the home and in our churches.[43]

I recommend that Bennett's idea be fostered as one of the most practical and pertinent answers to our educational dilemma.

A good book to read on options for educating your child is *Schooling Choices: An Examination of Private, Public, & Home Education*, by Dr. H. Wayne House, editor, with assistance from Dr. Kenneth Gangel, Dr. Greg Harris, and Dr. David Smith.[44]

Get Into the Books

Dr. Allan Bloom saw the reopening of the American mind as coming from getting back to the great books. This is also proposed by Nash, Bennett, and Kirk. Russell Kirk states:

> The aim of great books is ethical: to teach what it means to be a man. Every major form of literary art has taken for its deeper themes what T. S. Eliot called "the permanent things"—the norms of human action.[45]

Reading makes one a full person. The late James F. Byrnes of South Carolina was one of the greatest men produced by my state, but he never finished high school. By reading and studying on his own, he became a congressman, U.S. senator, justice of the U.S. Supreme Court, the "assistant president" for President Franklin D. Roosevelt during World War II, and finally, the governor of South Carolina.

Child experts say that reading to little children is one of the best exercises parents can practice to fulfill the heart desires of the little ones and to program their budding little computer brains.

Far too many Americans read far too little. People prefer fiction and entertainment over substantive works that build character and intellect. So parents, get yourselves and your kids in the habit of reading the right books. It may prompt *you* into doing what you too may be neglecting.

Watch Out for Their Peers

Running with the wrong crowd has destroyed so many young lives. Peer pressure keeps getting stronger and stronger. It is vital that parents help the kids get with the right crowd—like the Boy Scouts, Girl Scouts, Young Life, Youth for Christ, church, Sunday school, and Christian youth groups. I continue to thank God for directing that scoutmaster to me and also in directing me to the best young man in my hometown, David H. Banks, Jr., two years older than I. Both made a difference in the outcome of my life. Running with the right crowd! This is righteous peer pressure!

The Kids Must Know
You Love Them Unconditionally

Loving unconditionally is the first duty of all parents. Mom and Pop must love the Lord God Almighty, the two of them must become one in Christ for all to see, and then Mom and Pop must love their offspring the same way—unconditionally. The kids must know this beyond any question.

Spend Quality Time with Your Kids

This is how they will know you really love them. While spending time with your kids, answer their questions, teach them out of your own life and values, let them see some of the world about them, build up their self-esteem and hold down their personal egotism, and show them how to help other people. They should be getting their top value lessons at home. Today they are not only missing their value lessons at home, but they are not even getting proper time and attention there.

Never forget: the best teachers are supposed to be Mom and Pop!

Make It Your Goal to Bring Them to Christ

Finally, we are getting down to priority number one! We are to see to the physical and emotional maturity of our children. Most of all, we are accountable for the spiritual maturity of our children. You must be able to answer the first and foremost question: What did you do with what the Bible calls "a heritage from the Lord" (Ps. 127:3)?

We are to raise them up in the fear and admonition of the Lord so that they grow as Luke briefly described the development of Jesus' young life: "And Jesus increased in wisdom and stature and in favor with God and men" (Luke 2:52).

So, here is our principal duty to our posterity:

> Train up a child in the way he should go,
> And when he is old he will not depart
> from it (Prov. 22:6).

As glum as is the news coming out of our American system of education today, there is some good news. *The Day America Told the Truth* reports that 80 percent of Americans want to see morals and ethics taught in our schools. Also amazing, the majority of Americans are willing to sacrifice to make America stronger and better. Why? Because the survey also reveals that Americans fear for the future, and our posterity, of America.

Americans told the writers of *The Day America Told the Truth* that religious people are more moral, more willing to die for their beliefs, more at peace, more truthful, more committed to the family, and better workers.[46]

Hang in there! America can be turned around—if we can get our message into the hearts and minds of our posterity.

CHAPTER SEVEN

Right vs. Wrong in the Marketplace

Every person in the world is either a missionary or a mission field.[1]

The marketplace in America is the envy of the world. Our marketplace, or place of work, has produced the greatest quantity and quality of "golden eggs" in the history of the world. Our economic system is full of incentives designed to bring out the best thinking and work ethic in us. The person who can build the better mousetrap wins until a better one is invented and placed on the open market for sale at whatever price the traffic will bear.

The American economic system is a free market economy, or market economy where goods and services are traded according to basically free market principles of economics. The communist system, on the other hand, is one of total control, politically and economically. The control is exercised by the political party through use of a government apparatus.

While our free enterprise system has provided the most powerful and productive economic engine for producing economic prosperity, we are not without our economic highs and lows. We are subject to recessions and depressions because individual citizens and businesses have the freedom to spend our dollars when and how they please. We vote economically with our dollar bills in much the same way we vote politically with our ballots. All of our wise economists have not been able to agree on how to control the expenditure of those dollar bills in a way that would keep our economic engine rolling on the rails of prosperity. Thus there are times of employment and economic problems. We have been experiencing this in 1990–1992 after enjoying a healthy economy for more than a decade. This is the price we pay for having a free market economy and all of the blessings of personal freedom.

Freedom Can Bring Abuse

Another problem with this freedom of choice is that it allows cheating, deceit, lying, stealing, and all kinds of wrongdoing and crimes. Ours is an economic system that is highly competitive. Anytime we humans get ourselves into a competitive situation there is always the temptation, at the minimum, to cheat and skirt the edges of righteousness. The question for each individual is where is that line between what is Right and what is Wrong?

During the early days of the Watergate scandal John Ehrlichman was considered to be a "good" man with much power in the White House. John awakened one night realizing that earlier in the day he had crossed the line between Right and Wrong. As a lawyer and the counsel to the president, John knew that he could not get back across that line separating good from evil. He had broken the law. Subsequently he went through two Watergate trials and lost everything he had worked for in life. He served time in a desert prison in New Mexico.

When I visited John several years ago he told me and showed me that he is a different man. Out of all of his troubles John came to know Jesus Christ. Now he has an even higher standard of Right and Wrong to observe. John is a much better man today. He has found peace with God, with his peers, and with himself. He told me that he now thanks God every day for his two Watergate trials. He realizes that he might never have really known the Lord had he continued to live out his life only as a good man with power.

The scandals in America reach way beyond the marketplace of politics. Our highly competitive athletic programs are suffering the indignities of cheating and other wrongdoings. Professional and even college athletics have become big-time money-making marketplaces in recent years. This hikes the urgency to win at almost any cost. Professional baseball salaries have become unrealistically high. In 1991, 225 major league baseball players earned at least $1 million each. Heavyweight boxing matches are yielding multi-multimillion dollar purses, as much as $30 million. Athletes such as Mike Tyson evidently cannot handle so much fame, fortune, and favor. Big bucks can turn a person to big troubles, as with Tyson. Our sports heroes become idols to us and may become gods to themselves.

We read all about these excesses on our sports pages. Sports heroes can be great role models for Right, but they can also turn into role models for Wrong for our youngsters overnight.

The late Coach Vince Lombardi's famous quote, "Winning is everything!" vibrates all the way down to Little League sports. We all love athletic competition for our kids and grandkids. We all want them to be winners. That too is a part of the American Dream. But the question is what is the price of that victory?

Some of the athletes go so far as to injure their own highly prized bodies by using steroids to help them make first-team, to win, and become superstars. The problem can extend to winning cheerleader slots for our kids. Some get tempted to break laws and then cover up the criminal activities. Others do not bother with a cover-up because they see no Wrong in what they are doing. One mother was recently convicted for plotting to kill the mother of a rival to her daughter's election as a high school cheerleader.

While some see no Wrong, others have either rationalized the Wrong way or have what the Bible calls a "seared" conscience, known as psychopathy or sociopathy. They have no social or moral conscience. A 1987 book on child-rearing forecasts that the "future includes the high probability that greater numbers of psychopathic individuals are headed our way."[2]

Some people do not have enough intelligence, convictions, or education to understand the difference between what is Right and what is Wrong. All statistics also point toward an increase of people in this category. Some of the professional criminals feign insanity. A noted clinical psychologist with years of experience studying and working with hardened criminals maintains that the professional criminal does know Right from Wrong, but he prefers Wrong over Right. Dr. Stanton E. Samenow of St. Elizabeth's Hospital in Washington, D.C., says: "The criminal chooses crime." Thus Dr. Samenow declares that locking up this type of personality will not change him. What has to be changed, he says, "is how they think."[3]

The Apostle Paul said much the same thing in Romans 12:2, where he calls on God's people to be spiritually transformed so that they can move from being transformed by the ways of the world to being a transformer of people in the world to the ways of God.

It's Part of Our Sin Nature

People who best understand the high degree of the lack of reality—as well as the high degree of wickedness—that lurks in the human heart are law enforcement officers, prison guards, lawyers, medical personnel, counselors, pastors, anyone who deals with human problems. Not dealing with the truth and reality of a situation is another consequence of our sin nature. Innately we are tempted to deny that there is anything Wrong with us. However, we delude no one but ourselves. This is a big sign of IMMATURITY.

M. Scott Peck, M.D., a Christian psychiatrist and writer, covers this subject fully in his best-selling book, *The Road Less Traveled*. He says that people want a quick fix; they do not want to be changed. They refuse to see the reality of their sin and wrongdoing. He attributes this in part to the basic laziness of humans and sees laziness as a part of the sin nature of man. What has to happen for us to be changed, he writes, is that we must face our Wrongs and engage in constant self-examination as we seek to grow toward maturity. Humans must grow out of childhood and into adulthood. The Bible says this too, especially in the epistles.[4]

Keith Miller also deals with denial of any wrongdoing and the consequent deception, the two keys to deceitfulness and corruption. In most cases, no one is deceived but the deceiver. Miller says that denial leads to a lack of reality. This inability to face reality then issues into irresponsibility and wrongdoing.

With our moral values eroding, we are being confronted daily with national news reports of scandal after scandal in the marketplace. When commitment to a Higher Authority slips, crime and corruption rise. People tend to be more concerned about God's authority than man's authority. If they feel they are breaking God's Law they are more likely to stop, look, and listen. Both usages of the word *fear* convey our concern about God. In one use of *fear* we are expressing reverence and awe. In the other, we are conveying a fear of God's judgment and wrath, as has been posted throughout the Bible.

Ever since the days of the Enlightenment in the 1700s, man has increasingly sensed that he is smarter than he previously thought and that perhaps God may not be so supernatural after all. Maybe God is natural like man. Or perhaps God only has a touch of the supernatural.

Criminal Activities Stem from Increasing Explicit Sex

In an interesting book, *A Criminal History of Mankind*, Dr. Colin Wilson, a scholar in criminality, has made the same observation.[5] The history of criminal activities in the world continues to go up. One of the most startling conclusions from this study is the report that there is a direct correlation between the increase in the titillation of the sex drive in humans and criminal activity by humans.

Dr. Wilson contends that the sexual revolution and its explosive impact on sexual stimulation is a prime reason for the very high levels of crime in America today. Explicit sex is almost everywhere today, especially on television. The William Kennedy Smith trial on TV was most graphic about the sex act.

Pornography abounds on TV and in all kinds of publications. And pornographers in the United States are making billions of dollars by exporting some of their smut to the rest of the world. I was appalled to see the worst pornographic magazines on the streets of Cluj, Romania, soon after the revolution gave the people freedom. The publications were all marked "Made in the U.S.A."

Sexual stimulation and the breakdown in family values are directly responsible for this country leading the world in teenage pregnancies. The most volatile issue in America today is abortion. Abortion is M-U-R-D-E-R in the first degree. It is an abomination to God because it is coming out of sexual titillation and depravity that leads to m-u-r-d-e-r.

Sexual depravity is also directly responsible for the escalation of crime in America to the point where we lead the industrialized nations in the world in violent crimes. It is our young people who are committing most of the violent crimes. They are hyped up by sexual stimulation at the peak of their sex drives and emotional immaturity.

Unmitigated Greed

The two most shocking marketplace scandals in recent times have been the savings-and-loan fiasco and the "Greengate" rip-off on Wall Street. In both of these criminal enterprises the perpetrators had been wallowing in the slop of one of the seven deadly sins, unmitigated greed. Billions and billions of dollars were stolen and/or squandered. The taxpayers of America are paying directly for the S&L fraud because generous Uncle Sam has guaranteed bank deposits and many other fiduciary holdings, including company pension funds. Over the years Congress has approved many government-guarantee programs without comprehending the sin nature of man, the most elemental lesson in the Bible.

It is better to trust in the LORD
Than to put confidence in man.

It is better to trust in the LORD
Than to put confidence in princes (Ps. 118:8-9).

Jesus warned about this green-eyed monster of the marketplace in His parable of the Rich Fool.

"Watch out! Be on your guard against all kinds of greed; a man's life does not consist in the abundance of his possessions. . . . Life is more than food, and the body more than clothes" (Luke 12:15, 23 NIV).

Even the secular news media have been thumping their powerful pulpits in disgust about the loss of ethical values in our nation. The May 25, 1987, cover of *Time* magazine was adorned with a moral compass exemplifying Right versus Wrong and this big question:

What Ever Happened to Ethics: Assaulted by sleaze, scandals and hypocrisy, America searches for its moral bearings.

White-collar crime has been in the forefront of the crimes being given priority investigation and prosecution by the U.S. Department of Justice. And as the women in America become involved more and more in the workplace—65 percent of Moms are working outside the home today—the rate of incarceration of women escalates. The most common crime I see in the news regarding women is embezzlement of company funds. Today some Moms are nursing their babies behind locked prison doors. There was a time when the ratio of women to men in prison was negligible. Not today!

Civil rights issues have also become more prominent in the marketplace. In addition to race discrimination, there is now the matter of gender or sexual discrimination and harassment. The nation's attention was riveted on this question during the U.S. Senate Judiciary Committee hearings on the nomination of Judge Clarence Thomas to a seat on the U.S. Supreme Court in 1991. Even though sexual harassment is a Wrong, the American people had not focused on this as such a serious offense prior to the nomination controversy.

The Bible Lists Other Wrongdoings

The Bible is loaded with examples of wrongdoing in the lives of people. Perhaps the most descriptive list is set forth by Paul in Galatians 5:19-21, where he enumerates the works of the flesh.

Now the works of the flesh are evident, which are: adultery, fornication, uncleanness, licentiousness, idolatry, sorcery, hatred, contentions, jealousies, outbursts of wrath, selfish ambitions, dissensions, heresies, envy, murders, drunkenness, revelries, and the like . . . I tell you . . . that those who practice such things will not inherit the kingdom of God.

While our codes of laws list many Wrongs punishable by law, there are many Wrongs that are not recorded in the criminal codes of man. Despite the lists of Right and Wrong in the Bible, we will not be able to remember them by rote. But we can discern what Jesus Christ would and would not do under a given set of circumstances if we really know Him. He was not a legalist caught up in the jots and tittles of the law. My summary of what Jesus' life and sacrifice tells us is:

Forget your personal rights, but remember your personal responsibilities. You are to be givers, not takers; unconditional lovers and servants. The best summary of my law is wrapped up in the Golden Rule and the Great Commandment. Install these in your hearts. Then you can discern right from wrong. Any questions? Check the Good Samaritan. Forgetful? Hang my cross around your neck.

It is one thing to be holy or do what is Right in the church. We are expected to behave and be good in the church. Very few folks misbehave in or on the church premises. But what about out there in our workaday world? A different crowd works out there, and a different standard is expected out there. Right? No, Wrong! This is where we who call ourselves "Christ-i-ans," or as Martin Luther labeled church members, "little Christs," are "to be doers of the word" according to the Epistle of James and the overall thrust of the message of the Bible. Indeed, our purpose as members of the body of Christ is to get our spiritual tank filled at the church by "being hearers of the Word" so we can be "doers of the Word" as we go about our work in the marketplace.

This may seem to be crazy or too "churchie" to many on the church rolls. Yet being witnesses for righteousness in our actions and our words is what the priesthood of all believers and the ministry of all of God's people is about. This precept, called Marketplace Ministry, goes to the very heart of the gospel of Jesus Christ: ". . . and you shall be witnesses to Me" (Acts 1:8b). "Go therefore and make disciples of all the nations" (Matt. 28:19a). "Go into all the world and preach the gospel to every creature" (Mark 16:15).

Jesus commands His followers to win the world to His ways—in the beginning of the Book of Acts and at the end of each of the Gospels. No other teaching has received such prominent places of repetition as the Great Commission of Jesus Christ. The reason Jesus gives such a high priority and imperative to the implementation of the Great Commission is that *God's purpose is to save all humanity*.

This is what God the Father had in mind when He created the world. God wanted Adam and Eve and all of us living in right relationships with Him and with one another because God loves us, anyway!

The Great Commission is only one of many passages of Scripture that commands church members to be on duty as witnesses and ministers. The prime duty of all of God's people is to worship God in spirit and in truth. We are to be taught and trained to be mature saints who know what we believe and why. We are to fellowship together in love and help one another and pray for one another. But all of this is in preparation for evangelism, witness, ministry, and service in God's Army of Salvation. The mission of the church of Jesus Christ is to change the world from the ways of the world to the ways of Jesus Christ in order that all be saved.

And where and how can this aim be best implemented? In the world where we work, move, live, and have our being. Thus the importance of marketplace ministry and witness.

We Are to Be Fruitful

Church members need to hear the proclamation and teaching of the Word of God and must study the Word of God for all of these purposes. So the church is our recruit training depot, as the U.S. Marines would say. Worship is the first and foremost requirement. But even worship is designed, in part, to strengthen our personal relationship with the Lord so that we are better prepared to be Christians with mature character and to do God's Word in witness and ministry. Every purpose of the church is tied ultimately to the full witness and ministry of all of the people of God so that people who are spiritually lost may become spiritually saved. How is God glorified? Jesus answered this question in His Farewell Address at the Last Supper when He said, "By this My Father is glorified, that you bear much fruit; so you will be My disciples" (John 15:8).

Jesus used the word *fruit* in John 15 to mean bringing lost people into right relationship with Him and the people of God so that the words and works of Jesus may be implemented on earth. He used the analogy of the Vine-dresser (God the Father), the Vine (Jesus), and the branches (all the people of God). The spiritual life and love of Jesus flow from the Vine into and through the branches to produce new fruit. Spiritual life and love can move because of the right alignment or relationship between the Vine and the branches. John 15 is about right relationships that produce spiritual life and love to carry on the work of Jesus Christ in the world.

Jesus is concerned with the relationship between Jesus and His followers, among the followers, and the relationships of the followers with the hostile and unsaved people in the world. The aim is to use right relationships and the life and love of Jesus Christ to touch and change the hostile and unsaved people in the world. This is the plan of Jesus Christ for changing the world from the ways of the world to the ways of God in order to save all of humanity.

We Must Practice Real Stewardship

God commanded Adam and Eve to take dominion over all of His creation. The Scriptures tell us that God placed them in the Garden of Eden to keep and maintain it for God. This is the beginning of a major biblical teaching on the subject of stewardship. For years I thought that stewardship in the church was all about "picking people's pockets to pay the preacher and the mortgage," and I was even chairman of the church stewardship committee once. All of the sermons I ever heard on stewardship were directed toward meeting the budget or getting money for other causes of the church. Just as I did not understand the full import of this teaching, neither do most others in the church.

A *steward* is defined as one who is in charge of the large estate of another. In this case, the large estate is God's creation. God has the title deed to the world, and we are holding possession for Him as His trustees and overseers. We are in what lawyers would call a trust or fiduciary relationship insofar as the world is concerned. If a trustee violates his fiduciary relationship, the trustee is liable to be sued and/or imprisoned. This is serious business down here and also up there.

The earth is the LORD's, and all its fullness,
The world and those who dwell therein.

For He has founded it upon the seas,
And established it upon the waters (Ps. 24:1-2).

What is man, that you are mindful of him?
And the son of man that You visit him?
For You have made him a little lower than the angels,
And You have crowned him with glory and honor.
You have made him to have dominion over the works
    of your hands;
You have put all things under his feet,
All sheep and oxen—
Even the beasts of the field,
The birds of the air,
And the fish of the sea
That pass through the paths of the seas (Ps. 8:4-8).

In the well-known Parable of the Talents, Jesus expressed His concern for the serious nature of stewardship. He concludes with a stern warning about ignoring our duties as trustees.

My definition of stewardship is simply "It's all His 'un; ain't none of it our'n!"

Stewardship covers how a man uses his body and mind, what he does with His money, and how and where he spends his time. The big picture of stewardship is that God owns it all and is looking for righteous stewards. This spells accountability, responsibility, and stewardship.

God created human beings in a special way for a special purpose. He gave us a superior mind and the ability to think, to make decisions, and to choose. He endowed us with the power to communicate and to love Him and one another—to be able to live in right relationships vertically and horizontally. The supple hands He supplied for us are designed to enable us to grow food, to craft tools, to build buildings, and . . . to do the work of God!

Stewardship Includes
Bringing Others to Salvation

God's intention is that all of humankind serve Him, not just His chosen people. It is the duty of the chosen people to bring the lost people into God's Kingdom to take their place in God's Master Plan.

The mission, therefore, of the chosen people is to rescue the perishing and bring them into the church so they may be trained to do the work of ministry—to be stewards and witnesses for what is right in God's sight.

There is a certain sense of moral schizophrenia in us Christians who are privileged to be Americans. In the church we swear our fealty to God, the Bible, Christian values, and the work of the church. In the marketplace we are confronted with the idols of expediency, situation ethics, career success, pragmatism, and mammonism. This is like wearing two hats: one for Sunday and church and the other for Monday through Friday in the marketplace. Saturday requires a special holiday hat, and if we are not careful we may wear it on Sunday, God's Day.

But God did not create man and woman to "have a ball." And God did not intend for us to be able to take all of our accumulated material possessions with us when we die physically. Have you ever spotted a U-Haul trailer behind a hearse?

I see the beginning of the Great Commandment and the Great Commission all the way back in the book of beginnings, the Book of Genesis. These two teachings, loving and serving as stewards and witnesses for righteousness, run throughout all of Scripture. So our duty as members of the body of Christ is to bring the world under the Lordship of Jesus Christ. Our timing is to finish our part in God's master plan before we die, just as Jesus completed His mission before ascending to be with the Father. The final words Jesus uttered on the cross were "It is finished!" (John 19:30).

The Void We Have Makes Us Need God

Despite the commandments to do the Right Thing insofar as God is concerned, the marketplace is a different forum from the church place or even the home place. At home we can have our own little tribe thinking, believing, and doing what we wish. But in the marketplace things are different. Yet, God fashioned people much the same. He planted in every one of his human creatures so many similarities, including a void in our lives that cries out to be His residency.

God also gave us the best evidence of His existence, the vastness and beauty of all of His creation. In Romans 1 and 2, Paul tells us that we are without excuse if we do not believe in God and serve Him.

Adam and Eve had these evidences, but they chose to become the first humanists and relativists in the world. So, the "isms" of life, our philosophies of life, were born in the Garden of Eden and have been with us ever since.

In Genesis 3, the void that God had crafted in the lives of His human creatures as His place of residency was filled now with a new lord, man and woman, calling their own shots in life.

The Battle of Spiritual Warfare for all these years has been over who is lord in that void. Paul refers to our bodies as the holy temple for the residence of the Spirit of God to dwell and to lead and guide us past the rugged shoals and temptations of life and into the abundant life here and on into eternity (see 1 Cor. 6:19).

Death: Humanity's Biggest Fear

Man's biggest fear is physical death. God also has an answer for this morbid concern. It is that same spiritual transaction that takes us from living just in the temporal and sinful here-and-now to the Kingdom-living in eternity where that void is totally filled with the Creator. Thus man has this kind of desire for eternity beating in his heart. We usually only dwell on this thought during a funeral service.

That void is a head start for witnessing and ministering to people in the marketplace. There is no one out there who is not bedeviled by some trial, tribulation, or hurt. Here, again, God has designed hurts and fears to open the hearts of all people for a visitation by His Spirit upon prompting by God's ministering people.

We're Open to God When We Hurt

Reverend Charles Holland, pastor of Pleasant Grove Baptist Church near Bowman, Georgia, specializes in ministering to hurting people inside and outside of his church. He does so because the Bible commands him to reach out to people in distress. But he is also wise, realizing that when people are up against the wall with a problem they are more open to receive Jesus Christ as Lord and Savior.

The purpose of trials and testing is to mature us spiritually, to refine us spiritually, to strengthen us spiritually, to prepare us spiritually, to enrich us spiritually, and to save us spiritually. There is a most profitable book for hurting people. *Gaining Through Losing*, by Evelyn Christenson, has helped many people understand that the way down can well be the way up.[6] It is when we are down and out that we are more willing as humans to allow the presence and power of our

Creator into that void. There is one big cure for stubbornness and immaturity—a thorn in the flesh! Ask the Apostle Paul.

This is what happened to all of the president's men who came to Jesus Christ in the Nixon Watergate scandal. C. S. Lewis says every spiritual conversion experience is the product of a failure or crisis in a person's life. This is why so many alcoholics and other addicted people become Christians. There is healing in that personal relationship with our Creator through Jesus Christ as our Lord, Savior, and Mediator.

Peter, Paul, and James admonished us to count our trials as joy. Why? Paul answers the question in Romans 5:3–5.

> And not only that, but we also glory in tribulations, knowing that tribulation produces perseverance; and perseverance, character; and character, hope. Now hope does not disappoint, because the love of God has been poured out in our hearts by the Holy Spirit who was given to us.

Paul explains further in Romans 5 that our tribulations can lead us to reconciliation. In 2 Corinthians 12:9–10, Paul addresses the blessing that came to him:

> And He said to me, "My grace is sufficient for you, for My strength is made perfect in weakness." Therefore most gladly I will rather boast in my infirmities, that the power of Christ may rest upon me. Therefore I take pleasure in infirmities, in reproaches, in needs, in persecutions, in distresses, for Christ's sake. For when I am weak, then I am strong.

The apostle was making the point that we open up that void in our lives to the Presence and Power of God when we are hurting and distressed because that is when we depend on God instead of ourselves.

The reality of this teaching that "hurtin' helps" has been affirmed so many times in our ministry in prisons and behind the old Iron Curtain where the dear saints were persecuted for their faith for decades. This teaching has also worked in my own life. It is one of the reasons I am a full-time "minister of reconciliation" and "ambassador of Christ" today. In 2 Corinthians 5, Paul charged us all with being ministers of reconciliation and ambassadors for Christ.

Jesus Told Us Right and Wrong

Jesus also addressed this question of our tests, tribulations, and perspective in the marketplace and life in general. In the Sermon on the Mount, Jesus confronted His followers with His prescription for living the Right way instead of the Wrong way, wherever we are, including the marketplace. In fact, the Sermon on the Mount is a sermon on what constitutes real repentance before God. It contrasts God's ways with man's ways, and it contains the most detailed exposition of God's ethical standards.

The Sermon on the Mount established an entirely new system of values. The Beatitudes, the beautiful attitudes of life, set the requirements for the blessed life on earth. Jesus proclaims that blessings flow not from the values or conventional wisdom of the world but by the values that the world despises. Here is another example of down being up.

> Poor in spirit (realizing their spiritual destitution and thus dependence on God); mourners (sensitive to their spiritual faults and the need of God's help); meekness (openness and willingness to be changed by God); quest for righteousness (those up against the wall); merciful (forgiveness and compassion for others); pure in heart (devoted to God and sensitive to His presence in their hearts); peacemakers; those who are persecuted for the sake of God's righteousness (See Matt. 5:3-10).

Dr. Larry Richards sets up the sharp contrasts between God's view and man's view in *The Teacher's Commentary.*

Jesus' Values:	Countervalues:
poor in spirit	self-reliant
mourn	pleasure-seeking
meek	proud, powerful, important
hunger for righteousness	satisfied, practical, "well-adjusted"
merciful	self-righteous, able to take care of themselves
pure in heart	"adult," sophisticated, broad-minded
peacemakers	competitive, aggressive

Jesus' Values: *Countervalues:*

persecuted because   adaptable, popular, "don't rock the
of righteousness   boat"[7]

Jesus emphasized that the attitude in the heart of a person is as
relevant as the action by the person. In American law we call this
"willfulness" and "intent." The law of man distinguishes between
willful intent and lack of willful intent in the commission of a crime.
This can make the difference in staying free or being jailed. Righteousness is a matter of the heart and not just the action.

Jesus connected the importance of values being translated into
daily life actions: in other words, Believing and Behaving! He also
talked about the sensitive subject, especially in this country, of personal affluence. Jesus was very bold. It was this boldness in proclaiming the hard side of truth that took Jesus to the cross.

> "Do not lay up for yourselves treasures on earth, where
> moth and rust destroy and where thieves break in and steal;
> but lay up for yourselves treasures in heaven, where neither
> moth nor rust destroys and where thieves do not break in and
> steal. For where your treasure is, there your heart will be
> also. . . . No one can serve two masters; for either he will hate
> the one and love the other, or else he will be loyal to the one
> and despise the other. You cannot serve God and mammon.
> Therefore I say to you, do not worry about your life, what
> you will eat or what you will drink; nor about your body,
> what you will put on. Is not life more than food and the body
> more than clothing?" (Matt. 6:19-21, 24-25).

Jesus sums up His teachings about our material concerns with
this succinct imperative on priorities: "But seek first the kingdom of
God and His righteousness, and all these things shall be added to
you" (Matt. 6:33).

This teaching could be called "first things first!"

Again, Jesus addresses the subject of by whose value system are
His people going to live out there in that marketplace.

> "Whoever desires to come after Me, let him deny him-
> self, and take up his cross, and follow Me. For whoever de-
> sires to save his life will lose it, but whoever loses his life for

My sake and the gospel's will save it. For what will it profit a
man if he gains the whole world, and loses his own soul? Or
what will a man give in exchange for his soul? For whoever is
ashamed of Me and My words in this adulterous and sinful
generation, of him the Son of Man also will be ashamed when
He comes in the glory of His Father with the holy angels"
(Mark 8:34*b*–38).

Many People Have Heard What Jesus Taught

These tough teachings by Jesus may not be too well followed by
people, but many people—whether in church or not—are acquainted
with the message and can in whole or part quote these passages. The
teachings have a strong ring of reality with regard to the nature of
humans, but they are barely put into practice because of that same
marred nature.

Many people are also familiar with Jesus' story of the rich young
ruler. Here Jesus puts a "good" man, according to the standards of
the world, to the test. The rich young ruler wanted to inherit eternal
life, but he was not willing to pay the price set by Jesus in the test:
"Sell whatever you have and give to the poor . . . and you take up your
cross, and follow Me." The young man had asked for the test, but he
walked away from Jesus because his great wealth stood between him
and God.

Peter was rebuked more than once by Jesus for his worldly view-
point. "Get behind Me, Satan! For you are not mindful of the things
of God, but the things of men" (Mark 8:33*b*).

Peter meant well, but Peter did not always do well because he too
had a problem shaking the ways of man.

People who know the Bible can generally see God's perspective
on given subjects and questions, but the problem is in behaving and
living in accordance with God's perspective. This is why spiritual
growth is so vital in the life of the people of God. How is the world to
know the difference if Christians are doing business in the marketplace the same way as those who do not know Christ?

The Golden Rule

As Christians we have two hurdles to overcome. First, we must
know Right from Wrong in God's sight, and second, we must behave
in accordance with God's perspective. It is not easy being a Christian.

God has established a very high standard for His chosen people. However, I have become convinced that knowing and doing God's will is in our own interest even in the here-and-now.

The teachings in the Bible on Right versus Wrong make sense and are divinely designed to work in our interest because God loves us, anyway!

When we love people, such as our customers in the marketplace, they love us in return and we get more of their business. When we serve people after the sale as well as before the sale, our cash registers ring more times per day. Yes, the Golden Rule given by Jesus in that same Sermon on the Mount makes sense: "Therefore, whatever you want men to do to you, do also to them, for this is the Law and the Prophets" (Matt. 7:12).

In Search of Excellence[8] has been a best-selling book in the marketplace. The authors studied sixty-two American companies noted for the excellence of their operations and profits, and this book presents documented evidence as to the favorable impact of using corporate strategies similar to the Golden Rule.

The Golden Rule of Jesus also became the golden rule of Lee Atwater in the last year of his life at age forty. Lee was the controversial but very successful and youngest chairman in history of the Republican National Committee. Lee was a contemporary of some of my children in school. He trained in politics when I was chairman of the South Carolina Republican Party and in the White House. Lee's marketplace was wholly the world of politics.

One of his aims in life was to out-do one of his old political mentors, Harry Dent. So the morning after the 1988 election of George Bush, Lee called me. I had not heard much from Lee in the years since I had left politics and the practice of law. As with many others, Lee thought I had gone too far with religion.

Lee's message to me that morning was that he had achieved his first goal in life at age thirty-eight; he had run a winning presidential campaign. Then he called me again several weeks later when Bush selected him as chairman of the Republican Party. That, he said, was his second major goal in his life—both by age thirty-eight.

The next call I received from Lee was in the spring of 1990. He had just learned of a very serious brain tumor that would cause his death within a year. He exclaimed, "Harry, I looked into that dark abyss, and it scared . . . me! I want to know God. Will you come and help me find Him?"

Lee had been a church member for most of his life, but politics is a jealous mistress who wants all we've got. Politics had been my god also.

Lee Atwater's Third Goal

After Lee came to really know the Lord, he made it his third goal to give the rest of his life in service to Him. Lee's concern was that he might not live long enough to achieve that goal. But he served the Lord from his wheelchair and sickbed.

What kind of ministry could a new Christian have from his wheelchair and sickbed? The former "pit bull of politics" began testifying in the wheelchair, from his sickbed, on the telephone, by letters, and through the national news media. Through the phone and his mail he communicated with his friends and his old enemies. His ministry was a most unusual one; it was a ministry of repentance.

Lee called defeated Democratic presidential candidate, Michael Dukakis, and repented for his sins against him in the 1988 presidential contest. He didn't just apologize, he repented: "I am sorry, and I am never going to do anything like that again! Please forgive me. I am a sick man, but I am a new and different man. I have found Jesus Christ!" *The Chicago Tribune* carried a bold headline across the top of its front page: "GOP Bad-Boy—I Have Found Jesus!"[9]

A few months before Atwater died he asked his family to bring him home to Columbia so he could testify to his baby-boomer and blues-singing friends and also his old political cohorts. He wheeled himself into the big ballroom with a blues band playing his own song, "Bad Boy Blues." Then he stopped the music and began testifying to the several hundred friends present. He told them that he had found Jesus Christ and the Golden Rule and had begun loving his old enemies. He said: "I want you to find what I have found. I am giving the rest of my life to Jesus and His Golden Rule."[10]

Lee got rid of all of his old political enemies by loving them into friendship. Various political figures, including Governor Dukakis, publicly affirmed their forgiveness of Lee and paid tribute to his change. On the day of Lee's death the Democratic National Committee lowered its American flag to half-mast in loving tribute to their former nemesis.

The story of the repentance of Lee Atwater was featured in *Life* magazine and *Reader's Digest*. Lee's life is another chapter in God's book of Amazing Grace. Anyone can find Jesus Christ, and anyone can find a ministry for Jesus Christ.

Even the first and foremost Watergate culprit, G. Gordon Liddy, can be saved. This is the ex-FBI agent and White House pol who defied God during all of his Nixon Watergate trials and jailtime. He reasoned his way to Jesus a few years later with the help of some old FBI friends who showed Gordon some good doses of "salt" and "light" mixed with God's amazing grace.

Gordon told an audience in Arizona that it is no longer Gordon's strong will that determines the course of his life. Earlier he had written a book entitled *Will,* which stressed his own strong personal will.[11] Gordon says that every morning when he arises he asks God what is His will, not Gordon's once-strong and unbendable will.

Another "pit bulldog" of American politics also came to the Lord out of Watergate. He is noted today as one of the foremost Christian speakers and writers in the world. This is Charles Colson. Ask Chuck—anyone can be saved and turned into a servant of Jesus Christ.

God's Influence Is Needed in Our Workaday World

The saga of Lee Atwater is the story of one who, like the prodigal son in the Bible, came to his senses when he was forced to face the reality of life and death. Most of us never think of taking God to work with us because we think the workaday world is a different world. Today the presence and influence of God are more needed there than ever before. This is one world, and it all belongs to God. And work is a part of God's plan for humanity.

In this life we are responsible to God for our own individual lives, for our families (remember that the home is the first church), our duties to our fellowship with God, the church, and for our impact in our work.

The Apostle Paul addressed our responsibilities beyond God, self, and family. Paul says that "each of us shall give account of himself to God" for the way in which we handle our responsibilities toward our neighbors, our political authorities, our society as a whole, and especially our responsibilities to our families and to God.

We are accountable for our witness for good or evil. We are responsible to be stepping-stones instead of stumbling blocks for others, and to bear one another's burdens and to do good to all. What we sow out there in the world is what we will reap.

Believing and Behaving

Paul instructs us in Ephesians 4 and 5 how to "walk," or how to live before our fellowman.

> I, therefore, the prisoner of the Lord, beseech you to have a walk worthy of the calling with which you were called, with all lowliness and gentleness, with longsuffering, bearing with one another in love (Eph. 4:1–2).

Then Paul explains how we are to live in the whole of our worlds, and he sets the example for us in establishing our goals and priorities in life in the heart of his personal testimony.

> Brethren, I do not count myself to have apprehended; but one thing I do, forgetting those things which are behind and reaching forward to those things that are ahead, I press toward the goal for the prize of the upward call of God in Christ Jesus (Phil. 3:13–14).

He also calls us to humility, to have and exhibit in our lives the mind-set of Jesus Christ. "For it is God who works in you both to will and to do for His good pleasure" (Phil. 2:13). In other words, God is working through us in our work, our leisure, our home life—wherever. So, Paul commands us:

> Do all things without murmuring and disputing, that you may become blameless and harmless, children of God without fault in the midst of a crooked and perverse generation, among whom you shine as lights in the world (Phil. 2:14–15).

Our walk, how we put feet to our theology, determines our day-to-day witness everywhere we are. So as witnesses for Jesus Christ who call ourselves "Christ-i-ans" we are to walk worthy of our calling as servants of God in all aspects of life.

The major problem for Christianity and the church today is that people in the marketplace are not encountering much personal witness or ministry by Christians. But, worst of all, people at work are seeing hypocrisy instead of the Real Thing in the lives of too many so-called Christians.

Dr. George Gallup, Jr., himself a strong Christian witness in his marketplace of public opinion surveys, reports that people in the workplace see no significant difference between the churched people they work with and the unchurched people as to their values and actions.[12]

Your Work Matters to God

Some people who know bits and pieces of Scripture believe that God created work as a curse because of the sins of Adam and Eve. In their good book, *Your Work Matters to God,* Doug Sherman and William Hendricks emphasize that God cursed the ground and not the task of cultivating the ground. Indeed, God created man in the image and likeness of God and pronounced all that He had created as being "very good." Included is work, which God delegated to His created human beings. After the sin of Adam and Eve, God made the cultivation of the ground more difficult by cursing it.

Thus the two authors contend that *your* work matters to God. The world turns on man's use of his mind and hands. God's work, in part, depends on man's witness and ministry and also on man's stewardship of the bounties of his work. So Sherman and Hendricks rightfully contend that "work is a gift of God's grace."[13]

Sherman and Hendricks also make a valid distinction between self-interest in work and selfishness.

> Without question far too many workers (and customers) work from self-seeking, greedy motives. They cheat, they steal, they lie, they over-charge, they defraud, they rig the system.
> But these are sins of people, not flaws inherent in work. Instead, work as God has designed it anticipates a legitimate self-interest present in every worker. This is one reason why eliminating self-interest is neither possible nor desirable. To do so would contradict the nature of our humanity. . . . We are noble co-workers with Him, and He allows us to share in the product of our labor.[14]

In his 1991 book, Charles Colson decries the diminution of the American work ethic. The Puritans viewed work as a stewardship to God, and their primary rewards were spiritual and moral. The idea was to choose your profession or work based on your best service to God, not the most money and power you could accumulate.

Colson and his writing partner, Jack Eckerd of Eckerd Drugs, contend that the work ethic began to decline in 1950 when vocation was changed to occupation. Then came the relativism revolution with the advent of the Beatles, hippies, TV, and relativism.

> In a mere decade, the popular culture and student radicalism spawned by the existentialist writers had succeeded in bringing Western civilization full circle. Once again work had become a dirty word—something one did only if one must pay for pleasure. Work was no longer ennobling; it was again utilitarian—simply a means to an end.[15]

Jack Eckerd is another example of a positive marketplace minister. I remember when he called me to his home in Clearwater, Florida, several years ago to help him find his way through the Bible. He meant business for the Lord so much so that he sold his drugstore chain, the largest in America, in order to serve the Lord.

We Are Accountable

A helpful book on the Christian's dilemma in the marketplace is *The Man in the Mirror: Solving the 24 Problems Men Face,* by a friend of mine, a lay minister named Patrick M. Morley of Orlando, Florida.

Pat Morley concludes his book with an essay on the missing link, accountability. Our right to choose triggers our accountability to our Creator.

> Accountability is like nuclear fusion. Everyone has heard of it, everyone knows it's important, but very few people actually know how to explain it. Here's a useful working definition of accountability for Christians: To be regularly answerable for each of the key areas of our lives to qualified people.[16]

He says the key areas in which all of us need accountability are:

- Relationship with God
- Relationship with wife
- Relationship with kids
- Use of money and time
- Moral and ethical behavior
- Areas of personal struggle[17]

I would add one more area of accountability to Pat's list of priorities. We must have accountability to our work, meaning our employer, employees, fellow workers, and customers. Most people involved in work-related activities spend almost two-thirds of their waking time in the workplace. Work is most vital to the work of the church because the marketplace is a major mission field and also the producer of most of the tithes and offerings which keep the church afloat, financially speaking.

The Bible sets forth for us our responsibilities in all of our human relationships. They consist, in essence, in living out the principles of the Christian life as exemplified in the teachings in the Sermon on the Mount and the admonitions provided by Paul in the application portions of his epistles.

The salient teaching is to have the mind-set of Christ in our minds and hearts (see Philippians 2). In other words, we must be spiritually changed—born again as Jesus admonished us—and then we must connect our beliefs with righteous conduct. We must act and perform on the job just as we act and perform in the church. While we are being watched in our church life and our home life, we are being watched even more so in our work life. Most unbelievers work too, and they are watching to see whether Christianity and Jesus Christ are for real. As the Christian song says, "You May Be the Only Jesus That Some People Will Ever See."

God has blessed Betty and me in so many ways, especially since we have tried to be a blessing back to Him. God has put before us so many wonderful Christian lay witnesses and ministers. In fact, God has permitted us to help some people to become lay witnesses and ministers. The focus of our ministry shows in its very name, Laity: Alive & Serving.

President Bush Is a Marketplace Minister

Whether he realizes it or not, President George Bush is a prime-place and prime-time marketplace minister. He is an Episcopalian whose life has been spiritually refreshed since becoming vice president and then president.

When asked by a group of Christian leaders whether he had been born again in the 1980 presidential nomination race, Bush responded, "I don't think so, but I'd like to be." Ed McTeer told me of the Bush response, which he said was the "most honest answer."

Someone in that group reported George Bush's answer to Dr.

Billy Graham and his wife, Ruth. Soon after Bush became vice president, the Grahams and the Bush family spent a week together at Kennebunkport, Maine, the vacation home of George and Barbara Bush.

While I was chairman of the South Carolina Billy Graham Crusade, Dr. Graham informed me of these annual times of spiritual fellowship with the whole Bush clan. I walked into his crusade office to take Dr. Graham to the platform to give his evening sermon, and he was on the phone with Vice President Bush. When the conversation concluded, Dr. Graham commented to me that "the vice president is such a good man and good Christian." Having worked for and with Bush in politics, I agreed fully with the "good man" comment, but I had assumed that George was a nominal Christian as I had been for so long. So I inquired why he had come to that "good Christian" conclusion. Then he told me the story about the informal but serious ministry of Billy and Ruth Graham with the whole Bush family.

I was surprised but pleased that Dr. Graham had waded into the friendship business with a vice president of the United States after he was burned by what happened to one of his best presidential friends, Richard Nixon. Dr. Graham left the political arena after Watergate. Now here he was again in an informal and rather private manner helping to nurture the second family in America. It is a good example of marketplace ministry in the highest level of our society, the White House.

Since that time we have seen the Bushes and Grahams together publicly on many occasions, especially during Bush's inauguration as president in 1989 and later in the 1990 Mideast War. Today I always listen and watch for the spiritual side of George Bush to show up publicly. And it does—in the President and the First Lady. He almost always concludes his speeches with something like "God bless you" or "God bless America." The Bushes have responded to media inquiries that they pray together daily.

Other Leaders Stand Up for Christ

There are other public leaders who profess their faith in Jesus Christ: Vice President Dan Quayle and his wife, Marilyn; Secretary of State James A. Baker, III, and his wife, Susan; Secretary of State Dick Cheney and his wife, Lynn. From there the list is numerous; about one-third of the U.S. House meet every Wednesday morning for a prayer breakfast, and about the same percentage of U.S. Senators do likewise the next morning. There are prayer breakfast groups all over Washington, D.C., including the annual National Prayer Breakfast event. Here several thousand of the top leaders in Washington meet the first Thursday morning in February for breakfast, prayer, talks, and fellowship.

Every president since President Dwight Eisenhower has been present and speaking at each one of these breakfast meetings. Informally, it has become a command performance for the "most important man in the world."

James Baker gave his personal testimony before the breakfast group in 1989. I had given my book, *Cover Up: The Watergate in All of Us*, to the one thousand top leaders of Washington in 1987. A picture in the September 2, 1991, issue of *Newsweek* showed a copy of this book next to the president's bed at Kennebunkport. Jim Baker also received one. He wrote me a nice letter about the book and asked me to pray for him and come and visit him in his new role as secretary of state. Jim and I had worked together in politics for Nixon, Ford, and Bush, but I hesitated to bother the second busiest man in Washington. Then I got a call from a Washington friend, Don Dunlap, informing me that Jim had just given his personal testimony to the National Prayer Breakfast meeting.

It was then that I realized I should have accepted Jim's invitation to visit with him. So I set up a meeting with Jim and took the Episcopal evangelist and my good friend, Dr. John Guest, for the session. John and I were heading to Romania for our first mission behind the old Iron Curtain.

Jim told us that his prayer breakfast talk was the hardest talk he had ever given because he was making public his faith in Jesus Christ to the top people in Washington, including the whole diplomatic corps and his Soviet counterpart, Eduard Shevardnadze. What a marketplace ministry!

I later learned that my book *Cover Up* had helped Jim in his faith. His wife, Susan, has been involved in various lay ministries, and she received the best response we have ever had for a Governor's Prayer Breakfast talk in South Carolina when she spoke in 1991. Susan and Tipper Gore, the wife of Democratic U.S. Senator Albert Gore, Jr., of Tennessee, have been fighting pornography and heavy metal rock music with the support of their powerful husbands. Susan also has a big heart for ministry to the homeless people.

What mighty pulpits these ordinary lay folks have!

Ordinary Lay People Practice
Marketplace Ministry Too

Then there are the ordinary lay folks: people like Bob Stansell. He sends eighteen-wheel tractor-trailers across America with "Truckin' for Jesus" signs plastered on the rigs. Not only that, his Florida trucking company has a Christian chaplain to look after the families of the truck drivers, especially when there is a problem and the driver is on the road instead of at his home. When the drivers perform their chores properly and in a timely manner a bonus is provided—not to the driver, but to the mate of the driver.

Stansell is a member of a Christian organization of chief executive officers of corporations. The group, Christian Companies for Christ, is headquartered in Atlanta. There are many more CEOs like Bob Stansell.

There is our friend, Jack Barnes, of Anderson, South Carolina, an old Democrat who for many years ran J. C. Penney stores. Jack and his wife, Jane, have been volunteer teachers for Chuck Colson's Prison Fellowship Ministries for many years after Jack's working hours at the store. Equally important, Jack would always find a place of employment in his store for any pastor who lost his pulpit, for whatever reason. Jack and Jane also are heavily involved in church activities.

Then there is my prayer breakfast friend, Dick Smith of Columbia. As fast as the Lord provides it for them, Dick and his wife, Wilma, give away money to help others. They also have their own ministry for unwed mothers. The Smiths are such good stewards because they have no question as to who owns their businesses.

The man who puts my Bible teaching illustrations on acetate and in color for me is Milton Powell. Milton and Min Powell have long been strong church workers. In retirement they are keeping busy helping those of us who are on the front lines. They seek no applause as they use their time and gifts for the glory of God. Milton and Min help others also, including Columbia Bible College and Seminary.

There is a gifted lady Bible teacher, named Martha Linderholm, the widow of a former pastor, who teaches more than one hundred men and women in a Sunday school class at our church, First Baptist in Columbia. She and her helper, Norma Johnson, have been used by God to teach thousands of women the Bible, book by book. Martha and Norma and others, including Sara Petty and Betty Dent, have established twenty-seven marketplace Bible studies for working women.

In one of her two teaching groups, Betty has fourteen women. In talking about application of the teachings to their workplaces, Betty challenged the ladies to concentrate on "the mind-set of Christ" when people and problems plague them at work. One lady came back to the next study with this comment and big smile on her face:

> One lady at work really upset me today. Previously I would have let her have it straight from my mouth. But this time I just shut up my mouth and went on about the Lord's and my business! I felt so much better doing it God's way!

Ira and Betty Craft, also of Columbia, have had a most fruitful ministry for many years. In fact, they left the shoe-selling business and went into full-time lay ministry, like Harry and Betty Dent. They convinced the late Cecil Day of Atlanta to minister with them in planting new churches in the New England area, where the Crafts once lived. Subsequently, Cecil Day founded the Days Inn motel chain and became a multimillionaire. He established the Days Foundation before he died. Much of the proceeds from that foundation have been used to plant new churches all over New England and to do many more good works.

What better marketplace ministers are there than the football coaches, like Tom Landry, formerly of the Dallas Cowboys, Joe Gibbs of the Washington Redskins, and Mike Ditka of the Chicago Bears? In the college ranks there are many high-profile Christian coaches, including Bobby Bowden of Florida State University, Ken Hatfield of Clemson University, and Sparky Woods of the University of South Carolina.

Then there are the individual players themselves, so very many serving as role models for young admirers. One of the earliest Christian witnesses in big-time athletics was Bobby Richardson of Sumter, South Carolina. Bobby was a teenager right out of American Legion baseball when he worked his way up in the line-up of the New York Yankees in some of their greatest years. Bobby, not usually a home-run hitter, cleared the bases with a four-run homer in the last moment of the 1960 World Series to win for the Yankees and become "the most valuable player." Bobby has given his life to Christian witness and ministry. His principal project is the Baseball Chapel, featured on NBC-TV News in 1991. Here Bobby works with current professional baseball players and their spiritual lives and witness for Jesus Christ.

Their marketplace is the sports world, and their witness to young people is fabulous.

Lately there has been increased attention to the deployment of lay ministers all over the marketplaces of America. In part this move was begun by Pete Hammond, a senior leader of InterVarsity Christian Fellowship. Pete made a presentation at my conference center in the early 1980s. Reid Hardin, the lay ministry leader at the Southern Baptist Home Mission Board, heard Pete's presentation. Then the Southern Baptists began to move forward out of the Home Mission Board in holding conference after conference across America on the subject of Marketplace Ministry.

Pete suggests four ways to implement Marketplace Ministry:

1. To get to the nature of work according to God. Work is one of the ways in which we manifest God in us: as workers giving a full day's work for a full day's wage, honoring our employers and employees, earning our keep, and using the fruits of our labors to bless others. This is being conformed to His image again.
2. Another way we can infuse a healthy gospel into life is by restoring the ministry of the laity.
3. Another way we can breathe the gospel back into everyday life is by recapturing the concept of "the church scattered."
4. Finally, we can infuse life into the gospel by remembering that the biblical characters were marketplace people. (Over 75 percent never held a religious job.)[18]

More Lay Ministry Books Are Appearing

Because of the renewed interest in the ministry of all of God's people, more and more books are appearing on this subject. Robert E. Slocum, a Texas high-tech entrepreneur, has been heavily involved in Presbyterian Church lay renewal work. In 1986 he published a useful book on lay ministry entitled *Ordinary Christians in a High-Tech World*. He believes that it is up to the laity—ordinary Christians, not church professionals—to explore a new positive future for the church in the coming decades of high technology.[19] I agree!

Dr. Slocum is concerned that the arena of daily work is the least understood of the four major arenas of lay ministry. Yet this is the arena where lay folks spend most of their time. In addition to the marketplace, he lists these three other key arenas: the home, the government, and the church gathered. He is particularly concerned about the dwindling American work ethic. For this he takes us to Paul's teaching in Colossians 3:22–24 on holiness in the work life.

> Servants, obey in all things your masters according to the flesh, not with eyeservice, as men-pleasers, but in sincerity of heart, fearing God. And whatever you do, do it heartily, as to the Lord and not to men, knowing that from the Lord you will receive the reward of the inheritance; for you serve the Lord Christ.

In Chapter 4, Paul then addresses the bosses: "Masters, give your servants what is just and fair, knowing that you also have a Master in heaven" (4:1).

The heart of the message here is just that *it is up to God whether and how I am blessed.*

If only Christian businessmen, industrialists, and employees could think about this foundational truth from Scripture! This requires a special measure of faith, conviction, and commitment. Our problem as movers-shakers-doers in the world of commerce is that the American ethic comes in conflict with the Christian ethic. We are not the captains of our own souls and the masters of our own fates. It all comes down to the basic questions: Who am I? and Whose am I?

We have trouble with the first question, but our real problem comes with the lack of willingness to risk our own lives, fortunes, and fates on the answer to that second question.

This was the problem encountered by the rich young ruler. In America today the pull is toward self-reliance and self-gratification. We feel we're the ones who earned it, and we deserve to enjoy the fruits of our labor. This is just as American as apple pie and ice cream on the fourth of July.

Our Dilemma: Will It Be the American Way or God's Way?

The answer to this is wrapped up in the question raised by another good Christian book, *What Ever Happened to Commitment?* by Edward R. Dayton. This book calls Christians to all-out commitment to Christ and His real community. It reproves American individualism and selfishness and thus . . . Americanism. That was one of my cardinal sins.[20]

Commitment is indeed at the very foundation of all human relationships. It is the warp and woof of every society. Jesus was calling for commitment, not just a decision. Commitment implies that one is going to depend on something or someone. The message of the New Testament is our dependence, not on ourselves or any human being or human institution, but on the person of Jesus the Christ as our Lord and Savior.

When we get down to the ultimate weakness of the church of Jesus Christ it is simply that *people have been making decisions about Jesus Christ, for He's a jolly good fellow, but not commitments to trust in Him*. Our emphasis is on doing instead of being. It took me forty-eight years to discern how wrong I was to do for the Lord without first having committed my life to believe in and have a genuine relationship with Him. I have now learned that "being" is to precede "doing" if the "doing" is to bear real fruit.

Moses put the big question of choosing between good and evil and Right and Wrong before us in Deuteronomy 30:19 in the framing of the Palestinian Covenant between God and the first chosen people: "I call heaven and earth as witnesses today against you, that I have set before you life and death, blessing and cursing; therefore choose life, that both you and your descendants may live."

What Moses is talking about is eternal life over the temporal life and things of this world. His message is about God's Eternal Perspective, living in eternity with Him and forever and ever. This calls for far more than a decision.

Do we really believe in and trust in Jesus, the eternity He has promised, and the eternal verities He has proclaimed?

That is our problem. That is the graying of American hearts, even in the churches all across our land of the free and home of the brave. Our mission is to change the last word, *brave*, to *committed*.

CHAPTER EIGHT

Right vs. Wrong in Politics and Government

In the end more than they wanted freedom, they wanted security. When the Athenians finally wanted not to give to society but for society to give to them, when the freedom they wished for was freedom from responsibility, then Athens ceased to exist.

Edward Gibbon[1]

During the period of 1955–80 I devoted my life to politics and government. These were a fascinating and challenging twenty-five years for a boy from St. Matthews, South Carolina. Few people enjoyed politics and government as much as I did. I felt a calling—but it was my calling—to this venture of public service. It gave me the best opportunity to do what I found in school that I could do best, strategizing a game plan for victory and then implementing that plan. I wanted to be a part of America's plan to thwart the aim of world communism from imposing its will and ways on America and the rest of the world. Little did I realize that God could best handle communism in His own time and way.

We are told by psychologists, sociologists, and anthropologists that we humans have the desire to be somebody, the desire to have something, and the desire to do something. I plead guilty on all three counts, your Honor! These basic cravings of human beings can be fulfilled or used for Right or Wrong. I felt that my service in the Nixon White House could fulfill these aims for good and right. Little did I realize that the greatest opportunity could degenerate into a most perilous problem. Danger lurks everywhere, even in the White House. Who would have believed that the most notorious political scandal in American history would be waiting for the Nixon White House behind the taped door locks in the offices of the Democratic National Committee? Certainly not the Nixon White House, where President

Nixon seemed to be pushing all the right buttons in foreign and domestic policies.

Oh, how limited, fallible, and short-sighted we humans can be, even those who work at the most exclusive address in America, 1600 Pennsylvania Avenue.

After a few months of working in the Nixon White House, I was informed by John Ehrlichman that my duties were being changed. No longer would I be his assistant and the "Southern strategist." Now I would be the political liaison for the White House and continue as the "Southern strategist." I would report to the president through the chief of staff, Bob Haldeman. I was to oversee the Republican National Committee, all of the state GOP organizations, and all GOP election contests. This meant that I would be sitting in on cabinet meetings and the president's political sessions. I would be strategizing and implementing again. But the top strategist would always be the president. There was none better at strategizing than Richard Nixon.

When I came back to the office from my first cabinet meeting, my secretary, Rose Smith, saw me pinching myself. She asked why. I told her, "Rose, I just can't believe that at thirty-nine, I, Harry Dent from St. Matthews, am sitting in that room with the most important and powerful people in America and perhaps the world." Rose responded, "Don't worry, you'll get over that."

After three cabinet meetings Rose proved to be right. She walked in my office and inquired, "Why aren't you pinching yourself anymore?" I responded, "Rose, I finally realized that those important folks are no smarter than I am, and, frankly, that scares the devil out of me!"

I had worked among senators and congressmen and had become accustomed to their fallibilities and limitations. But the White House is close to being the capitol of the world. Now I was seeing the same fallibilities and limitations in the place where they keep the "football," whose buttons, when pushed, can blow up the world in a nuclear holocaust. For the first time in my life I came to realize that all of us folks in this world are fallible and limited human beings.

I had not yet comprehended the great potential that all of us have when God puts His saving and healing hands upon our hearts and calls us to Himself to serve God and our fellow citizens in the implementation of God's government and God's Master Plan through Jesus' politics of loving and serving. This is the highest election of all.

Jesus Is Truth

People involved in politics and government need to understand what I misunderstood but now understand, believe, and serve. "What is truth?" is what I misunderstood. It is *the* most critical question of life! Pilate put that question to Jesus before crowning Him with thorns and submitting Jesus to scourging and then the cross. (See John 18:38.)

He posed this question because Jesus had just responded to a previous question by telling Pilate:

"You say rightly that I am a king. For this cause I was born, and for this cause I have come into the world, that I should bear witness to the truth. Everyone who is of the truth hears My voice" (John 18:37).

One of the reasons the Jews had turned Jesus over to the Roman authorities for prosecution and crucifixion was because Jesus had made what is known as a number of "I am" statements that equated Him with God. He had claimed to be the authority of life, the bread of life, the water of life, the judge of life, the light of life, the shepherd of life, the door of life, and the resurrection and the life. John the Baptist called Jesus the Messiah. Jesus had also told His followers in His Farewell Address that He was the truth and that people can know the truth and be set free by this truth.

"I am the way, the truth, and the life. No one comes to the Father except through Me" (John 14:6).

"If you abide in My word, you are My disciples indeed. And you shall know the truth, and the truth shall make you free" (John 8:31–32).

In introducing Jesus in His Gospel, the Apostle John presented Jesus as being God:

In the beginning was the Word [Jesus], and the Word was with God, and the Word was God. . . . And the Word became flesh and dwelt among us, and we beheld His glory, glory as of the only begotten of the Father, full of grace and truth (John 1:1, 14).

Jesus Is God

Jesus is God is the thrust of the Gospel of John. It serves as a commentary of the three synoptic gospels—Matthew, Mark, and Luke.

I remember riding with Jack and Betty Matthews one day when Jack asked me, "Don't you know that Jesus is God?" Well, I did not know that Jesus is God. I told this dynamic lay witness for the Lord that I thought that God is God. It never occurred to me that Jesus is God. I had taught all of those Sunday school lessons and did not ever have an "aha!" experience on that point. If it was in any of the lessons, I missed it or totally ignored it. I have found that most people in the church see Jesus as the Son of God but not as God. Today I understand that Jesus *is* God!

As are love and righteousness, truth is one of the attributes of God. There are several definitions of truth. Dependability and uprightness in character is one definition, and this applies to God. There is the definition of truth in the absolute sense of that which is real, Right, and complete as opposed to what is Wrong, false, and wanting. This also applies to God, thus Christianity is truth. Jesus claimed that He was truth personified, as noted above. This truth is more than a creedal formula. It is God's active Word which must be obeyed. Psalm 31:5 and Jeremiah 10:10 refer to God as the God of truth. Our Creator is the one who created everything, including truth and reality.

So what is truth? Jesus Christ is truth!

The Old Testament testified to His coming as the Son of God. The New Testament affirmed the deity and lordship of Jesus Christ. His death on the cross for our sins and His resurrection from the tomb affirm that Jesus is the life everlasting. In the Bible the word "life" has two meanings: physical or temporal life and spiritual or eternal life.

Jesus Christ is the Real Thing! Not a soft drink, not anything else in the world. Not Buddha, not Allah, not any other man of god lying in a grave or tomb. Jesus is the God of righteousness. What He says, what He does, tells us what is Right as opposed to what is Wrong. Our standard for Right and Wrong is the word and life of Jesus the Christ of the Holy Bible. This is the message of the Holy Bible which Americans revere so very much but know so very little about, according to Dr. George Gallup, Jr.

Of all the people in the world who should know the truth, reality, and right, it should be the people who hold earthly power over the crucial matter of life and death of human beings. These are "the governing authorities" that Paul commands us to obey in Romans 13. Peter makes the same demand in 1 Peter 2:13–17. They are saying to us that we should:

DO WHAT IS RIGHT BECAUSE IT IS RIGHT, NOT BECAUSE YOU HAVE TO.

Christians Are to Honor the Government

God introduced the institution of human government for a purpose, just as He established the home for a purpose and the church for a purpose. The purpose is to restrain wrongdoing so that righteousness and peace shall reign on earth and in our homes, communities, and nations. So God permits human authorities to have limited authority. Christians are commanded to subject themselves to the governing authorities for conscience's sake and not just for fear of possible punishment. The Christian is commanded to live as a good citizen of righteousness of his country and community. The aim of God is righteousness, and God's aim is in our interest because God is love.

The function of human government is to protect people from harm from each other, to punish evildoers, and to promote the general welfare of the community. This is similar to the stated purposes in the Preamble to the United States Constitution. These are good purposes for good ends, so we are commanded to pray for our governing authorities.

Peter also has instructions for Christians regarding our responsibility to human government. We are to recognize and accept that the powers-that-be are ordained by God, we are to pay taxes—as Jesus did, and we are to pray for the leaders of human government. And they do need prayer!

In Ecclesiastes 8 the old pol named King Solomon also has some wisdom to dispense on the subject of human government. His exhortation may be of a subjective nature since he was a governing authority himself, but Solomon suggests that we can't fight city hall because "where the word of a king is, there is power." So go with the flow, and "do not take your stand for an evil thing, for he does whatever he pleases." He counsels us to obey also "for the sake of our oath to God."

A noted French observer of human governments, Alexis de Tocqueville, left us with an insight into the principles upon which our constitution rests. He calls it "those principles of order, of the balance of powers, of true liberty, of deep and sincere respect for the right."[2]

We are living in a time when truth, reality, and right are questionable. They have become very subjective. We interpret this in our own selfish interests rather than the more objective "common good" or the Word of God. We, especially our governing authorities, need to be very objective about truth, reality, and what is right in God's sight.

The God of the Bible is an absolutist God; He is not a relativist. But He is very relational in that He majors in Right relationships. He is incomparable to anyone or anything else. As He tells us in Isaiah 55:8-9:

"For My thoughts are not your thoughts,
Nor are your ways My ways," says the LORD.
"For as the heavens are higher than the
    earth,
So are My ways higher than your ways,
And My thoughts than your thoughts."

In his classic book, *Evidence That Demands a Verdict*, Josh McDowell states, "He [Jesus] is either a liar, a lunatic or the Lord. You must make a choice.[3]

We are commanded in the Bible to make a choice, indeed a commitment to the reality of this absolutist God in the person of Jesus the Christ. The consequence is:

LIFE versus DEATH,
RIGHT versus WRONG,
HEAVEN versus HELL.

There is no wonder that this question framed by Pilate to Jesus is the most important question in the history of the world! Yet 67 percent of the people in America claim that they do not believe in absolute truth. And worse, 52 percent of people who call themselves born-again Christians agree with them.[4]

This book has been written to put these questions to you:

WHAT DO YOU SAY IS TRUTH? WHO DO YOU SAY
REPRESENTS OR IS THIS TRUTH? ARE YOU
CONNECTED TO THIS TRUTH?

These questions are similar to the question that Jesus asked His disciples at Caesarea Philippi, His last retreat with key followers before returning to Jerusalem and the final week of His life on earth. The first question to his disciples was "Who do men say that I, the Son of Man, am?" The response was that Jesus was seen as a good guy and great prophet. Even most of the other major religions acknowledge this description of Jesus.

Then Jesus asked the critical question, "But who do you say that I am?" And Simon Peter answered and said, "You are the Christ, the Son of the living God" (Matt. 16:13–16).

That was and is *the question* for humankind. The Bible is emphatic that calling Jesus a "good guy" and/or a "great prophet" misses the mark by light years. The answer has to do with heaven and hell. Human beings will not stop existing just because we die physically. Each of us will keep on thinking and knowing and keep on being ourselves—forever and ever. We do go around twice! Our choice, our commitment in the here-and-now determines our choice for our abode in eternity.

I agree fully with Paul and Peter that we should pray for all in authority over us and that we must obey the laws of man. God does have a valid purpose for human government. We also are to be subject to the "Government of God." This is His Kingdom on earth that is being built by the church of Jesus Christ. One of the principal purposes of the Bible is to make us knowledgeable of God's views regarding Right versus Wrong. As Americans and Christians we are accountable to human government and God's Government. Therefore, it is vital that we be informed of and subject ourselves to our duties, responsibilities, and accountability to both the kingdom of man and the Kingdom of God.

In my experiences in working in the kingdom of man and the Kingdom of God, I find superficial knowledge and understanding and thus superficial commitment and limited participation and action in both. Approximately one-half or less of the American people vote in a presidential election. Too many people cannot identify their elected representatives.

Not only are the problems similar, but some of the methods are similar. In humanity's politics, when we are campaigning we are seeking to persuade people to vote our way by pulling a lever in support of our candidates and causes. In God's politics, through evangelism we are seeking to persuade people to vote with their hearts by accepting our candidate, Jesus Christ, and committing to live by His teachings and to minister in His causes. In both scenarios we are asking people to do something they are not required to do; they only have to choose "yea" or "nay."

It Takes Committed People

In earthly politics there is a small corps of people who are so committed that they make the difference in the outcome of elections. Thus they have political clout when their team wins—maybe even a chair in the White House. There they can make a contribution for Right or Wrong, good or evil. In God's politics, there is likewise a small band of very committed people, according to Dr. George Gallup, Jr., and they too can make a vital difference in the here-and-now. But the difference is that they can also make a critical difference in the eternal destiny of humanity. Earthly politics can only get us to the White House; God's politics can get us to heaven in eternity.

That is why I now feel such personal fulfillment in being involved in God's politics. My time in man's politics provided temporal fulfillment, a bigger than normal ego trip limited to the here-and-now, which I discovered could get me in trouble, even in the White House.

There is no area of life that is tougher on the family and where self-ism is more rampant than in the arena of politics and government. In order to be a winner—and that is the name of the game in American politics—the conventional wisdom dictates that a politician must be a workaholic and his or her career must come first over everything and everybody else.

Government service is one of the higher callings in America. Yet politicians and government servants are not held in the highest repute by the public. The basic reason is that the voting public tends to believe that most politicians are selfish, greedy, and crooked to some degree. Politicians and lawyers rank toward the bottom of professions in the public opinion polls. Congress only had an 18 percent approval rating in late 1991. The House of Representatives was caught up in a check-kiting scandal at the house bank, a scandal in the house post office, and in failures by some members of congress to pay their house restaurant charges. People in congress should know better than to abuse their privileges. In fact, they should not have privileges forbidden for their constituents. This is bad politics—if you get caught!

Politicians Are Seen as Self-serving

Why are politicians rated so low in the polls? Because people just cannot abide self-serving people. It can also be that the people are just as selfish as their political leaders. The much-quoted Christian writer, the late C. S. Lewis, summed up this public view this way:

> There is one vice of which no man in the world is free; which every one in the world loathes when he sees it in someone else; and of which hardly any people, except Christians, ever imagine that they are guilty themselves. . . . There is no fault which makes a man more unpopular, and no fault which we are more unconscious of in ourselves. And the more we have it ourselves, the more we dislike it in others. The vice I am talking of is Pride or Self-Conceit: and the virtue opposite it, in Christian morals, is called Humility.[5]

Pride or self-conceit is at the core of politics and thus in much of government service. It is the father of self-ism. There are those who run for public office and serve in public office who are truly humble and oriented to serving people. However, the politicians, the bureaucrats, the officeholders, the lawyers, are looked upon, by and large, by the populace as the very epitome of what C. S. Lewis described.

As a lawyer, political operative, and public servant, I recognize that conceit and self-ism are the order of the day in politics. Those who run for and serve in the top elective positions can rationalize all the glory and press clippings because he or she must be elected. The top folks will not countenance selfishness and personal glory by those who surround them as assistants, however. The glory belongs exclusively to the winner and officeholder.

As a consequence, the weakness of American politics and government service is the original sin nature of man. Politicians and government servants need to know the Lord as much or more than any other Americans. They must understand the human condition of a sinful, selfish nature that can only be harnessed by the power and work of the Spirit of Jesus Christ as Lord of even the lords of this country.

An Example of Wisdom from the Bible

In Old Testament times, young Solomon prayed for wisdom from God as he approached the throne of Israel. This son of King David had good intentions. His prayer of humility is recorded for us in 1 Kings 3:5–14.

At Gibeon the LORD appeared to Solomon in a dream by night; and God said, "Ask! What shall I give you?" And Solomon said: "You have shown great mercy to your servant David my father, because he walked before You in truth, in righteousness, and in uprightness of heart with You. . . . Now, O LORD my God, You have made Your servant king instead of my father David, but I am a little child; I do not know how to go out or come in. . . . Therefore give to Your servant an understanding heart to judge Your people, that I may discern between good and evil." And the speech pleased the LORD, that Solomon had asked this thing. Then God said to him: "Because you have asked this thing, and have not asked long life for yourself, nor have asked riches for yourself, nor have asked the life of your enemies, but have asked for yourself understanding to discern justice, behold I have done according to your words; see, I have given you a wise and understanding heart, so that there has not been anyone like you before you, nor shall any like you arise after you. . . . So if you walk in My ways, to keep My statutes and My commandments, as your father David walked, then I will lengthen your days."

Every person taking public office should follow the example of Solomon in praying for wisdom and then exercising God's kind of wisdom in judging and serving his people. They also should learn from his mistakes. Solomon did not finish the race of life as a winner. During his reign as King of Israel the chosen people of God experienced the greatest time of wealth and power in the history of Israel, the Golden Age of Israel. In the end, Solomon could not handle all the power, wealth, women, and wisdom, false gods, and the things of the world. That is the weakness of the powerful. Pride, conceit, and self-ism lead to immaturity and a poor understanding of reality, which in turn lead to irresponsibility and self-destruction.

As with too many people in public office, Solomon turned his back on God. He became caught up in his own ego, his own wealth, his own power, his own harem, and his own pomp and circumstance.

King David Confessed His Sin

His great father, King David, had set the right example for all to see, including his son Solomon. David was guilty of adultery and murder. As with the Nixon White House in the early seventies, his first reaction was denial and then the cover-up of the crimes. Fortunately, God sent a friend and wise man named Nathan to rip off David's cover-up. One of the most famous quotes in the Bible is attributed to this brazen and brave member of David's court (2 Samuel 11 and 12).

After Nathan told him a story of an injustice administered by one man to another, David condemned the bad guy. In doing so, David said to Nathan, "As the Lord lives, the man who has done this surely shall die!" Without hesitation, Nathan condemned and uncovered David, saying, "You are the man!" David immediately confessed and repented: "I have sinned against the LORD." Then Nathan responded, "The Lord also has put away your sin; you shall not die" (2 Samuel 12:7, 13).

This is known as confrontation with the truth, repentance, and then forgiveness. Here is the gist of what Christianity is all about. This is what public service should likewise be all about. But the biggest failure of the vast majority of public servants is that they never admit or repent.

The major lesson from the Nixon Watergate scandal is that covering up the crime can cause more damage than the original crime. The cover-up of the burglary crimes put many of the Nixon men in prison and the president out of office. The fallout from the break-in at Democratic Party headquarters in June 1972 could have been minimized had the truth been told from the beginning.

In my book, *Cover Up: The Watergate in All of Us*, I wrote in the preface in 1986:

> I am not sure that we have learned much from the history lessons available to us in Watergate. There has been little change in political, corporate, social or individual behavior in our nation.[6]

Since writing that commentary, the scandals in government, the marketplace, homes, and elsewhere have proliferated considerably. I was shocked when I saw the beginnings of the Iran-Contra scandal in the Reagan Administration. It followed the path of our Watergate saga in almost every respect, including the cover-up, except that it was a direct violation of a new law by Congress to thwart President Reagan from doing exactly what his people did. The other difference is that the Iran-Contra scandal directly involved the president's most important responsibility, the conduct of foreign policy. While the Watergate scandal was domestic politics, its consequences did reverberate adversely all through domestic policy, foreign policy, and American politics.

When will public officials in Washington understand that there are no secrets and no successful cover-ups in the nation's capital? In the past many keystone-cops capers were likewise conducted at the highest levels of government, but FBI Director J. Edgar Hoover usually handled the political hanky-panky for the incumbent president. Having "J. Edgar" handle the chore was almost foolproof. No one dared investigate the great investigator because he was *the* investigator and he had "the goods" on most of the powerful people in Washington in his highly guarded secret files, which were destroyed upon his death.

When it was the Nixon White House's time for some illegal breaking and entering, Mr. Hoover was not available. He was in his old-age mental dotage and was also peeved because the president had tried and failed to retire him. The result was the biggest political scandal in American history, Watergate.

Another handicap helped uncover the Watergate scandal. Bob Haldeman knew that Nixon wasn't very good with his hands. When the taping system was installed, Haldeman made sure it operated automatically, not manually, for the president's ease. But evidently, both Haldeman and Nixon eventually forgot the system recorded every phone call. This proved very damaging as they plotted to cover up the break-in.

So today if the law enforcement people don't get you, the whistle-blowers in government will report you to *The Washington Post*. If not *The Post*, some foreign, unheard-of publication might expose the story, as in the Iran-Contra scandal. Or you might even give yourself away.

Humans Refuse to Grow Up

But humans are stubborn when it comes to disciplining their own personal wills. Cover-ups are a natural part of the human psyche because we limited and fallible human beings habitually hide and/or rationalize our dark sides. This is a prime reason why we must know the truth! Nothing is worse than to be charged with the original crime and then add the crimes of perjury and/or obstruction of justice. There is only one cure for unrighteous behavior: We must come under the supernatural governance of the Commander-in-Chief of the universe, become spiritually changed, and then grow up spiritually.

There are too many pandering assistants in public service who are not willing to tell their employer that he is not dealing with reality. Why? Because the aides seek to curry favor by telling their "emperors without clothes" what he or she wants to hear. Also the "emperors" want to do what they want to do in accordance with their human condition and their fallibility because of their basic immaturity. Just like their kids, they believe that they "can handle the situation" or "it won't happen to me."

This is exactly what happened to "emperor" Adolph Hitler and his sycophantic minions. History has other similar examples. Man just cannot handle unchecked power at either the emperor level or the assistant level.

M. Scott Peck, M.D., writes that far too many of us supposed adults are in reality immature kids. In addressing the subject of people handling power, he asserts:

> Most of us are like children or young adolescents; we believe that the freedom and power of adulthood is our due, but we have little taste for adult responsibility and self-discipline.[7]

In his books, Dr. Peck is constantly challenging people to grow up emotionally and spiritually. In *People of the Lie: The Hope for Healing Human Evil*, Dr. Peck focused attention on two supreme evils that can engulf people in politics—malignant narcissism and pathological lying. I do not mean that all people in politics are in love with themselves or are liars. However, there is no profession better equipped to lull or draw people into habitual extreme self-love and lying. The addiction can develop gradually.

Dr. Peck calls people of the lie "evil people." "The fact of the matter is that some of us are very good and some of us are very evil, and most of us are somewhere in between."[8]

Erich Fromm says that we move in the direction of good or evil, Right or Wrong, as a matter of personal choice and usually over a period of time through a succession of choices.

> If the degree of the freedom to choose the good is great, it needs less effort to choose the good. If it is small, it takes a great effort, help from others, and favorable circumstances. . . . Most people fail in the art of living not because they are inherently bad or so without will that they cannot

lead a better life; they fail because they do not wake up and see when they stand at a fork in the road and have to decide. . . . At each step along the wrong road it becomes increasingly difficult for them to admit they are on the wrong road.[9]

Dr. Peck corrects Fromm in part by averring that:

There are only two states of being: submission to God and goodness or the refusal to submit to anything beyond one's own will—which refusal enslaves one to the forces of evil. We must ultimately belong either to God or the devil.[10]

Peck checked out other worldviews or religions before finally settling on Christianity because he found it to be the Real Thing. He also found Satan to be the Wrong Thing and has been involved in exorcisms of demons.

He states in *People of the Lie*, "In common with 99 percent of psychiatrists and the majority of clergy, I did not think the devil existed. . . . I now know Satan is real. I have met it."[11]

C. S. Lewis was right in his comment:

There is no neutral ground in the universe: every square inch, every split second is claimed by God and counterclaimed by Satan.[12]

Betty was concerned about every moment of my involvement in politics. And she could see me moving down that road to self-love and the evolution from white lies to black lies. The human rationalizer works overtime in politics. The built-in filter system that screens out the unwanted signals that seek to warn of Wrong thinking and doing works hand-in-glove with the human rationalizer, which assures one to "Go ahead. Actually this is the right thinking because the right end will justify whatever wrong thinking is involved—if any. Besides, it won't happen to you!"

The next step in that faulty decision-making is the resort to a cover-up.

What we need in politics and government today are more Davids and more Nathans! More Josephs. More Daniels. More Nehemiahs. Cover-ups and scandals would take a nose-dive.

If I were permitted to provide one passage for all people entering political activities or public service it would be the teaching of King Solomon in Proverbs 3:5, 7:

> Trust in the LORD with all your heart,
> And lean not on your own understanding; . . .
> Do not be wise in your own eyes;
> Fear the LORD and depart from evil.

Oh, how I wish I had understood and applied this very practical and powerful wisdom to my heart before moving to Washington, D.C., in 1954, and even more especially when I went back there again with the Nixon White House in 1969.

The powerful tend not to realize that their feet are made of clay. They also tend not to understand God's Word and Wisdom. Too many of them are guilty of my big error: playing with God instead of praying to God and listening to His wisdom.

Voters Add Pressure

Politicians and elected officials are also infamous for passing the buck in order to protect themselves from the pressures of selfish voters back home. Indeed, the genesis of the selfishness in politics and government is with the voters themselves. They telegraph their *wants* into *oughts* by letters, phone calls, petitions, personal requests, or indirect requests through their lobbying groups.

When an individual voter's vested or personal interest is involved, the voter can be very selfish, demanding, and unrealistic. Politicians or public officials are rewarded or punished according to their response to the wishes of the voters. Many issues generate petitions by the voters, and many issues stir much controversy. So the politician or public official has to make many choices in the course of his or her duties.

Whenever the buck can be passed to another body of government many of the politicians will vote for the more popular side of a question and force the president to veto a bill that should be defeated. I remember President Nixon fuming in a cabinet meeting one day because the Congress was forcing him to veto bad legislation. This was one of those times when Nixon resorted to what the media came to call "expletives deleted." The members of Congress knew that the president could not permit the legislation to be enacted into law. They voted "yea" to feather their own political nests back home.

Today the United States Government is saddled with almost four trillion dollars in national debt. One of the reasons for this monumental indebtedness is such buck-passing and so many amendments to bills in the interest of getting special projects for back home at the expense of the overall common good. Politicians who specialize in bringing home government dollars profit in votes and/or dollars for re-election campaigns. The problem lies in the fact that legislators from all fifty states are "bringing home the bacon." The taxpayers ultimately lose.

In preparing to leave the United States Senate in disgust because of the catering to special interest groups by Congress and the White House, Senator Warren Rudman advised his colleagues, "Put partisanship aside and put your own careers aside and do something for America."[13]

President Nixon warns in his book, *Seize the Moment*, about "the rise of that new despotism under the cover of 'entitlements.'" These are government subsidy programs that are voted by Congress under the rationale that by virtue of living in the U.S. certain groups of people are entitled to various benefit programs at the expense of the U.S. Treasury.[14] Our form of government is meant to provide for the rights of people as individuals, not as groups, especially not special interest groups who seem to be claiming most of the rights and entitlements.

Dr. Robert J. Samuelson, an economic writer for *Newsweek* magazine, refers to our time as "the Age of Entitlement." He writes:

> We came to believe that prosperity was inevitable—and that it would automatically create the Good Society. On these two pillars of faith rested our national identity and hopes for the future. Every age has its illusions. Ours has been this fervent belief in the power of prosperity.[15]

Entitlement programs serve to entitle politicians to re-election victories on the notion that we are all entitled to financial prosperity.

The ungoverned ego is the fountainhead of our problems in human government by the people and the politicians!

We are equally to blame. We vote our own selfish interests. Private virtue is lacking in public officials, and private virtue is likewise lacking in private officials, the individual electors. Also, "We the People" must not be too concerned about government debt because personal debt and corporate debt are beginning to rival government debt.

Today, America is the number one debtor nation in the world—in trade deficits and national debts.

Political Campaigns Cost Too Much

Another horror in our political life today is the ever-increasing fund-raising in political campaigns. Money is the mother's milk of politicians, so the pundits opine. Millions and millions of dollars for the presidential campaigns, and even millions for state-wide campaigns. Political campaign contributions border on out-right bribery in too many instances. The politician may rationalize that the contributor expects nothing in return, but, by and large, the contributor *is* expecting something. These campaign contributions are corrupting the governing authorities. The bigger the donations, the bigger the ultimate tendency to corruption!

Yet government funding of elections is not a good alternative. It adds to the deficits at the Treasury Department and gets the government directly involved in election campaigns. The money we check off on our tax returns to be used in the matching election fund would otherwise go into the Treasury. Fortunately, only 27 percent of the tax filers are providing for the matching election funds.

The only answer is to severely curb fund-raising and campaign-spending. TV advertising should be very limited—in the interest of TV viewers and the misinformation that is produced through short and slick political commercials.

In politics the name of the game is winning, and winning big—preferably without opposition. This attitude is connected to that primary problem running throughout the Bible, pride, the very bottom-line of the original sin nature of man. Remember, these people at the top of politics are looking to be part of the history books, especially those in the White House.

But hold on! There is some good news! There are politicians who are very earnest about public service and stewardship of the resources of our government.

U.S. Senator Warren Rudman of New Hampshire has become noted as a very forthright and righteous Senator. In his political campaigns he faces the tough questions and tells his people the hard truth about what is Wrong and what is Right even when his positions cut across the self-interest of his voters. They evidently respect his candor because they have elected him to public office several times with hefty majority votes.

Many people across America lament his decision to retire from
the Senate after twelve years of service. He was the first Washington
insider to break cover on the gridlock in the nation's capital city. He
told *Time* magazine:

> We ought to tell (people) what the real facts are. We
> ought to do what we have to do, go home, and try to defend
> it. The worst thing that can happen to a politician is to get
> defeated. . . . But people here don't seem to want that; for
> reasons of ego, they've got to hold on to power. And frankly,
> I'm not sure the power is worth holding on to if what we're
> doing is bankrupting America.[16]

It's Harder to Avoid the Lobby Groups Today

There are many powerful lobby groups in Washington that can
generate tons of mail to Capitol Hill in short order. I also remember
once when U.S. Senator Strom Thurmond of South Carolina was being importuned by most of the well-to-do automobile dealers in South
Carolina to vote against legislation requiring car dealers to put sticker
prices on the windshield of each new car. The idea was to protect the
consumers from the possibility of being tricked on the sales price.

The Senator gave the car dealers a courteous and attentive ear.
That is all they got. When they concluded their presentation he gave
them all of the reasons why he and they should be for the proposed
legislation. With his usual candid style, the Senator informed them
that he would be supporting the bill against their wishes. The car
dealers left the meeting praising him for his candor and courage. This
is why he has the longest tenure in the Senate and is the oldest member
today.

I also saw him fire a legislative assistant for misleading a constit-
uent on the Senator's vote in a committee. He was doing this in what
he thought was the interest of the Senator.

The Prophet Daniel Is a Good Example
of Public Service

The prophet Daniel was an outstanding example of public service at its best. He outlasted two empires, three dynasties, and the
lion's den. Daniel had been hauled off into captivity in Babylon as a
young man with his friends, Shadrach, Meshach, and Abed-nego.

Daniel was so committed to his Lord God Jehovah that he refused to defile himself. So God granted Daniel favor and compassion in the sight of the commander of the Babylonian officials. (See Daniel 1:8–9.)

This young Jewish boy was greatly blessed and protected by his God. He became a leader under three kings and the author of one of the greatest books of prophecy. The Book of Daniel provides the basic framework for Jewish and Gentile history from the time of King Nebuchadnezzar to the second coming of Jesus Christ. An understanding of Daniel's prophecies is essential to the proper interpretation of Jesus' Olivet Discourse, Paul's doctrine of the man of sin, and the Book of Revelation.

What an example for our people in public life!

Governor Nehemiah is another sterling role model for our public officials. He too was a man of solid faith and a reaper of high favor with God. At first he was like the chief of staff in our Nixon White House, in title and duties in his role as the cupbearer to King Artaxerxes I of Persia. His memoirs in the Book of Nehemiah constitute "must" reading for all public officials—believers or not. If they study the life of Nehemiah they are most likely to become believers in the truth and THE Real Thing.

Nehemiah's strengths lay in his personal integrity, loyalty, stability, concern for others, and proper discernment of his mission. He was dedicated to his God and the people God had provided for Nehemiah's mission. He was unselfish, enthusiastic, tactful, and equally as courageous as Daniel. What's more, this Governor of Jerusalem rebuilt the walls in a record fifty-two days under enemy attack. He surrendered all of his perquisites and privileges of office and worked with his men with a trowel in one hand and a sword in the other. He even permitted his troops to eat first.

Another great model politician for our governing authorities is Joseph. He is compared in some respects to Jesus Christ. Joseph was ditched by his jealous brothers, but he became the prime minister of Egypt at the time when his family and people back home in the promised land needed food.

Joseph may best be cited as a role model as to how one can avert a sex scandal. This continues to be a special problem for some of our governing authorities today. Joseph was made overseer of the house of Potiphar in Egypt. The Egyptian leader's wife sought to seduce Joseph, but he demurred, saying, "How then can I do this great wickedness, and sin against God?" (Gen. 39:9).

Subsequently when she further pursued him and grabbed at

him, "he left his garment in her hand, and fled and ran outside" (Gen. 39:12).

There are several answers to all of these problems.

Politicians Should Depend on God

All people involved in politics should become involved in God's government as well as man's government. One of the aims should be that ultimate trip to eternity. The purpose in the here-and-now is, frankly, a matter of good common sense. Politics is a dangerous game, but a very fulfilling and necessary game—especially in a republican or democratic form of government. People in politics tend to become very pragmatic. So why not think in terms of real practicality. That human rationalizer and that human filter system will not work as well in the life of a committed member of the Government of God. They will be blinded by Holy light.

The Bible calls reality and truth the light. In a Christian's life there is a special light that shines in our hearts and minds. This light is much more powerful than human conscience. It is the reality light. Jesus introduced this light in His Sermon on the Mount.

> "The lamp of the body is the eye. If therefore your eye is good, your whole body will be full of light. But if your eye is bad, your whole body will be full of darkness. If therefore the light that is in you is darkness, how great is that darkness!" (Matt. 6:22–23).

This teaching reminds me of the word processor I am using to write this book. If I put garbage in my computer, garbage comes out; if I put in the Right Thing, the Right Thing comes out. In other words, what goes in comes out for Right or Wrong.

Paul also challenges us to turn on the light in his chapter on our responsibilities to higher powers. "The night is far spent, the day is at hand. Therefore let us cast off the works of darkness, and let us put on the armor of light" (Rom. 13:12).

One of the top complaints against President Richard Nixon was that he had a dark side. True! We all have a dark side, but God has made provision for our dark sides. He provides the Holy Spirit, the Spirit of Jesus Christ, to come into our hearts and minds and to shine so brightly as to shed light (reality and truth) on ourselves and others about the darkness in our inner being. With the supernatural help of the Holy Spirit, we get supernatural insight into our own lives and the world around us. I call this double vision: Man's limited perspective and God's unlimited perspective.

In particular, every person involved in politics and government must have double vision. We need God's perspective correcting man's perspective—like our bifocals correcting our astigmatism or limited sight. I believe that once people perceive the Real Thing in politicians and the governing authorities there could be a change in those who cast the ballots on election day. There is something catching and fetching about selfless people who have the courage to stand for truth and reality.

We Must Pray for Those Who Don't

If a person involved in politics chooses to go it alone, believing that he or she can handle themselves and politics, then we should all pray that they may become persuaded to yet put their trust in God. Any other suggestions could be futile. Politics is so important and so dangerous that my recommendation extends beyond just being a *child* of God to being a *mature child* of God.

Politicians Must Understand the Law

Each person in politics and government must be fully educated on the laws that apply to them in their duties. Even as an attorney I did not make that my first order of business when I entered the White House. Had Richard Nixon, Bob Haldeman, John Ehrlichman, or John Mitchell understood what could happen to them in just covering up the original crime, I do not believe that they would have chosen to obstruct justice. John Dean, counsel to the president, had to consult a Democratic attorney to discover that a cover-up amounts to the crime of obstruction of justice. When he so informed Haldeman, Ehrlichman, and Nixon of this problem, they were dumbfounded. All were attorneys except Haldeman.

G. Gordon Liddy, the instigator of the scandal, has emphasized that he would have committed the crime anyway. He knew the risk and accepted his punishment.

Politicians Need to Take Reality 101

People in politics and government should take a special political competence course that I would call Reality 101. This course should be required at least once a year. At higher levels of government the reality batteries really should be re-charged daily because the higher one goes, the less reality exists. This is why top assistants have on occasion ignored presidential orders that were out of touch with reality. Joseph Califano pleads guilty to having trashed some of the orders he received from President Lyndon Johnson.

And They Need Humility 101 Too

People in politics and government should take a special character competence course that I would entitle Humility 101. This should be a daily checkup. How do we get these daily checkups? On our knees consulting with God. Public officials consult with all their assistants and others. So why not God?

"Dare to Be a Daniel"

The voting public is almost as selfish as their public servants, but there is in most people a quality that admires courage in people who "dare to be a Daniel." This is the reason that Gordon Liddy profited so much from his Watergate experience. He refused to be "a rat" as he explained in accepting a maximum sentence for refusal to tell on his comrades in crime. It is ironic that the one who conceived and executed the original crime seemingly ended up with the most public favor. It was because he was willing to pay the price of his misdeeds.

Political leaders who do live an exemplary life and stand for basic principles despite the pressures can expect to be returned to office. People do not trust politicians, so when they sense one who is honest and earnest about his or her duties they tend to applaud.

For good examples, read the late President John F. Kennedy's book, *Profiles in Courage*. These were government leaders who "dared to be a Daniel."[17]

Is It Smart Politics or Dumb Politics?

Doing favors for your constituents is noted as "smart politics." It can also be dumb politics. Selfish and deceitful constituents can destroy you in politics and government. Many have fallen or been sullied for going too far in "smart politics." I shudder to think about how many people might have destroyed me in politics and government.

Politicians must look for the hidden agendas!

Politicians Must Choose to Work with People of Integrity

Staff your office with people of integrity who love people. Politics is people. Loving people pays because God made people to want to be loved. My senator-boss had a standard operating code for our staff. It was one of my duties to enforce the code, but he best enforced the code with his example: no smoking or drinking, doing Right by people, etc. The personal discipline of this senator is one of the reasons he is the oldest in age and tenure in the United States Senate. People admire leaders of discipline and integrity, regardless of their politics.

Loving people means that politicians must serve their family as much as they serve their constituency.

Politicians Should Limit Campaign Donations

Set strict policies regarding campaign donations. Former Senator Lawton Chiles of Florida is today the governor of Florida. In returning home he campaigned on the basis of a limit of no more than one hundred dollar contributions. It was expected that he would not be able to win because he would be short of funds. He won, in part, because of the limit on contributions. People do respect integrity.

Voters Must Vote Righteously

Every voter should set up his or her own code of righteous voting, remembering that selfishness begins at the bottom and moves up from there.

Voters should vote and do so with information, intelligence, and integrity. This is one of the greatest rights conferred on humans. It is basic to the operation of our form of government.

Voters should recognize that their elected officials represent a broad constituency with diverse interests. Be careful not only of your selfish interests, but also of one-issue politics. It is good to become involved in a special issue, like the abortion controversy or some other cause that you know comes down to Right versus Wrong. But do not limit your political vote and actions to just one issue.

Ascertain the basic character of the candidates, and make this a signal part of your criteria in choosing who will receive your vote. And yes, adultery is a terrible character defect. God despises it and so should we. It is helping to destroy the family.

All people should become involved in politics to some degree. The people who determine the nomination of the candidates for president from the Democratic and Republican political parties constitute a relatively small core of the national constituency. I was amazed how quickly I became the chairman of a state political party. My actions at two national conventions made a critical difference in the outcomes and also in Nixon's squeaker victory in 1968. I would never have believed this to be possible for me. So become involved in a political party and make not only your vote count but your political action help make the difference.

Christians should be involved in politics but not pastors. God's work comes ahead of man's work. Pastors and people in key positions of Christian work must be careful they don't dilute their influence for the Lord. If such a person is solicited or feels compelled to use his pulpit or position in a political campaign, make certain that this is God's will. But *everyone should vote!*

CHAPTER NINE

Church vs. State Questions

The political and social practices of our civilization derive from their Christian content—and they will not long survive unless they are replenished by faith.

Arnold Toynbee[1]

Americans have not been able to resolve how to maintain public virtue and public values in an increasingly diverse public without establishing religion in the public square.

Americans basically agree that no one religion should rule over the government of man. Americans also generally agree that religion promotes private virtue and values and thus good public virtue and values. Americans are very concerned today for our future because of the reality that private virtue and values have dimmed and public virtue and values are at an all-time low. The vast majority of American people love America profusely, and we want God to continue to bless America!

Many of us want God to bless America by saving America!

Virtue is defined as "general moral excellence" and "goodness of character." Value has to do with "the worth of a thing" and "acts, customs, etc., that are regarded as especially favorable by a people." The founding fathers of America's unique form of government were concerned about private virtue and values because they knew that they ultimately find expression in public virtue and values. And they believed that virtue and values were most essential to keeping this republic with its guarantee of personal freedom.[2]

Ben Franklin's famous comment at the end of the Constitutional Convention sums it all up: "We have a Republic, if we can keep it."[3] For more than two centuries generations of Americans have been able to keep it. But we have now moved past the historical mark which some writers of history have described as the beginning of the end for most of the great civilizations. The American Dream is about to become the American Nightmare!

We Need to Learn from History

Today more than ever, Americans need to study our past. The nature of man has been the same since the days of Adam and Eve. Thus the behavior and actions of humankind can be charted because there are cycles of history. George Santayana is best known for his warning that "those who forget the past are condemned to repeat it."[4]

Why do we fail to learn from history? It's because of our basic immaturity as human beings. This is the cardinal failing of our kids today: "But it won't happen to me!" Unfortunately—fortunately—it can happen to you, to me—even to all Americans! Yes, even nations die. There is a time for everything, including the decline and fall of civilizations, empires, and nations. King Solomon told us that there is a "time for every purpose under heaven: / A time to be born, / And a time to die . . . to break down . . . to weep . . . a time to lose . . . A time to keep . . ." (Eccl. 3:1-8).

Alexander Tytler and other great historians have charted a course that civilizations and nations have followed in winding their way from nowhere to somewhere and then back again to nowhere. The average age of the world's greatest civilizations is two hundred years.

These nations progressed through this sequence: From bondage to spiritual faith, from spiritual faith to great courage, from courage to liberty, from liberty to abundance, from abundance to selfishness, from selfishness to complacency, from complacency to apathy, from apathy to dependence, from dependence . . . *back into bondage*.[5]

We are living in a different day when what was the principal religion in America is no longer "king of the hill." For many years the Protestant churches provided much of the private virtue and values that were translated into public virtue and values for much of America's history. The Catholic Church also played a prominent role in the establishment of American virtue and values.

We Have a Mixed-Bag Religion

Over a period of time this Christian ethic was broadened to a Judeo-Christian ethic. Now the Judeo-Christian ethic is receding. Today we have a new ethic. I call it the Humanism-Situation ethic. It is composed of a mixed-bag of all kinds of religions, including the religion of secular humanism and relativism. Perhaps this latter religion is moving into the lead as we turn the corner on the transition from the Second to the Third Millennium.

This mixed-bag religious ethic resembles the one that tripped up Adam and Eve with this seductive appeal, "You can be as god!" That Garden of Eden serpent, the original dirty trickster, did not retire when he triumphed over our first Mom and Pop. He kept on keeping on until he prevailed over God's first chosen people, the nation of Israel in the Old Testament. Despite the fact that they had pledged their all to the Lord God Jehovah at Mount Sinai, they eventually succumbed to the same "siren song" of the serpent along their trek to the Promised Land. What evolved was a new religion for Israel, the First Channel of Redemption, called syncretism.

Syncretism equals pluralism equals mixed-bag religion. This means something like a tossed salad. Throw in a piece of God from the Old Testament nation of Israel, add a dash of the New Testament Jesus Christ, stir in Allah's jihad mentality à la Muammar Qadhafi and Saddam Hussein, add a touch of the wise sayings of Confucius, a portion of reincarnation from the Hindus of India and the New Age movement, a smidgen of Buddha, and turn up the heat with a mite of Satanism.

America is a land of Rights, so even those with their own individual religion, as with the late Ron Hubbard and his dyanetics and with the Moonies, expect to be represented in coming up with just the right portion of syncretism.

Then there are all of the divisions within each of these individual faiths, not to mention all of the other faiths not listed here. As in man's politics, there is always the left-wing and the right-wing. In some cases there is the north-wing and the south-wing. Beliefs vary among the various Protestant denominations. Then there are the differences between Protestants and Roman Catholics and also between Roman Catholics and the Orthodox Church. Southern Baptists have a special problem in nailing down individual beliefs so that there is a consensus or anything like unanimity of opinion on even the cardinal doctrines of Christianity.

So who is to specify what is to be the creed, prayer content, or doctrines of our national or civil religion? Dr. Martin E. Marty expresses the dilemma this way:

> No one has the sole key to the ways that religion and the public should meet in a kinetic, pluralistic society. The mix

is too rich, the set of situations is too volatile, and the reposi-
tory of plausible proposals from many sources is too well-
stocked to permit anyone's sense of having arrived at full
resolutions.[6]

What Is Civil Religion?

Civil religion is a way of thinking which makes sacred a political
arrangement or governmental system that provides a religious image
of that society for many of the people. It is also denoted as civil, public, political, or societal religion or as public piety. Some would say
that it is the general faith of a community or nation that focuses on
widely held beliefs about the history and destiny of that people. In
effect, it is putting a political twist on religion, or *vice versa*. Usually
this is not done by a specific denomination.

In America we call it God and Country religion. Some folks are
so big on God and Country religion that they are really emphasizing
Country and God more than God and Country. I once did this.

Civil religion has no central authority or formal organization as
such. However, "God," whichever god that may be, is usually the
focus along with the country or community. In the U.S. the authority
figure is usually the president because it has substantially been our
presidents, from George Washington to George Bush, who have made
and molded our civil religion.

The genesis and revelation of civil religion in America is best set
forth in a book called *Civil Religion & the Presidency* by Dr. Richard
Pierard and Dr. Robert Linder of the University of Iowa. In this book
they give special focus to the private faith and public accomplishments
of nine presidents: George Washington, Abraham Lincoln, William
McKinley, Woodrow Wilson, Franklin D. Roosevelt, Dwight D.
Eisenhower, Richard M. Nixon, and Ronald Reagan.

The authors state that all presidents have been friendly to religion. And why not, as politicians? After all, the very liberal Supreme
Court Justice William O. Douglas once aptly observed in a Supreme
Court decision, "We are a religious people whose institutions presup-
pose a Supreme Being."[7]

The American civic faith did not begin with Washington. It goes
back to the old English civil religion as understood and revered by
the early Puritan settlers of New England. Our civil religion probably began with Governor John Winthrop of Massachusetts. In 1630
he challenged his Puritan brethren to build "a city upon a hill." He

proclaimed this to be their divine calling. Many years later a former movie star named Ronald Reagan would become Governor Ronald Reagan of California and subsequently President Ronald Reagan. He is the one who used that Winthropian phrase so eloquently and often in his trek from Hollywood to the White House. He gave Americans a vision for virtue and values for our beloved land. With this he attracted the biggest following of Christian political campaign workers ever.

Those Puritans out in the wilderness of the new America were to be shining lights and godly models for the world to see and accept as the Right way to live. The other key stepping-stones for America's civil religion were the Mayflower Compact, the Declaration of Independence, the United States Constitution, and President Abraham Lincoln's great Gettysburg Address. Taken all together, they form the essence of the sacred scriptures of the national religion of America.

National holidays, special ceremonies—such as the Fourth of July, Thanksgiving Day, Memorial Day, Martin Luther King, Jr., Day, and even Christmas Day would all become noted on our national calendars. In every war, including the Civil War, the troops were exhorted to win the victory for the civil faith—whether above or below the Mason-Dixon line. In World War I and World War II many patriotic songs became famous and so beloved because they wrapped God and country together for a great cause.

The most cherished song was made famous by the late Kate Smith. "God Bless America" may be more used and loved than even "The Star-Spangled Banner," which is still sung at the opening of many athletic events across America. Other favorites are "America" (or "My Country 'Tis of Thee") and "America the Beautiful." The latest rival for leadership in patriotic songs is Lee Greenwood's new hit, "God Bless the USA." President George Bush and other national leaders pushed this new song throughout the Mideast War of 1991 and thereafter. Nothing thrills Americans more than patriotic music with a smattering of God and Country flavor.

What Is the Ideological Base of Civil Religion?

It is rather amazing that in this day of religious pluralism American civil religion seems to continue to transcend separation of church and state and permeates every level of national life. What is its ideological base? *The Dictionary of Christianity in America* defines it this way:

(1) there is a God; (2) his will can be known and fulfilled through democratic procedures; (3) America has been
God's primary agent in modern history; and (4) the nation is
the chief source of identity for Americans in both a political
and religious sense.[8]

Dr. A. James Reichley of the Brookings Institute is another expert in the area of civil religion. His 1985 book, *Religion in American
Public Life*, is one of the most informative works on this subject. He
lists seven value systems that serve to motivate individuals and social
groups. Four are religion-based, and three are secular-based. The first
four are based on transcendental reality, looking beyond the here-and-
now. The other three relate only to the here-and-now. Reichley raises
this pertinent question:

A critical question for all modern democracies is
whether the three secular value systems, either separately or
in some combination, can provide sufficient moral basis to
maintain the cohesion vitality of a free society.[9]

He argues that if the answer is "no," as Presidents George Washington, John Adams, and Thomas Jefferson evidently believed, then
the four value systems based in one way or another on religion must be
scrutinized in depth. The question to be answered, he writes, is:

How transcendent moral authority or inspiration can be
maintained in a democratic society while minimizing the
risks of bigotry, fanaticism, irresponsibility, and obscuran-
tism that some tendencies within religion have all too often
fostered.[10]

The three secular value systems are egoism, which reduces all
value to the drives and appetites of individual humans; authoritarianism, which bases value entirely on the welfare of the social group; and
civil humanism, which attempts to balance the rights of the individual
against the needs of the group without relating either to transcendent
moral law.

Realistically, none of these can work, and especially "egoism."
That alone is the key to the human problem. The other two are mere
extensions of that fiction.

Religious Values Are Vital

Religion and politics are both concerned with the pursuit of values at the personal, social, and transcendent levels. Values are based on moral authority and intellectual interest and/or physical appetite. It is easy to see how values that originate with self or the group will of necessity sink into self or group interest. Actually, human values originate in either the individual human, the group or community, and the realm of Eternity.

The transcendental arena fosters piety, humility, and right relationships—in other words, selflessness and a bent for doing Right instead of doing Wrong. Here is the vital difference! This is not just documented in the Holy Scriptures. This has been established as a reality throughout history. As a consequence our founding fathers hooked their hopes for a successful republic on religion flourishing in the hearts of individual people. Dr. Reichley agrees that religion and capitalism need each other:

> To the extent that it promotes theist-humanist values, religion supplies moral values that capitalism needs for survival and that counter its dehumanizing tendencies. . . . From the standpoint of the public good, the most important service churches offer to secular life in a free society is to nurture moral values that help humanize capitalism and give direction to democracy.[11]

Despite all of this good, trouble surfaces in the human conflict between "what I want" and "what that other 'selfish' guy wants." There we are again—right back in the Garden of Eden, me versus thee. Reichley agrees:

> Public moralists in all societies, speaking on behalf of one or another of the competing value systems, have regularly condemned concentration on self-gratification as an end in itself.[12]

Self-awareness is one of the great gifts bestowed on human beings. It is the essential quality of humanness and is the key to human community and society. Dr. Billy Graham says that the deepest hurt in humanity is loneliness. We were made to want to live in right relationships with God and with one another. But human consciousness is also the bane of our existence. It is when we become aware of self that we become selfish. And when we discover that we cannot handle life by ourselves we then begin to look for supernatural and thus transcendental help.

Religion has been around for ages, and it is in vogue in some form or another all over the world. The people who seem to ignore religion do not make up a large percentage of the population. They tend to be those who have higher intellect and who have come to believe that they can handle life by their own wits. It can lead to ego inflation and the temptation to play god. This is what happened to Karl Marx and others who have dreamed big pipe-dreams that produced the "isms" or philosophies of life that have turned civilizations and nations into graveyards.

The current best example to study is the Marxist-Leninist "ism" called communism, which turned the vast empire of the old Soviet Union into its present-day chaos. Marx concocted a most idealistic plan that excluded God and placed the new communist comrade at the center of the universe. That new communist turned out to be the communist party elite, not the proletariat for whom Marx dedicated his existence and dreams. The party elite lived like kings, and the working people and the intellectuals paid the price for their fun and frolicking.

It is the here-and-now "ism" dreamers who have jeopardized the future of America.

History Documents Humanity's Rebellions

Since the beginning of time man has been seeking to get around God. That is the essence of man's rebellion against the authority of his Creator. The creature seeks to devour the Creator so the creature can have the power and authority. But the universe was created to work God's way and not ours.

Dr. Larry Richards has provided us with a convincing argument against theories regarding evolutionism as the answer to the existence of a God, who is Creator. In his book, *It Couldn't Just Happen*, Dr. Richards asks:

> Is it reasonable to think that something could begin without a cause; that the universe could begin without a Creator; that natural laws present from the beginning could govern our universe without their being designed? Not really. Every reasonable conclusion requires God! And no reason-

able explanation other than God has been offered! . . . The more we learn about the universe, the more strange and awesome it appears. Yet everything is ruled by natural laws whose only possible source is God![13]

Dr. Richards, author of more than one hundred Christian books, teamed up with Dr. John N. Moore, a founding member of the Creation Research Society, and Dr. John N. Clayton, the author and producer of the popular film series, "Does God Exist?" to refute the theory of evolution.

They point out that the exact spin and tilt of the earth gives us our days and nights and also our seasons. Our earth is the perfect size. If it was smaller the law of gravity could not hold either our air or water. Thinner air would provide no protection from the thousands of meteorites that rush toward earth daily. With thinner air temperatures would drop, and life could not exist.

Their book also makes these interesting observations:

> If the Earth were twice as large . . . everything would weigh eight times as much, and that weight could crush most living things. If Earth were twice as far from the sun . . . living things would freeze during winters. If the Earth were half as far from the sun, its surface . . . would become a burning desert. If Earth did not have a moon . . . there would be no tides in the sea . . . waters of the oceans might grow stagnant, unable to provide the oxygen that fish need to live. . . . Any of these changes would make life on earth impossible.[14]

All scientists and medical doctors should have little difficulty seeing beyond self to the existence of the Creator of the universe. When I studied through the Time-Life series of books on *The Human Body* I became even more convicted about the reality of our Creator-God. How could any medical doctor accept evolution? And how could any woman who has given birth to a baby not believe God was behind that miracle?

Civil Religion Has Been Our Strength and Weakness

One of the great strengths of American life is civil religion. It has been the spiritual and patriotic glue that has united America and motivated America to do its best and be its best. Ironically, civil religion has its weaknesses too, especially for the religious side of the equation. For one thing, people can worship country over God. For another, politics, public-interest groups, and ideologues can take advantage of religion and use and/or pervert religion or religious groups in all of their piety and naiveté.

Many people in churches may be as confused as I was about my faith. I now believe I had more of a civic faith than a real Jesus faith and did not understand the difference. My faith now is centered in Jesus Christ as Lord and Savior. I have spoken at many "God and Country" rallies and church services. My concern has been which one ended up on the throne: Jesus Christ or the U.S.A.?

This kind of public faith is more in the nature of a Deistic Unitarianism, which leaves Jesus hanging on the cross as a common criminal who was guilty of blasphemy against the Lord God Jehovah. It also leaves Jesus without His resurrection experience. The Unitarian prayers are directed, in effect, "to whom it may concern." This kind of civil religion ignores sin, guilt, judgment, punishment, humility, and hope.

No, Christianity and civil religion are not the same. Yet so many Americans with superficial understanding and superficial commitment equate Christianity with civil religion. The losers in this mistaken notion are the superficial members, their families, the church of Jesus Christ, the United States of America, and the world.

The pastors must clarify this critical distinction for their members so that they fully comprehend that civil religion can be a good thing but is not the Real Thing!

Politicians Sometimes Use Religion

As to the second problem with civil religion, there is no question in my mind but that all of the presidents have used religion for their political ends. I can certify to this regarding President Richard Nixon, for I was a co-conspirator. We took civil religion for a ride with our occasional Sunday morning ecumenical services in the East Room of the White House. Dr. Billy Graham was the unofficial pastor to Nixon in elections and also in the administration. This is documented in a 1991 book on Billy Graham by Dr. William Martin, in a friendly biography, *A Prophet with Honor*.

The Democrats' selection of Hubert Humphrey [in 1968 as the presidential nominee], another old friend [of Graham], kept some check on Graham's expressions for enthusiasm for Nixon, but his preference was transparent. At a September crusade in Pittsburgh, he read a telegram of greeting from Humphrey, but he invited Nixon to take a prominent seat in the VIP section, where the television cameras could easily find him, and he lauded him from the platform, citing his generosity, his "tremendous constraint of temper," and his "integrity in counting golf score," and calling their friendship "one of the most cherished I have had with anyone."

Nixon described the occasion as "one of the most moving religious experiences of my life." The telecast of that particular service, broadcast just before the election, was added to Graham's TV schedule at the last minute because of "the urgency of the hour."[15]

The author cited the fact that Harry Dent, as the "Southern strategist" and campaign leader for the South, had exploited Billy's absentee vote for Nixon in TV ads all across Dixie. We also used a videotape showing Billy Graham at a special Nixon TV show in the Bible Belt. All we needed was what was captured by one camera: the presence of BG. That communicated Billy's blessing for RN in a very close race whose outcome was determined below the Mason-Dixon line as we were stiff-arming Governor George Wallace of Alabama with our TV commercials that proclaimed: A Vote for George Is a Vote for Hubert! Our political strategy was to indirectly transfer this winning punchline from Senator Strom Thurmond and Harry Dent to Billy Graham. It worked! And it made the winning difference for Nixon in 1968.

The book about Graham also cites the use of the Nixon White House Sunday worship services for our political gain. Dr. Martin rummaged through the Nixon files in the archives and found exactly how the tickets of admission were allocated. That alone tells the real story. Charles Colson, then a pagan, received fifty tickets to distribute among his constituency, the business and labor leaders. Pat Nixon and I received ten each. Mine were primarily for use in the South. A memo from the chief of staff's office—which usually meant from Nixon personally—ordered that "non-VIPs" be limited to no more than 25 percent of the congregation.[16]

President Nixon spoke to each National Prayer Breakfast meeting during his time in the White House, as have all presidents since its inauguration in 1953 by President Dwight Eisenhower.

Skin-Deep Religion

Yet when we survey the damage of the Watergate scandal, it is apparent that whatever religion there was in the White House was mostly skin-deep. I was chairman of the Prayer Breakfast Group that met each Wednesday morning in the executive staff mess situated under the office of the Nixon's chief of staff, Bob Haldeman.

Skin-deep religion could be said to apply to President Reagan's White House. The First Lady was consulting star-gazers to better be able to pull the strings from behind the Oval Office. The president barely missed his own Watergate experience in the form of the Iran-Contra scandal. Lieutenant Colonel Oliver North now publicly suspects that the Commander-in-Chief was a part of that problem. Reagan testified at the 1982 National Prayer Breakfast that "God was carrying me on His shoulders" when he narrowly escaped assassination in 1981. Because of his brush with eternity, President Reagan promised the top leadership of Washington and God:

> I've always believed that we were, each of us, put here for a reason. That there is a plan somehow—a divine plan for all of us. I know now that whatever days are left of me belong to Him.[17]

These remarks were extemporaneous. Reagan made many comments like this. His talks to the annual convention of the National Religious Broadcasters Association were loaded with God and Country punchlines that won great applause and high favors for one of the most fervent God and Country presidents in history. He did more to enlist Christians into political action than any other president in history. Some might call Ronald Reagan the high priest of civil religion, for he was the figure for whom numerous religious-rightist political organizations were initiated and used.

President Reagan was fuzzy in the specifics of his spiritual convictions, very limited in his church contributions (one tax return showed 1 percent), and seldom turned up in church. But he outpolled Jimmy Carter for the Christian born-again vote in 1980, the year when all three presidential candidates were running as born-again Christians. Carter had won in large part over President Gerald Ford by attracting so many evangelical Christians into his fold. In 1980 he was defeated by the born-again vote. And in 1988 the high priest of civil religion walked away with the great majority of the Christian vote as he exceeded even the huge Southern Bible Belt victories that Nixon won in 1972.

These are examples of how politicians can make use of religion for various purposes, especially their own election. Today ex-President Jimmy Carter and his wife, Rosalyn, are directly involved in Christian ministry as carpenters building homes for the needy. This is the prime reason Jimmy Carter has risen from the ashes of defeat to become called by some media persons and some historians the best ex-president America has ever had.

The Carters dropped some of their piety in defeat, but they eventually regained their spiritual legs and have become lay ministers and witnesses for righteousness in the marketplace of Christian home-building through Habitat for Humanity.[18] I have noted little if any direct Christian activity and real witness for righteousness by Nixon or Reagan, and I am an ex-Republican activist. However, I no longer permit partisanship to cloud my view of what is the Right way to minister and witness—even on the part of an old Democrat foe.

Make no mistake! Politicians use religion, and religion is a most profitable tool to use when it comes to winning elections.

Religion Is Used for Good by Some Politicians

At the same time, religion can be used for good. I believe that these presidents have put religion or public faith to work for the common good, as did President George Bush, especially in the Mideast War. In most cases, religion is important in encouraging public order, public freedom, and public justice. And there have been times in American history when religion in one form or the other has intervened in the public affairs of our country for good. One specific example is the determined belief of President Abraham Lincoln that the Union must be saved—indeed, if for no other reason than that it was the will of God. Drawing upon his fondness for the Puritan conviction that God had chosen America to implement His plan, this rough-hewn backwoodsman linked divine destiny with the preservation of the United States of America.

On December 1, 1862, Lincoln directly addressed the question of slavery and domestic strife with a warning that "we cannot escape history" in his Last, Best Hope Speech:

The fiery trial through which we pass, will light us down in honor or dishonor, to the last generation. We say we are for the Union. The world will not forget that we say this. We know how to save the Union. The world knows we know how to save it. We—even we here—hold the power, and bear the responsibility. In giving freedom to the slave, we assure freedom to the free. . . . We should nobly save, or meanly lose, the last, best hope on earth. Other means may succeed; this could not fail. The way is plain, peaceful, generous, just—a way which, if followed, the world will forever applaud, and God must forever bless.[19]

Lincoln articulated a new and stronger civil religion in speech after speech. Although he quoted no Scripture in his most famous speech, the Gettysburg Address, he did drop a most powerful phrase which was later inserted in the Pledge of Allegiance in 1954: "One Nation Under God." In the understatement of American history, Lincoln declared, "The world will little note, nor long remember what we say here, but it can never forget what they did here."[20]

One of the sixteenth president's most meaningful phrases was coined out of his belief that God both shaped and judged America. In a meeting with a group of clergymen in 1862 he corrected one who expressed the hope that "the Lord was on our side." Lincoln remarked:

I don't agree with you. I am not at all concerned about that, for I know that the Lord is always on the side of the right. But this is my constant anxiety and prayer that I and the nation should be on the Lord's side.[21]

I must confess as a good ole Southern boy that my forebears were not on God's side in the controversy that culminated in what we in the South have insisted on calling "The War Between the States." After my life was spiritually transformed, I publicly repented of my previous political actions that could be termed anti-black in word or deed.

Nixon Did It Right

When I was in the White House I initiated the idea of establishing and implementing a plan to desegregate the public school systems in the South by moral persuasion, instead of "bullets, blood and bayonets."[22] Former Nixon and Reagan cabinet-member George Shultz was the chairman of Nixon's Cabinet Committee on Education. My task was to assist Shultz, along with the help of my assistant, now the Reverend Wallace Henley, a Baptist pastor in Houston. This committee greatly facilitated desegregation in Southern schools. The story of the committee's work is recorded in my political book, *The Prodigal South Returns to Power.*[23]

The key player in this plan was Nixon himself. *New York Times* writer Tom Wicker has recently applauded Nixon's desegregation program in a 1991 biography of Nixon.

> There's no doubt about it—the Nixon Administration accomplished more in 1970 to desegregate Southern school systems than had been done in the 16 previous years, or probably since. . . . perhaps the most significant of his administration's domestic actions.[24]

We had only one tense moment in handling integrated black and white delegations of persuaders from Southern states. The Mississippi delegation was composed of white Citizens' Council members and black NAACP members. A fistfight almost broke out in the ante-room to the Oval Office, but once inside the president's office, his presence brought the old enemies together for a common cause.

Bush Did It Right

During the Christmas season of December 1990, President George Bush took a note from Lincoln's eloquent comment about the Right side as opposed to the Wrong side. The national news media reported that Bush spent twelve days at Camp David walking through the woods trying to ascertain God's will regarding the question of war or sanctions against Saddam Hussein of Iraq. Apparently this forty-first president was rethinking the civil religion comments of that other lanky president, Abe Lincoln. Soon thereafter Bush concluded that he would be on God's side in moving against the Iraqi despot. He must have been Right because America won a world war in record time with limited casualties and with the assistance of the United Nations and twenty-seven other nations.

On the evening before issuing the order to attack, President Bush had his friend Billy Graham lead a prayer meeting at the Pentagon and spend the evening at the White House.

George Washington initiated civil religion from the White House, and Abe Lincoln emblazoned it into the history books of America and into the hearts of Americans for years to come by using it for much good.

Former Education Secretary under President Reagan and Drug Czar under President Bush, William J. Bennett is a strong proponent of civil religion. Here is Dr. Bennett's case for having a semblance of a national religion in the public square:

> Let me be clear: The virtues of self-discipline, love of learning, and respect for family are by no means limited to the Judeo-Christian tradition, or to any religious tradition. My point is that, in America, our civic virtues are inseparable from our common values. And values such as courage, kindness, honesty, and discipline are, to a large degree, common to almost all religious traditions.
>
> But it is the Judeo-Christian moral tradition that has given birth to our free political institutions and it is the Judeo-Christian moral tradition that has shaped our national ideals. . . . But what is agreed upon is important: It has content and power. It infuses American life with a sense of transcendence. All profit from it, although none is forced to assent to it. And, as the Founders predicted, the constitutional order depends on it.[25]

We Must Be Careful Not to Put Country Before God

Charles Colson believes that civil religion is nothing but idolatry, while privatized faith is really no faith at all. I disagree with my old colleague in his comments against civil religion, but I agree that for too many Americans civil religion has become a form of idolatry that puts country ahead of God. Pastors have a duty to make this distinction crystal clear to believers. By and large, this has not been done.

I agree with Colson about privatized faith. There is no way we can implement the Great Commission by hiding our faith. This is the major message of the Bible to all who profess to be God's people. We are to let people know that "I am not ashamed of the gospel of Christ, for it is the power of God to salvation for everyone who believes . . ." (Rom. 1:16).

I would be one of the last people in America to belittle civil religion, but I would be in the forefront of those making that vital distinction between the faith of Jesus Christ and the civic faith. There is that vital difference, but there are also the commonalties of values that Dr. Bennett denotes.

Our Rotary, Exchange, Kiwanis, Lions, Sertoma, Ruritan, and other civic clubs perform a vital service to our God and our country by continuing to champion the values of our Judeo-Christian tradition. In order to provide this valuable service, it is necessary that they highlight the common values addressed by Dr. Bennett above. Wherever I have spoken before civic clubs I have had no hindrances in quoting Scripture or mentioning Jesus Christ. I am sensitive to using discretion in speaking to these civic clubs; they too must be discreet in managing the meetings of their clubs because of the diversity in their membership. They appear to be handling this duty with aplomb.

God has established His church for a particular purpose: to provide a special place for worship as the body of Christ, to edify and equip the saints to do the work of ministry, and to implement the Great Commission. Civil government was provided for the people by God to provide order, justice, peace, and the common good for the welfare of the people. God created us humans to be free, responsible, and creative as good stewards of all of His creation.

Justice Is the Goal of Human Government

So, justice, in effect, is the main aim of human government. Righteousness or morality is the main aim of God. It is vital that justice and righteousness march together in step as much as possible, for there will be no real justice without righteous hearts being involved. And there will be little room for morality and righteousness if justice is not maintained and enforced by human government. Justice is to ensure that each person has freedom and opportunity, and righteousness and morality are to ensure that freedom and opportunity are to be exercised and explored in accord with righteous and responsible behavior and actions.

What we Americans must have guiding our governance of others is individual responsibility connected with every individual right granted to every individual American. This is what is out of kilter today: too much exercise of our rights and too little exercise of our responsibilities. For with every right we have been granted comes a concomitant responsibility. Only people with a finely honed sense of Right versus Wrong can be expected to be restrained in the exercise of our precious human rights as American citizens. This is where religious values play such a vital role for the common good.

The question of what to do about court decisions that nudge God further and further away from the public square has been addressed most cogently and consistently by a Lutheran leader, Richard John Neuhaus. The classic book on this subject is his work *The Naked Public Square: Religion and Democracy in America*. He heads the Rockford Institute and its Center on Religion and Society in New York City.

Dr. Neuhaus states his concern about the wider wall of separation of religious values from the realm of what he called "the naked public square" that court decisions have forced in recent years.

The naked public square is the result of political doctrine and practice that would exclude religion and religiously grounded values from the conduct of public business. The doctrine is that America is a secular society. It finds dogmatic expression in the ideology of secularism. I will argue that the doctrine is demonstrably false and the dogma exceedingly dangerous.

Central to the story is the claim that the public square will not and cannot remain naked. If it is not clothed with the "meanings" borne by religion, new "meanings" will be imposed by virtue of the modern state.

As will become evident, I am skeptical about the alarms and crisis-mongering that marks so much writing about American society and America's role in the world. It is therefore with reluctance, joined by modest hope, that I set forth the reasons for believing that ours is indeed a period of crisis throwing into severe jeopardy the future of religion and democracy.[26]

Pastors Should Avoid Politics

Pat Robertson of the CBN-TV network invited me to write his program and run his campaign for president in 1988. He felt that his manager had to be either Charles Colson or Harry Dent, and he was convinced he could not get Colson. After two visits with him in Virginia Beach, Virginia, I refused to return. I had given him my best advice: don't run! He has one of the largest congregations in the world on CBN. His candidacy brought more Christian lay people into political activism.

Dr. Mark Noll shows in his 1988 book, *One Nation Under God?*, that when Christianity became more directly involved in man's government, Christianity suffered. He cites the Christian involvement in the American Revolution. Then he points to stronger influence by Christianity when its leaders were less involved, such as in the writing of the United States Constitution.[27] In 1800 Christians returned to the political fray against Thomas Jefferson with a vengeance, only to be humiliated. The problem was that the Christians had "more fire than light." So Noll's teaching is that Christians must beware of superficial knowledge in politics. "Amen!" I say to that.[28]

Charles Colson and I agree with Noll and Blaise Pascal, that brilliant French scientist and Christian of the 1660s, in his much-quoted book, *Les Pensées*. He said, "Men never do evil so completely and cheerfully as when they do it from religious conviction."[29]

This is why pastors and church leaders must be very careful about jumping or being lured into political frays. For one thing, pastors are not trained in politics; they are trained in theology. Second, when a pastor uses his pulpit or his position to back one political party or politician over another he is risking not only his pulpit and position but also his message to the people who come to hear him proclaim the gospel.

I recall a young pastor telling me after I had spoken in his church service that he was going to rip the Democractic Party's national platform to pieces in the pulpit the next Sunday. He thought I would appreciate his stand. Over lunch that day we discussed the necessity for abstinence by pastors and especially regarding political party platforms in the pulpit. I asked him what percentage of the people in his pews were Democrats. He responded, "Most of them." I did not have the gall to check back to see if he had peeled his Reagan-Bush bumper sticker off of his car bumper in the pastor's parking spot.

Preaching about subjects that affect morality and righteousness, such as abortion, alcohol, or adultery is another matter. But even here caution and discretion must be exercised. For instance, the Democratic or Republican candidate backing abortion rights should not be attacked from the pulpit in the course of preaching against abortion rights.

God Calls Pastors

Politics did not call pastors. I pray that God called them. The reason I am not directly involved in politics today is because God called me to do something else—His work. One of the marks that stands in history against Southern pastors in the Civil War is the fact that most supported a cause that would have kept human beings in slavery. I do not condemn those who did so because I probably would have been on that side based on what I did in modern-day American politics.

In his book, *Kingdoms in Conflict,* Colson provides this advice to Christians regarding involvement in politics:

> While I believe an open pulpit endorsement of a candidate is improper, I feel that—if made responsibly from the right motivations—a cleric's statement that Christians should not support candidates who reject basic human rights is justified.
>
> Within these limits, then, we can conclude that Christians, both individually and institutionally, have a duty, for the good of society as a whole, to bring the values of the Kingdom of God to bear within the kingdoms of man.[30]

I agree with Colson on his suggestions. Christians should become very involved in politics, most of all, as "salt" and "light," but also in seeking to influence the governing authorities about issues which affect the important Bible subject of righteousness. Individual Christians will have their own matters of interest to support. In everything that a Christian does in politics or any endeavor it is vital that the Christian conduct himself or herself as a mature Christian. It is possible for Christians to do more harm than good when they use the same improper behavior and tactics that others may employ.

NEVER FORGET THAT YOU TAKE THE NAME OF JESUS CHRIST WITH YOU WHEREVER YOU GO—IN POLITICS, GOVERNMENT, THE MARKETPLACE, THE HOME, AND EVEN THE CHURCH.

The church is to use its moral persuasion to influence the governing authorities for moral righteousness. However, there is a dividing line between taking over the kingdom of man in the name of Jesus

Christ and forcing non-Christians to believe and do as we Christians believe and do.

There Are Different Levels of Christian Participation in Politics

Dr. Reichley establishes four categories of religious participation in the affairs of man's government: the separationists, the social activists, the accommodationists, and the direct interventionists.

Separationists hold that churches should confine themselves to nurturing spiritual and moral values, leaving individual church members to apply these values to concrete public issues.

Social activists agree that church and state should be kept institutionally separate, but argue that moral imperatives springing from the Judeo-Christian tradition, which provides the common religious heritage of most Americans, require that religious bodies work actively to promote virtuous causes in public life.

Accommodationists insist that religion should maintain at least a symbolic presence in most areas of public life (like the frieze depicting the Ten Commandments above the Supreme Court dias) and that the church should help set the moral direction of civil society.

Direct interventionists recommend that the church, or at least its leaders, should plunge into the deals and stratagems of practical politics, winning for the church and its constituents a share of the benefits that issue from public power.[31]

Thus the separationists and social activists believe in strict separation of church and state and a small role for the churches in politics. The social activists also are strict on separation but large on church participation. The accommodationists are moderate on the question of separation, as are the interventionists. But the accommodationists are moderate on church participation, and the interventionists are large on church participation in politics.

I find myself torn between being a separationist and a social activist. However, if the United States Supreme Court does not become more realistic—and it is beginning to do so—I could move up one notch to an accommodationist, but never to be a direct interventionist.

The American Civil Liberties Union and other very liberal groups have pushed the Supreme Court to go too far too fast and to engage in nit-picking religious involvement on questions such as a prayer by a speaker at commencement exercises in a school and Christmas scenes celebrating what America acknowledges as a holiday season, Christmastime.

This is what troubles Dr. Neuhaus and those who stand with him in publicly expressing concerns about efforts and actions to smother religion and religious values which have played a dynamic role in making certain that we keep Ben Franklin's republic.

The day that prayer was bounced out of our public schools marked the beginning in a downturn of public virtue and public values. Public opinion polls continue to show that 78 percent of the American public favor allowing religious activities in public schools.[32]

Individual rights should be balanced with the public good.

Many scholars who do not qualify for the Christian fundamentalist tag sense the necessity to find a way to get back to the view of the founders in writing the First Amendment:

THAT FUNCTIONAL SEPARATION BETWEEN CHURCH AND STATE SHOULD BE MAINTAINED WITHOUT THREATENING THE SUPPORT AND GUIDANCE RECEIVED BY REPUBLICAN GOVERNMENT FROM RELIGION.

This is the exact view of Dr. Reichley, a scholar from the liberal Brookings Institute in Washington, D.C.[33]

Although the U.S. Supreme Court is not a politically elected body, it is politically nominated and confirmed by the president and the senate. Thus the election of a president is vital on this subject. The election of individual U.S. Senators carries significance for this subject but less so than the person who does the nominating. The Senators only confirm, and sometimes they do not vote to confirm.

The philosophical and political orientation of the Supreme Court has been changed in the past few decades, beginning with Richard Nixon and carrying on to George Bush. Very few liberals have been nominated and confirmed; mostly those with more conservative orientations have been seated on the Court since 1969. So political involvement in the Right way is important in determining whether "we can keep it," meaning the republican form of government announced by Ben Franklin.

The great American political experiment is based on that precious principle and privilege of personal freedom. Dr. Paul Johnson, an eminent Catholic historian, credits the very basis of human freedom to Christianity. He sees Christianity's strength as lying in "its just estimate of man as a fallible creature with immortal longings" and its "outstanding moral merit" as being God's investment of man with a conscience, "and bid him follow it." He adds:

> The notions of political and economic freedom both spring from the workings of the Christian conscience as a historical force; and it is thus no accident that all the implantations of freedom throughout the world have ultimately a Christian origin.[34]

We Must Remember the Importance of God's Government

As much as we prize our freedom, we Americans and Christians must ever remember what Jesus had in mind about the importance of His Kingdom as compared to the importance of living the good life in the good society on planet Earth. Dr. Johnson captured the difference in these remarks:

> "My kingdom is not of this world." Those seven words go to the heart of the Christian faith. The truth is not a truth about worldly Utopias. It is not a mandate for socialism or capitalism or democracy or kingship or social welfare. When Satan took Jesus to the high mountain and showed Him the kingdoms of the world, and Jesus rejected them and told Satan to be gone, He was rejecting the worldliness not only of wealth and privilege, but the worldliness of political programs and politicized theology, and of morals preached to attain political ends, however speciously high-minded they may be.
>
> When a historian looks at Jesus Christ and Christianity, his final conclusion must be, I think, that Jesus was not concerned with this world at all, except insofar as it forms a threshold to the next; and that Christianity is quite literally *like nothing on earth*.[35]

So man's politics is important, but it really isn't all that important when we move from man's perspective to the perspective of God Almighty! That is what Betty kept trying to tell me during all those years I was in the political arena.

CHAPTER TEN

Pluralism: The Rival to Christianity

But our faith is true for different reasons—in the ultimate sense, that what Christianity teaches is the correct explanation of reality.

Michael Scott Horton[1]

There are many human views of what is Right versus what is Wrong. America's foremost dilemma today, this is the reason for all the multiplying problems that plague the moral character of a nation whose major religion has been Christianity. Whether we know it or not, or like it or not, our nation is a witness to the world for Right or Wrong. We do not look too good or righteous.

Harry and Betty Dent's visits to every continent in the world except Antarctica have indelibly inscribed in our hearts the reality that Americans are appearing to be witnesses for Wrong more and more. This kind of witness adversely reflects on the character and teachings of Jesus Christ and the Christian worldview. The purpose of this book has been to set forth succinctly and simply why we as Christians have a duty to our country and an even higher duty to our Christ to re-think and change so that we may truly become *witnesses for righteousness* to a world that is spiritually lost.

On my second mission to Australia in 1989 I was confronted with a cute comment by an immigration official when I noted on my entry form that my profession is "Christian Ministry." He laughed and commented, "Oh, so you're one of those, eh!" I asked what he meant. Then he retorted, "Jim Bakker and Jimmy Swaggart!" He told me that they had been the most-watched religious programs on TV "down under." So I asked him to permit me to change my entry card. I struck out "Christian Ministry" and substituted "Lawyer." He smiled and said, "That's much better."

This is some different day in America when foreigners rate lawyers over Christian ministry. The last survey I saw on the worst professions in America had "TV evangelists" rated third with lawyers close behind. The lesson is to *watch your witness because others are even if we aren't.*

Not all of us are called to be foreign missionaries, but we are all called to be domestic missionaries to the people within our borders. We may stay here and continue to enjoy the rights, privileges, and great blessings of living "in the land of the free and the home of the brave." But our day-to-day witness extends far beyond our borders because our freedom enables us to be individual governors of our land and thus the governors of the actions of our country for Right or Wrong.

We do hold the levers of political power and moral authority in this country as Americans and Christians. One day we will answer for what we did or did not do with all this power and authority vested in us as American citizens and as citizens of the Kingdom of God on earth.

We have a dual duty to the kingdom of man and the Kingdom of God. We also have another duty to the people of the world who watch the witness of America for good or evil, Right versus Wrong.

Now that we accept service on the Great Commission's worldwide import, let us look at some of the views regarding Right versus Wrong confronting our people at home and the people scattered throughout the world. We are living today with pluralism, or a wide variety of religious beliefs.

Satanism Is the Most Menacing

The most menacing one is Satanism or devil worship. Would you believe that this is a problem even in the Bible Belt of America and among our schoolchildren? In this diabolical worldview, Wrong is Right and Right is Wrong. Even secular TV shows have exposed the extent of this problem in America.

Animism Is a Part of Most Religions

Then there is the basic religion in the boondocks of the world, animism. This is the principal religion that influenced the Israelites to straddle the fence with the Lord God Jehovah by also worshiping the spirit gods of animism. Animists believe that all life is produced by a spiritual force.

Basically, animism is totally self-centered. Our actions are not ultimately our responsibility. While humans have a fear of the spirit world, the name of the game in this religion is to manipulate the gods of power to do humanity's will instead of the other way around. Animism is a forebear of the "isms," such as relativism, and also of situational ethics. Sin and basic morality are of little concern because humans manipulate the spirits that inhabit us and everything else through voo-doo and other odd rituals. What makes it appealing to us is that it is a power religion.

According to Dr. Phil Steyne, there is some animism in all of the major world religions, including Christianity. It claims to produce success, security, happiness, and man as the master of his own destiny, what is most appealing to the human heart.[2] Some of the TV evangelists have been using potions and portions of animism because of this special appeal to the selfish nature of humans. This is one of many reasons why we as Christians must know our own faith.

Eastern Religions Are Making Inroads

We also need to know what we believe and why because the Eastern religions of Hinduism, Buddhism, and Islam have been making more inroads in the Western world, especially in America. Trappings of various teachings of these religions can be seen in cultic religions springing up here, such as the New Age movement, its relationship to Hinduism, and its teaching of reincarnation in lieu of the resurrection experience of Jesus Christ.

The fact that so many cultic groups are taking root in America, particularly from the influence of Eastern mysticism, signifies an increasing spiritual hunger in the lives of many people, and, perhaps, a disillusionment with the principal religions. In particular, this search for meaning and purpose is in response to public alarm about the disintegration of the family, the problems in our schools, the violence and vulgarity on television, and the scandals in politics, business, and even in the church. In addition, all of the "isms" discussed in this book, plus hedonism—the extreme and unethical search for pleasure—have left Americans with an increased sense of uncertainty and insecurity.

Communism Is Failing in the West

One of the world ideologies and religions that is on the blink these days is communism. It too had made inroads into America in various ways and degrees. But it never stood a solid chance here because of its total opposition to religion in any form, except that of communism. Its totalitarianism was another negative for the communist hope of "burying" America. Now we are helping to dig the grave for communism.

The Hindu Religion Encourages Fatalism

The Hindu religion of India has made progress here, but the tenets of Hinduism have been spread even further through the New Age movement. Buddhism has had minimal impact in America, but over time more units have been established. This religion has spread all over the Far East and has been a missionary faith much like Christianity.

The Hindu religion tends to keep people living in poverty and slums, as we see in India. They accept their status or fate in this life, good or bad, because this was supposedly determined by their conduct in the previous life. The big term for Hindus is the word *karma*, which rewards them in the next life for their good deeds and penalizes them for their evil deeds. The idea is to follow the flow of the customs of society. In American politics we call this going along to get along. The problem is that their view of truth and Right is muddled because the one great reality of their culture may have a mixture of good and evil or Right and Wrong. So they have their form of relativism too. A visit to India will signify to anyone why the religion must be wrong because the culture certainly appears to be a failure. Most of the people have been locked in poverty for generations.

The New Age Movement Has Had the Greatest Impact

The cult having the most impact in recent years in the U.S.A. is the New Age movement. It is recruiting many mover-shaker-doer types. In effect it is a combination of pantheism (God is in everything—you are god) and Hinduism. Shirley MacLaine is noted as its foremost celebrity and channeler. Channeling is related to reincarnation, which is a doctrine that the soul of a person reappears after death in another and different bodily form. A vast number of Americans see some credibility in this supposed answer to future life. This is one of the reasons why the New Age movement has prospered here in recent years. The idea is that you can do as you please until you get to the final phase of reincarnation—whenever that may be. And doing your own thing as and when you please is very popular in the American mind-set. It goes hand in hand with our individual freedom without responsibility, postponing the pay-up day for some future time.

Hindus and New Agers believe that man's problem is that he is living under an illusion that he is limited and finite. What man needs is what the gnostics of the Bible days advocated, illumination through knowledge. This is likewise popular in America, especially among intellectual-types and those who are attracted to elitism.

Many books have been written on the New Age phenomenon. The movement consists of a network of individual groups bound together by common assumptions and a common vision. Its aim is to replace secular humanism and traditional religion. Humans are in the driver's seat since we can determine our own transformation. Humans are not depraved or dependent on any outside source of deliverance. We are all individual gods. We need to realize our oneness and divinity so we can make use of our spiritual power and well-being. The New Age movement (NAM) is big on human pride.

The Information Age has helped propel the NAM into the business community. Many corporations are providing seminars which use NAM thinking. Public schools looking for teaching materials to promote values have been charged with instructing school students in New Age concepts. Some of the NAM ideas sound good, but most people do not understand that this movement has no ethical guidelines or a God to be the judge. Each person is his own god. *Time* magazine called the NAM a religion without religion.[3] People who become caught up in any of the NAM groups have good intentions and are searching for meaning and help in solving major life crises.

There are many other cult groups moving up in America in the new age of relativism, such as the Moonies. However, the most vibrant and growing faith among cultic groups today is the NAM. Americans need to better understand their own faiths as well as the "siren song" groups that have strong appeals to the American way of life.

Islam Is the Second Greatest Challenger

Aside from the New Age movement, Christianity is being challenged most by the forces of Islam, who hate the West and Christianity. Judaism and the Muslims have some commonalities with Christianity, especially Judaism. All three go back to Abraham in the Old Testament and they claim the most holy site in Jerusalem, the Temple Mount. While the Muslims dislike us, they hate the Jews more. This is what the Middle East turmoil is all about because the Jews likewise hate the Arab Muslims.

Some people blame the problem in the Middle East on the impatience and lack of faith of Abraham in producing a son, Ishmael, by his wife's maid, Hagar. Abraham and Sarah became anxious about the implementation of God's covenant with Abraham since the covenant promise turned on having a son named Isaac, and Sarah was barren. The Book of Genesis tells the story of the subsequent miraculous birth of Isaac to Sarah and the resulting banishment of Hagar and Ishmael from the household of Abraham and Sarah. God had promised to make both Ishmael and Isaac the fathers of two great nations. Ishmael became the father of the Arabs and Isaac the father of the Jews. There has been bitter enmity and hatred ever since.

The ultimate founder of the Islam religion, Muhammad, placed a curse on both Judaism and Christianity as "infidels." After demanding their repentance and change, he condemned both of the rival religions. So there has, in effect, been a holy war against Jews and Christians for all these years. Amazingly, President George Bush was able to forge an alliance with some of the Muslim Arab countries in the 1991 Middle East War, and Israel was also a member of the alliance. Secretary of State James A. Baker, III, convinced the Jews and Arabs to sit down and talk peace in late 1991 and early 1992. Ironically, Baker and Bush are noted to be Christians by the Jewish and Arab leaders. Miracles are still very much a reality!

The Muslim view of Right versus Wrong focuses substantially on how one relates to and obeys Allah and the Koran. To enforce Allah's aims, any kind of power, including a holy war, is fully justifiable. For the fundamentalist Shiite branch of Islam the taking of hostages is a moral Right—as we in the West have come to realize in recent years. The Muslims are concerned with social sins, but these sins fall below the sins against Allah. They are at their best in personal discipline regarding the observance of the revealed law of Allah through creed recitals, fasting, prayer (five times daily wherever they may be), almsgiving, and travels to Mecca.

We Christians could learn from their devotion and discipline. My travel in Arab countries has impressed me with the dedication of the people to their faith, especially in kneeling to pray in public five times each day. What a change this might bring in the U.S.A. if we Christians were as public with our faith!

Allah is a god who offers no grace, no helping hand, only the back of the hand. Another problem with Allah is that his people will take over your country in the name of their view of right, which could mean a holy war. They also may turn off your oil in the name of Allah. The religion seems to major more in hate and terrorism than love. Jesus commands us to love our enemies.

The U.S.A. and Christianity have a problem with all Muslim nations: our friendship with Israel and the prominence of Christianity in American life. Most Americans probably fear the Arab Muslims today more than communism. The more we favor Israel the more the Muslims dislike us. We are not pitted against all Muslim countries today, but the ones that oppose us are moving into the vacuum left by the communist threat which haunted us for almost five decades.

The most difficult people to convert to Christianity are Muslims. They may be making more progress in winning Americans than Christians are winning Muslims, particularly among black Americans.

Jews and Christians Have Been Able to Live Together

The Jewish and Christian faiths have been able to live together in America in an amicable fashion despite their differences, which are primarily over Jesus Christ, the centerpiece of Christianity. In the Jewish faith Jesus is a "no-no." But the Jews do not pose a significant threat to Christianity because so many seem to have lost their faith but not their identity as members of the Jewish race. An increasing number of Jews are marrying into Christianity or otherwise outside of the Jewish faith.

Indeed, the United States and Israel have been strong allies with intervening spats. The U.S. played a significant role in the establishment of the Jewish State of Israel in 1949. Many Jewish people are among the most wealthy, successful, and influential people in America.

Native Chinese Religions Pose Little Threat

Christians are not particularly challenged by the native Chinese religions in America except where their tenets show up in some of the syncretistic movements. Taoism has surfaced in the New Age movement. As with the NAM, the Taoists are strong on harmy, the dialectical forces of Yin and Yang. Tao means The Way. Tao claims that it can maintain the antithetic but complementary rhythms of the universe in harmony so that they correspond with and counterbalance each other in a way that can control the destructive forces of nature. The idea is to live in harmony with Tao, first and foremost.

In America we quote Confucius occasionally because he left us with a number of wise sayings that seem to have served the Chinese families well. Confucius had his own version of Jesus' Golden Rule. But Confucius missed out on the proper understanding of the sin nature of man—as do many of the religions of the world. After all, man does not want to hear about his innate flaws. And Confucius told them that we are basically good. This is what most Americans wrongly believe today, even people in the church of Jesus Christ. One of the reasons the Chinese ultimately fell to communism and are still there today is because of their basic belief in humanism and the "good" nature of man.

Shinto Religion Is Not Spreading in America

The Japanese have very little in the way of formal religion, including Christianity. But they are a religious people. Their own Shinto religion is the worship of various gods of nature with some animism thrown in. As with most other religions, it does not come to grips with the sin nature of man. Its biggest strength in the past was the idolatry of emperor worship. In large part, this led to the instigation of war with the U.S.A. in World War II and the kamikaze attacks by Japanese pilots and troops. Shintoism developed a fervent patriotic religion. It really put religion and the state together.

General Douglas MacArthur put an end to much of this evil when he became the occupation boss of Japan after World War II. As a Christian and strong believer in the American system of government, he established a system of government and industry that has evolved into one of the strongest economic powers in today's world. General MacArthur called on American Christians to hurry to the white fields for harvest after the war and during all of that time of reform, but we missed most of that great opportunity. We were resting on our laurels and the three Bs, big buildings, budgets, and body counts in our churches.

Other Cults and Religions Offer Various Threats

As more religions and cults arise and grow in America the problem of syncretization likewise rises. This was in large part the undoing of the nation of Israel in the Promised Land. We have been syncretized in varying degrees already.

Superstition is a silent religion which abounds in the lives of people who are caught up in the various religions, including Christianity. I remember being controlled to some degree by superstition as a church member. Today I rebuke myself when even the thought of a small superstition pops into my mind.

People are also subject to black magic and forms of voodoo. This is why some people will empty their bank accounts to send money to corrupt TV evangelists who give the impression that they directly represent some deity who wants viewers to send in immediately no less than $1000. This is also why people—even church people—favor the lotteries being voted into existence in one state after another in America. P. T. Barnum warned us years ago about so many suckers being born into the world.

Efforts to manipulate God to do our will instead of His will constitute another example of the way the basic tenets of animism and other religions have seeped into modern-day Christianity. The prosperity theology of television is a prime example of seeking to manipulate both God and the people in the studio or in the viewing audience. The Bible is so clear on the fact that Christianity is all about getting people to do God's will because God has us to obey Him. It is also because His will is so much better for us than our own self-destructive tendencies in our fallible and fallen nature. Yet people are still being swindled out of their money and allegiance by false prophets, even after Jim Bakker was jailed for doing this.

Paul warns us in 1 Timothy 6:5 to stay away from those "who suppose that godliness is a means of gain." That is the aim of "prosperity theology."

The Biggest Obstacle to Faith Is Idolatry

Despite the superstitious nature of Americans and our other failings as to what we believe, our biggest obstacle to real faith and commitment to God is our rabid addiction to the dreadful disease of idolatry. This was the downfall for Israel in Old Testament days. What is idolatry?

IDOLATRY:
THE VERY EPITOME OF SIN
DENOUNCED IN THE TEN COMMANDMENTS
AND ROMANS 1
THE BEGINNING OF HUMAN DISOBEDIENCE
WORSHIP OF THE CREATED, NOT THE CREATOR
FALSE WORSHIP AND IMAGING
USURPING GOD'S PLACE

It is the nature of us humans to act on the basis of our beliefs. God certainly had this in mind when he handed down the Ten Commandments. At the top of His dislike list God put idolatry. "You shall have no other gods before Me" (Ex. 20:3).

What is the basis of the first sin in human history? Adam and Eve bought the serpent's lure to rebel against God and to thus become their own gods. So the first sin was idolatry. It has been our downfall ever since. Eminent historian Arnold Toynbee surveyed civilizations and warned us of the pitfalls of humankind and civilizations. He concluded that self-worship is our paramount religion, although its guises are numerous and diverse.[4]

What was the principal warning of the Old Testament prophets? Idolatry! What are the other idols of our day? In the best work on idolatry in this day, Dr. Herbert Schlossberg lists these major areas of idolatry:

> The idols of history; of humanity; of mammon; of nature; of power; of consequences and expectations; and also the idols of country and even religion.[5]

These idols can be extrapolated into the thousands and thousands of idols that we can choose to put between us and God. Israel had idols, but nothing like the number we have today, especially in this land of the affluent.

When we examine what is Right as opposed to what is Wrong in the big and little judgments we make on a day-to-day basis we must ever keep in mind that first and greatest commandment issued at Mount Sinai. Will this create an idol that will obstruct my view of my Creator and Savior? When I was involved in presidential politics I had so many idols standing between me and God. They came substantially out of ignorance and immaturity—both caused by insufficient belief and commitment. Looming largest was man's politics. Today that is no more a problem, although I am still a watcher of political events—as we all should be. What a difference is made in our lives and our destiny when we finally focus on God's eternal perspective as against our own limited, fallible, and selfish perspective!

We must ensure that America does not become the idol that stands between us and God. This is my concern about civil religion and God and Country religion. Our fear is that too many people in America, even in churches, may be choosing in ignorance, lack of faith, and commitment to permit our dearly beloved country to become an idol for destruction. That is the title of Herb Schlossberg's book, *Idols for Destruction: Christian Faith and Its Confrontation with American Society*.

The whole question of the religious nature of humanity as well as our sin nature goes back to the earliest days. Wherever one goes in the world people can be found to be worshiping some religious god or spirit or idol. God empowered us with the gift of choice. We are always caught up in the dilemma of searching for the Right Thing to fill that void in our life as described by St. Augustine. So there is a hunger for right relationship with a spirit power embedded in people. Through ignorance and selfishness many seek to fill that void with the idols of the world. This is but another reason why the fields are so ripe for potential harvest, as Jesus challenged us in John 4.

Today We Are One World

Today we live in a global village. Whether we like it or not, we are one world. We have moved in the history of man from the First Wave where humans basically lived off the land, to the Second Wave which began with the Industrial Revolution in Europe and which has now culminated in the Third Wave, the Age of Information and Knowledge. The man who conceived of the three waves of history is Dr. Alvin Toffler.[6] He has written three books on the future: *Future Shock, The Third Wave*, and *Powershift: Knowledge, Wealth, & Violence at the Edge of the 21st Century*. Each book took ten years to write.

In *PowerShift*, Dr. Toffler describes the big powershift as moving from the struggle over the distribution of wealth to the distribution of and access to knowledge. "The control of knowledge," he writes, "is the crux of tomorrow's worldwide struggle for power in every human institution." He says that today's powershift will transform virtually everything.[7]

Dr. Toffler makes another interesting prediction. He sees secularism as being in retreat in the twenty-first century.

Today in country after country, secularism is in retreat. What do advocates of democracy have to put in its place? So far the new, high-tech democracies have renovated neither their outdated mass democratic political structures nor the philosophical assumptions that underlie them.

Religion is not the enemy of democracy. In a secular multireligious society, with a clear separation of church and state, the very variety of beliefs and nonbeliefs adds to the vibrance and dynamism of democracy. . . . Religions that are universalistic, that wish to spread all over the world and embrace every human being may be compatible with democracy. . . . What is not compatible are those religions (and political ideologies as well) that combine totalitarianism with universalism.[8]

What Dr. Toffler is saying is that Christianity's principal rival, the Muslims, will not do well with their totalitarian ideology and religion as the world moves faster toward our American form of government. The Muslim religion is the law in Arab lands. It is more than a religion. It is a way of life, a code for social behavior, a political system, and even an economic system.[9]

Dr. Toffler, John Naisbitt of *Megatrends* fame, and other prognosticators of the future are alerting us to the fact that the world is changing rapidly. The speed of change is even accelerating. All of the vast networks of communications and transportation have shrunk the size of the world, especially since the United States was established. As the world changes, the major religions continue to exist. For many centuries religion virtually dominated and influenced all other interests. In recent years, however, the rise of secular humanism and the other "isms" that grew out of the Enlightenment period have challenged religion's role in the world. But Dr. Toffler says there is a trend developing in our favor.

Of all the major religions, Christianity has the best hope for influencing the future world for good. Christianity best fits the emerging and increasing trend toward democratic forms of government. This is why the fields are ready for harvest behind the old Iron Curtain for Christianity.

The Future Belongs to Christianity

Here are the reasons why I believe that the future could well belong more to the Christian faith.

Human beings are the only part of God's creation that have a sense of self-awareness and self-transcendence. Thus the number one quest of humans is to discover the meaning and purpose of life. Christianity best answers that big question. Man can live again and forever. Indeed, the gospel of Jesus Christ permits us to see and experience reality beyond the limited bounds of history. Our purpose here is to serve God and to live in right relationships with God and one another. God fashioned us to be gregarious, to love, to serve, and to find our place in a movement bigger than ourselves.

As humans we have the capacity to know Right from Wrong. We are called upon to make value judgments every day of our lives. We need to live by transcendent values framed not by humans but by a God who is not only the God of history but also the God of creation. What is so appealing about Christianity is the fact that it was given birth out of actual and factual history. It is the only religion that centers its case in historical events. This is the place to discern the answers to the critical questions of life—in the human experience in history.

Christianity provides the only real answer to the human condition, the sin nature of man. Through sending His "only begotten Son," the God of creation has provided an escape for us from a life of guilt and shame here on earth and then, upon physical death, we find our ultimate place in Eternity. The Christian worldview includes a sense of meaning in life, values by which to live and principles by which to act.

When God the Father sent Jesus Christ from heaven to earth, His purpose was to provide the only way to get from earth to heaven. And when Jesus began His ministry, instead of pomp and circumstance, Jesus came as a servant, a suffering servant. Instead of hate, Jesus came with a new unheard message about the unconditional love of God the Creator. Instead of conquering with power He conquered with a love that the world had never experienced. He put together a channel to change the world for good and eternity. And He entrusted its mission and care to ordinary people who were willing to live and die for this cause based on their experiences in walking and living with Him under adverse conditions.

The leaders of the other major religions are dead and are lying in a tomb somewhere on earth. Jesus is the only man to be raised from a tomb to new life and to exhibit Himself to hundreds of people in that resurrected state. His followers were radically transformed by His resurrection. Jesus' rag-tag followers were used by God to build a universal church that still stands and holds sway all over the world, especially in the most industrialized parts of the world.

Archaeologists continue to find new evidence that validates the truth of the Holy Scriptures that constitute the Right versus Wrong Handbook for living on Earth and escaping to heaven and eternity. The Holy Bible is the greatest and the most printed book in the history of the world! And people are still living by its precepts today. As a consequence they are finding a peace that surpasses all understanding and enables them to ride out the storms of life, knowing that this life is but the warm-up for eternal life with this miracle God-Man, Jesus the Christ.

The Christian faith has touched more lives for good than any other worldview or faith. The magic touch is God's love mediated into the lives of Jesus' followers by Jesus' Surrogate on earth, the Holy Spirit. There is supernatural power and love made available to the followers of Jesus Christ on earth. Thousands of books have been written about the ministries and good works of people who have decided to follow Jesus and His precepts as set forth in the Holy Scriptures.

The greatest value system as to Right versus Wrong is the legacy that Jesus Christ left behind on earth on His way back to heaven to be our Intercessor at the Throne of Grace. The teachings of Jesus were tailor-made to meet the deepest needs of humanity. These teachings were best set forth by St. Francis of Assisi in his oft-quoted prayer:

> Lord make me an instrument of Your peace;
> Where there is hatred, let me sow love;
> Where there is injury, pardon;
> Where there is doubt, faith;
> Where there is despair, hope;
> Where there is darkness, light;
> Where there is sadness, joy.
>
> O Divine Master, grant that I may not so much seek—
> To be consoled as to console
> To be understood as to understand;

To be loved as to love;
For it is in giving that we receive,
It is in pardoning that we are pardoned,
It is in dying that we are born to eternal life.[10]

Our God is so preeminently correct in His diagnosis of what in the world ails humankind. It is the original sin nature of humanity. And our God exposes us to the only way to really change human beings from habitually doing the Wrong Thing to habitually doing the Right Thing by changing humans from the inside out. This is unlike the secular world which tries to change people from the outside in. The failure of the communist worldview is proof of the failure of man's ability to grasp the reality of the human condition and the impossibility of changing someone else from the outside in. Our will is truly changed when it responds to the Will of God rather than the will of limited, fallible humans.

Christianity Makes Sense

The biblical worldview makes the most sense and thus most reflects reality, the Real Thing. There must be some form of reality to any cause which claims to be a worldview. The Bible illustrates a supernatural perspective above and beyond that of any other world religion. All the way through we see such enduring—indeed, eternal—values and virtues in doctrinal form and also in the lives of the principal characters who serve as visual aids as they flesh out the Right Thing in their lives. These are qualities such as righteousness, truth, honesty, humility, character, compassion, sacrifice, repentance, forgiveness, and redemption.

There is nothing but goodness in these virtues. The number one visual aid for inspection is the only begotten Son of God, who possessed the same attributes as God the Father. When we see Jesus in the Bible we discern the same basic moral character, the Real Thing. When we see a person in which there is no guile we say: he is for real! That is what Jesus said when He met Nathaniel, a man of no guile. (See John 1:47.)

The church of Jesus Christ has continued to stand and grow all over the world for two thousand years. In the most powerful and prosperous country in the world, the United States of America, more than 80 percent of the people profess belief in Jesus Christ and half of the people in America are in church on any given Sunday.[11] The church has staying power and saving power because it has spiritual power from a supernatural God.

Christianity's greatest appeal is to the people that Jesus called "the least of these." It is a faith that majors in touching, encouraging, healing, and loving the broken, the sick, the poor, the prisoner, the unlovable, and unloved people on earth. It is the beacon of faith, hope, and love that offers the free gift of God's grace and ultimately eternal life to all who believe on the name and work of Jesus Christ.

Christianity Is Relevant

No other religion provides man's greatest need for a love that is absolutely unconditional and everlasting. Here is the answer to the question of whether or not it is RELEVANT. The evidence—what we lawyers call the "best evidence"—of the availability of this special kind of love is exemplified in the life and work of Jesus the Christ. People were created to need and to want to be loved with no holds barred. It is our biggest desire and need. This is the healing balm of Christianity. The other religions have admired Jesus for His unconditional love, but none can match the greatest legacy that Jesus Christ supplies through the indwelling of His own Spirit in the very heart of every person who submits to His leadership and lordship.

Our God was relevant in the Old Testament days, He is relevant today, and He will be relevant tomorrow because God never changes. He is the same yesterday, today, tomorrow, and for eternity. His kind of love falls into the same category because as the Apostle John reminds us, God is love. Righteousness and love are God's foremost attributes. And it is this kind of supernatural, everlasting love that man was created to need and want and to enjoy and give while living in right relationships.

The question we need to consider on a day-to-day basis is *Who is my God (or idol) today?*

The answer to the problems and challenges posed in this chapter is that every person who calls himself or herself a "Christ-i-an" must face up to his or her duty to the Lord and to fellow humans here and all over the world.

There is only one way to translate our good intentions into concrete results. We must invite Dr. Holy Spirit to get out His Holy Scalpel and cut out that old heart full of idols and syncretistic misbeliefs and install in each of us the heart of Jesus Christ as Lord and Savior.

We must come under His authority and stay under His authority by beginning every day of our lives in His instruction book and on our knees talking to Him and listening to Him. Otherwise, the idols and misbeliefs that block our view of our Holy God will continue to grow and never be destroyed.

CHAPTER ELEVEN

The Case for Christianity as Our Worldview

Of the 22 civilizations that have appeared in history, 19 of them collapsed when they reached the moral state America is in now.

Arnold Toynbee[1]

Who would have predicted or even believed that in two years, 1989 to 1991, the biggest enemy in the history of America—the U.S.S.R. and its principal "ism," communism—would be wiped out before our own eyes without the U.S.A. firing one shot? Former President Richard M. Nixon confesses that even he was surprised by these world-changing events. Now he is campaigning with a new book, *Seize the Moment*, and a new cause. His message is this: We must seize the moment to win victory for peace and freedom in the world.

I agree with my old boss. But for his cause to become a reality, the church must also seize the moment for Jesus Christ—behind the old Iron Curtain and in the United States.

Secretary of State James A. Baker, III, told me that none of the expensive and expansive intelligence services forecasted the cataclysmic events that knocked down the Iron Curtain, opened up Eastern Europe to freedom from communist rule, dethroned the U.S.S.R. Communist Party, and then disintegrated the Soviet Union. Miracle after miracle after miracle.

Jim Baker further explained, "Harry, the president and I have talked about this. We have concluded that it was the hand of God Almighty!"

While we have a great opportunity as a nation to prove freedom and democracy to the world as President Nixon exclaims, we also stand in a time of grave internal danger. What has happened to the

U.S.S.R. and communism can happen to the other great and surviving superpower of the twentieth century, the United States of America!

IT IS TIME TO WAKE UP, AMERICA!
IT IS TIME TO GET RIGHT WITH GOD, AMERICA!

It is time for the church of Jesus Christ to wake up, train up, and go *show and tell* the people in "the land of the free and the home of the brave" that Jesus Christ is Lord!

The failure thus far in America is the failure of the church to implement God's Master Plan here. We are trustees of the plan with the answers. We must unlock the plan, explain the plan, and implement the plan by turning loose all the saints in the homes, the churches, the marketplaces, politics, government, and wherever we are, as citizens of the government of humans and the government of God.

Paul's Words Are Pertinent Today

We can sell everything in this country from better mousetraps to Cadillacs. Why can't we sell Jesus Christ and the Christian worldview and master plan?

Before he submitted his head to the chopping block at the Mamertime dungeon in Rome, the Apostle Paul wrote his young protegé, Timothy, about the signs of "the last days." Two of my favorite chapters in the Bible are 2 Timothy 3 and 4. Betty and I have visited Paul's final place of incarceration. You have to look down into the dungeon underground. A visit to this spot will strengthen your faith when you realize the vitality of Paul's faith right up to the release of the chopping blade onto the back of his neck.

We American Christians need to take note of Paul's last instructions to Timothy and to us:

> But know this, that in the last days perilous times will come: For men will be lovers of themselves, lovers of money, boasters, proud, blasphemers, disobedient to parents, unthankful, unholy, unloving, unforgiving, slanderers, without self-control, brutal, despisers of good, traitors, headstrong, haughty, lovers of pleasure rather than lovers of God, having a form of godliness but denying its power. And from such people turn away! For of this sort are those who

creep into households and make captives of gullible women loaded down with sins, led away by various lusts, always learning and never able to come to the knowledge of the truth (2 Tim. 3:1-7).

Does this read like today? Exactly! We are living in perilous times with conduct exactly like this. And too many people in the church have "a form of godliness but deny its power," as I did for too long. Some people are "always learning and never able to come to the knowledge of the truth." This truth is the Real Thing, Jesus Christ.

Paul warns Timothy against getting caught up in these ways of the world and thus apostasy. He reminds Timothy that his best defense is a good offense:

> But as for you, continue in the things which you have learned and been assured of, knowing from whom you have learned them, and that from childhood you have known the Holy Scriptures, which are able to make you wise for salvation through faith which is in Christ Jesus. All Scripture is given by inspiration of God, and is profitable for doctrine, for reproof, for correction, for instruction in righteousness, that the man of God may be complete, thoroughly equipped for every good work (2 Tim. 3:14-17).

In his farewell address, Paul gives this charge to Timothy and all of us Christians today:

> Preach the word! Be ready in season and out of season. Convince, rebuke, exhort, with all longsuffering and teaching. For the time will come when they will not endure sound doctrine, but according to their own desires, because they have itching ears, they will heap up for themselves teachers; and they will turn their ears away from the truth, and be turned aside to fables. But you be watchful in all things, endure afflictions, do the work of an evangelist, fulfill your ministry. For I am already being poured out as a drink offering, and the time of my departure is at hand. I have fought the good fight, I have finished the race, I have kept the faith. Finally, there is laid up for me the crown of righteousness, which the Lord, the righteous Judge, will give to me on that Day, and not to me only but also to all who have loved His appearing (2 Timothy 4:2-8).

Nowhere in the Bible was our mission more eloquently, clearly, and succinctly recorded than in that underground dungeon in Rome. Some of the best writings in history have come out of prison, for there a man's heart and soul are opened wide in search of the Real Thing and the Right Thing. Paul had found the blessing and the truth, so he had trained young Timothy to pass it on. We have been confronted with the truth throughout this book. So what are we going to do with it and about it? We in the church have been, like Esther, called "for such a time as this."

The previous chapter in this book compared Christianity to our basic competition in America. This chapter will focus our attention on why we have the answer and why we have such great potential in putting the answer into action.

Religion Answers the Big Questions

Religion is substantially concerned with the big question of what is the ultimate meaning and destiny of our lives as human beings here on planet Earth. There is no more important question that we must pursue in our limited time of pilgrimage in preparation for what happens to us, not only here, but on into eternity.

As humans we have been endowed above all the rest of God's creation with a capacity for self-awareness or self-transcendence. We have been blessed with the ability to be able to discern who we are, whose we are, and why we are. Our most important duty therefore is to prepare ourselves to be able to make value judgments between what is Right and what is Wrong. We are accountable here on earth for our choices concerning Right versus Wrong, and we are accountable as to our ultimate destiny in eternity for choices we make here.

One of the principal purposes of this book is to challenge each reader to choose for certain whose we are. The answer to this question will determine how we live here on earth and where we live in eternity. It is just that simple, and yet, just that profound. I wish I had understood this many years ago. I have had a good life, but I could have had a better life. I would have been able to help many more people see with full reality the meaning and purpose of life. And I could have served my country so much better in the military, in politics, in the United States Senate, in the White House, and with my vote.

Reality means the truth and thus the Real Thing. There are so many obstacles to discerning the real truth about most everything on earth, especially in our highly pluralized and relativized culture. There are many idols to pull us away from the Real Thing. The Bible tells us the Real Thing is God, the Creator. The prime teaching in the New Testament focuses on God's only begotten Son, Jesus the Christ, as the object of our worship and belief. This is why this major religion is called Christianity.

So the biblical worldview is that Jesus Christ died on that cross for our sins and was raised to new life from that empty tomb. We must submit to die to our sin nature and be raised (born again) to a new nature that will help us in our battle against the old sin nature as we daily make the choices in life between Right and Wrong.

We Need Supernatural Help

Because of our limited, fallible, and selfish nature, we need this supernatural help in the continuing battle of spiritual warfare during our time on earth. So many people are unaware of spiritual warfare— the war between good and evil and Right versus Wrong. By and large, they recognize that there is a Right versus Wrong, but they do not see this as being a continuing battle of good versus evil because they do not have spiritual sight or discernment. I missed this for forty-eight years of my life, much of that time as a church leader.

Dr. Paul Johnson has spent much of his life studying and writing about history and Christianity. He is convicted as to the reality of the Christian faith and the fact that it works in the interest of what is Right, good, and practical for humanity on planet Earth. He has risked his own faith by delving into the depths of ancient history looking for the truth of his faith. He has emerged with a "strengthened and reinforced faith in Jesus Christ and Christianity." Here is a portion of his testimony:

> Such a history [of Christianity] is marked by the folly and wickedness of leading Christians on almost every page, but I came to realize . . . that men have done evil not because of their Christianity but despite it—that Christianity has been not the source of, but the supreme (often the sole) restraining factor on, mankind's capacity for wrongdoing.
>
> It is now a solid part of my belief, both as a Christian and a historian, that true religion, by which I mean religion based upon Judeo-Christian revelation, is the essential mitigating factor in human depravity.[2]

As a practical matter, Christianity is the greatest moral force for good the world has ever known. It is the answer to what is Wrong in this world and it is the catalyst for what is Right in this world.

Dr. John P. Newport of Southwestern Baptist Theological Seminary is one of the most respected professors of the philosophy of religion in the world. Dr. Newport has written many books on this subject. The peak of his writings is *Life's Ultimate Questions: A Contemporary Philosophy of Religion*. Here he examines the human experience in relation to what he deems to be the eleven most important questions of life, "those issues that raise themselves over and over in life because they touch on matters that are basic to life."[3]

In his book he places the biblical worldview alongside the other major religions and worldviews. He concludes that "the biblical worldview—far from being irrelevant to the twentieth century—is indispensable." I agree, especially after studying his and other books on this subject and also repeatedly experiencing God's way as the only answer for not only the questions of life but the hurts of life.[4]

Religion Is in Every Country

Religion is a universal phenomenon. All of the various peoples of the world have some type of religion and ways and means for dealing with the various aspects of life that are beyond human control. We have a need for the supernatural.

The difference between a system of philosophy or ethics and a religion lies in relating to a higher power. With philosophy and regular ethics, it all stops with humans and humans alone. Religion is the glue that holds together the socio-cultural structures of society. It provides a set of beliefs and a value-grid whereby an individual or people in a society can deal with life's experiences like those discussed by Dr. Newport in his book.

Christianity has provided the basic underpinning of the ethics and values of the Western world. In America the teachings of the Holy Bible have had a particular impact in past years. The problem is that the Christian values have been fading as the philosophies and ways of man are holding more sway than ever before. This includes what some call "modernity" and others call secular humanism. This revolves around the conviction that man is the measure of all things, and there is no god—or if there ever was, this god is now dead.

Today in America the biblical worldview has many worldviews

with which to compete. There was a time when it was prevalent nationwide. But not today. Religions and "isms" abound all around the Christian churches that continue to dot the landscape of America.

While Gallup polls continue to show that 95 percent of Americans believe in a god, the question is *which god*. In the past there was not much question about the God of the Bible being the God that American people believed to be the Creator of the universe.[5]

The Ten Commandments of Exodus 20 and Deuteronomy 5 was considered to be the basic law of the world. The sin nature of man was an accepted fact. That is why the founding fathers of our republican form of government were so careful to separate and divide powers of government. They were convinced that for people to govern themselves they must be educated and people of virtue who would vote for the overall common good.

Statue of Responsibility

Responsibility was considered a heavy duty. With every right conferred upon the individual citizen by this new experiment in people-rule, there was to be a concomitant responsibility and accountability.

I have proposed to President Bush the construction of a Statue of Responsibility in San Francisco Bay, to complement the Statue of Liberty in New York Harbor.

Today Right versus Wrong is blurred. Individual rights are predominant over the common good. The Ten Commandments have been turned into "the ten suggestions." There are no more moral absolutes. Everything is relative.

Dr. Newport has a most realistic answer for Americans oriented toward Christianity as their worldview.

Because human reason ever seeks to assert its proclaimed autonomy, [the late Herman] Dooyeweerd sees a continuing tendency for the Christian mind to accommodate itself to the world. This means that those who wish to remain true to the fullness of the biblical worldview must do more than properly relate their hearts to God; they must also seek a biblically directed global vision of the world and life. This means they must constantly guard against the dilution of biblical truth.[6]

It will not be enough for the "old" Harry Dents to keep going to church. It will not be enough that they serve as deacons, elders, or stewards—or even as Sunday school teachers.

Jesus may have best summed up our duty, responsibility, and accountability when He related the Parable of the Faithful Steward to His followers with this conclusion:

> For everyone to whom much is given, from him much
> will be required; and to whom much has been committed, of
> him they will ask the more (Luke 12:48b).

What a warning for the most blessed nation in history! And what a stern challenge for the church of Jesus Christ!

The Answer Is Simple

So, what do we do? Where do we begin?

We must open up the stained-glass windows of the churches and blow out all the soot of superficial Christianity, apostasy, church strife and divisions, and the things and ways of the world that are all stifling spiritual growth and the ministry of all of God's people.

The "saints" must become serious about the focus of the Christian religion. This focus is on the saints living out our lives as "living epistles" and "ambassadors for Christ" as Paul prescribed and as "salt and light" as Jesus commanded—in the home, the workplace, the recreational places, and wherever we are on earth. Our duty is to "Let your light so shine before men, that they may see your good works and glorify your Father in heaven."

Taking over the White House, the Congress, and the Supreme Court in a spiritual coup through political action will not provide the answer because American sentiment against church over state is very strong, and the Bible does not sanction such actions.

We are going to have to do it by Jesus' prescription. This means penetrating the lives and hearts of those who profess belief in a Supreme Being, and especially those who say Jesus is the One, by fielding salty and turned-on "salt" and "light" Christians. This is what Bible professor James Hatch prescribed for Ginny and Alton Brant in witnessing to me. Professor Hatch called this "the hard way—with your lives." The potential and also the problems we must overcome are set forth in one of my color overhead transparencies set forth below in black and white:

the COMMITMENT BAROMETER *of* AMERICANS

The obstacles to be overcome are the differences between the 95 percent who profess belief in a God and the 32 percent who say, "I've been born again." Another obstacle is the difference between the 81 percent who profess Jesus to be that God and the 32 percent who profess to be born-again Christians.[7] These two big gaps in numbers of people can make the difference in turning around America if we can turn around the professors and make them possessors of Jesus Christ as Lord and Savior. Because of the weakness of many born-againers it may be that we should drop down below that 32 percent to the 10 percent who are described as "highly committed."

Jesus' charge to His disciples at Jacob's Well, as recorded in John 4, is the charge we should have ringing in our ears and hearts today:

In the meantime His disciples urged Him, saying, "Rabbi, eat." But He said to them, "I have food to eat of which you do not know." Therefore the disciples said to one another, "Has anyone brought Him anything to eat?" Jesus said to them, "My food is to do the will of Him who sent Me, and to finish His work. Do you not say, 'There are still four months and then comes the harvest'? Behold, I say to you,

"Lift up your eyes and look at the fields, for they are already white for harvest!" (John 4:31-35).

Jesus' mission is defined by Him as doing the will of God the Father who sent Him to earth to die for our sins and to be raised to new life, and to complete this mission before His death. Our duty is to focus on Jesus, His life, His mission, and the mission that He prescribed for all of His followers in the Great Commandment and the Great Commission.

**PASS ON THE BLESSING,
GOD'S SALVATION AND RIGHTEOUSNESS,
AND GOD'S LOVE!!!**

The Harvest Is Ready

The fields are so white unto harvest everywhere—here in the United States, there behind the old Iron Curtain, and wherever people are hurting. Dr. George Gallup, Jr., showed the potential here in a 1988 Gallup Poll. While 40 percent of the people in America say they are unchurched, here is what that 40 percent say they believe and do:

- 72 percent say they believe Jesus is the Son of God.
- 63 percent say they believe the Bible.
- 77 percent say they pray to God.
- 58 percent say they are open to the church.[8]

BUT IS THE CHURCH OPEN AND AVAILABLE TO THEM?

Our mission as Christians is to grab the biblical worldview, to know it, to be trained up for ministry in this worldview, and to pass it on in love and service for the glory of God and the good of all of humankind. Jesus made it clear that this duty is to extend "unto the least of these" and "unto the uttermost parts of the world."

It Is "The Greatest News"

We are to pass on to others what the Father passed on to His only begotten Son, the "Greatest News the World Has Ever Heard and Experienced."

Why do I call the gospel the Greatest News? An intellectual citizen of Kiev in the old Soviet Union and new country of the Ukraine corrected me when I called it the Good News. Two months before the collapse of the Soviet Union in 1991 I was ministering in Kiev. This is the area of old Russia where Christianity got its start ten decades ago.

I asked this gentleman, Dr. Vladimir Afonichkin, why there is such deep spiritual hunger in the streets to know Jesus and why there is such deep spiritual hunger to know the Bible in the churches. He responded:

> Mr. Dent, you Americans must understand what it was like here living on the road to nowhere for seventy-four years. Our communist bosses sought to install and instill in all of us a mind-set that said there is no God and that if we found anyone talking about God or worshiping God we were to report them and/or to be a part of the persecution of that person.
>
> But, Mr. Dent, I had a hunch down deep in my heart that there must be a God. Now I have found that indeed God tells us in Ecclesiastes 3:11 that He has put "eternity in the hearts of all people." I wanted to get affirmation of my hunch about God. So I thought I would ask my friend, Ivan, if he had the same hunch. But then I caught myself, realizing that Ivan might report me. So I could not get my hunch affirmed.
>
> And then you American Christians came to us and you affirmed my hunch. You told us that we could even have a personal relationship with this God through accepting His Son, Jesus Christ, as Lord and Savior. And, what's more, when we surrender our lives to Jesus, His Spirit will come and live in our hearts to help us through this life and on into eternity.
>
> Oh, you American Christians call this the Good News. But this is not the Good News. This is the Greatest News the world has ever heard!

Vladimir is now our pen pal, but soon we will return to Kiev in the Ukraine, now an independent republic and country. We will be staying with Vladimir if his Chernobyl wounds have not taken him home to Jesus.

What Vladimir explained to me affirmed what all I had been experiencing in ministry in Romania and the Soviet Union after the fall of the Iron Curtain. As one who had spent much of his adult life in politics fighting the biggest former "ism" of our day, communism, I just had to answer the call "to come over to Romania."

I had witnessed that revolt against Nicolae Ceausescu, the worst communist dictator in Eastern Europe, on CNN television in December of 1989. Duty called. At the Yalta Conference after World War II, our Western powers had permitted the Soviet dictator, Stalin, to take the Romanians and others in Eastern Europe behind his Iron Curtain.

Those people had lived under the heel of communism without freedom and prosperity while I had been growing up in "the land of the free and the home of the brave." So, I joined Dr. John Guest in an evangelistic crusade in Cluj, Romania, in July 1990. Then I returned with a team of my own in December 1990 and again in May 1991, including a mission to Kiev, Moscow, and St. Petersburg in the old Soviet Union. We returned again in May 1992.

I was amazed at the spiritual hunger of the people outside of the church to receive Jesus Christ and to get Bibles and tracts. While street preaching for the first time ever on my first mission, I had been overrun by a few hundred Romanians at their statue of liberty in the city of Cluj when I gave the invitation after only ten minutes of talking.

In the churches, the spiritual hunger to know the Bible was fully evident. My first experience in a church lasted for three and one-half hours on a Friday night. I later came to understand this to be rather routine. Here were these formerly persecuted saints sitting on boards with no arm rests and no backs to their rugged and ragged pews—and for three and one-half hours!

On my first mission I had some of my two thousand color overhead transparencies translated into Romanian so I could teach the church members the big picture of the Bible from cover to cover. The Baptist church in Dej was packed to overflowing.

People were sitting in each other's laps. The aisles were filled. The door of the church had people standing in it. The windows were open and people were looking in. It was a hot July evening, and I was dressed in a suit. After two and one-half hours of preaching and teaching, I stopped. I was about to fall over, and I was concerned for the people holding others on their laps. The pastor jumped up and yelled, "Why you stop?"

The pastor then put up another visitor to speak. I thought, "Oh, Lord, if my Southern Baptist friends back home could see and experience this! What a difference it might make in America!"

On my second and third missions I had plenty of Southern Baptists and people from other denominations with me. Everyone was mesmerized by the spiritual staying power of the Romanian saints and also by their loving and serving hearts. We were experiencing the Real Thing in these people who had only recently been getting thin New Testaments without any notes or explanations. We realized that while we knew the Bible better than they did, they clearly knew the Lord better.

On these missions we have sought to be "salt" and "light" not only in street preaching and our preaching and teaching in the churches. We have established sister-city relationships, sister-church relationships, sister-hospital relationships, and so many brother and sister personal relationships. We have helped Romania get most-favored-nation trade status with the U.S.A. and hospital help to train sixty doctors in heart surgery and angioplasty procedures. Now we have a ministry for collecting and shipping critical-need supplies to the orphanages and our needy Christian friends. The freight is free, thanks to Presybterian layman, Bill Cassels of Columbia, and missionaries Roger and Liisa Finch in Belgium.

This political, economic, and medical help has enabled us to give translated copies of our other books, *A Layman Looks Through the Bible for God's Will* and *Cover Up: The Watergate in All of Us* (the big picture of salvation) to political leaders across Romania and especially in their parliament. Senator John Babos, a strong Baptist layman from Arad, Romania, has provided access to many political leaders in Romania, including the president and national TV and radio.

These political leaders, mostly ex-communists, can better digest the books and Bibles when they know that even Christians from America are willing to help them and their people. These are the leaders that have invited Christian teachers to teach the Bible in their public schools in Romania. In July and August of 1991 we had a contingent of Romanian political and industrial leaders visit South Carolina and Washington, D.C.

These leaders brought along John Achim, our best friend and a deacon in First Baptist Church in Cluj, one of our sister-churches. John told me how much the political and industrial leaders were impressed with the fact that everywhere they visited American Christians were in charge, whether it be the Mayor's Office, the Chamber of Commerce, the Technical College, or at industrial plants.

John said to me, "Brother Harry, you cannot realize the wonderful impact these visits are having on our political and business leaders. They have looked upon us Romanian Christians as next to nothing. Here they see Christians in the leadership positions. They were especially impressed when First Baptist Church in Spartanburg had the Chamber of Commerce to lunch with us in the church. That has never happened in Romania!''

We Can't Even Do What the Ex-Communists Do

Our experiences behind the old Iron Curtain have convicted us of the fact that there is overwhelming spiritual hunger where people have been persecuted for the sake of Christ and where people have been denied the freedom to even talk about their spiritual hunches in the streets.

But there are even stronger signs of the opportunities for witness for Jesus Christ behind the old Iron Curtain. Hugh Sidey reported in the September 9, 1991, issue of *Time* magazine[9] that Mikhail Gorbachev and also Boris Yeltsin informed Dr. Billy Graham that religion is needed in Russia to restore the moral corrosion brought about by communism for seventy-four years. In Romania, public officials are permitting Dr. Josef Tson of the Romanian Missionary Society and Dr. Nick Gheorghita, Reverend Paul Nagrut, and Dr. Phil Roberts of Second Baptist Church in Oradea to provide Bible teachers for public schools in Romania. The government pays the teachers to teach Christianity as an elective course.

Behind the old Iron Curtain the leaders realize that Christianity builds moral character and discipline in the lives of their people so that they better know Right from Wrong and how to behave in a righteous manner.

The irony in this is that the communist leaders under Ceausescu's orders threw Tson in prison for preaching "the greatest news" in the early eighties. The Queen of England convinced Ceausescu to release him, so the fiesty Tson landed in Wheaton, Illinois, where he expanded the Romanian missionary organization to keep pastors posted by short-wave radio broadcasts and by smuggled Bibles and Christian books.

Even more ironic is that in today's America we cannot do what the old communist leaders in Romania are permitting in Romanian schools—just an optional course on Christian moral values.

The American Public Knows the Value of Christianity

The 1991 secular book on the views of Americans, *The Day America Told the Truth*, states that Americans believe that "religious people are: more moral, more willing to die for beliefs, more at peace, more truthful, more committed to the family and are better workers."[10]

So the public does not have to be sold on the utilitarian value of Christianity. That is a given!

What the American public needs is to see authentic Christianity—the Right Thing and the Real Thing—being lived out by people who profess to be "Christ-i-ans." If people are going to profess Jesus they should possess Jesus and present Him as the Lord and Savior of the world.

The authors reveal that the people of America are concerned about the future of America. The majority say they are willing to sacrifice and volunteer "to make America stronger and better."[11] Eighty percent believe that morals and ethics are needed in our schools. Almost half of unchurched adults would like a close relationship with God. And—get this—70 percent of people ages eighteen to twenty-five agree that the Bible is accurate.

Thus, we have come to see the problem in "Christian America." And I do put this in quote marks. Our problem is simply this:

WE, THE MOST BLESSED NATION IN THE HISTORY OF THE WORLD, HAVE TURNED OUR BACKS ON THE GOD OF OUR UNIVERSE.

Our problem is that Jesus is so familiar to us so that we hardly know Him. We are in and out of His churches on most every corner in America, but we take Jesus for granted! We do not hunger and thirst after Him and His righteousness, which He tells us in the Sermon on the Mount is our first priority. "But, seek first the kingdom of God and His righteousness, and all these things shall be added to you" (Matt. 6:33).

Notice that Jesus is talking about righteousness and thus against wrongness. Jesus is referring to our needs, not necessarily our wants.

It is our wants that are destroying our value system, our priorities, and our relationships—vertically and horizontally.

At age forty-eight I took Jesus into my heart as Lord and Savior. Then Jesus began to take me seriously. I surrendered my personal lordship over my life to the lordship and leadership of Jesus, His Spirit coming to live as Lord over my spirit, honest to God!

This is unconditional surrender. Yet we proud Americans cannot stomach the word *surrender* because we pridefully see ourselves as winners. But this should be the first priority for our lives. Jesus took command of the strengths He had vested in me. I had been using these strengths for my pursuit and enjoyment of the Great American Dream.

The number one priority of most Americans is the Great American Dream: to do as I please and live as I please.

The number one problem of most Americans is the Great American Nightmare: to burden our posterity with the price for doing and living as we please.

Today I can look at my life and the life of my country with 20/20 vision because I now have God's sight overlaying my faulty sight. I can see and perceive God's everlasting perspective while I am also focusing on man's temporal perspective. Now I know which one is to get the right-of-way in my life—and, what's more—in my own interest and that of my family.

As a sign of a country church marquee says:

**MAN SAYS SEEING IS BELIEVING; BUT
GOD SAYS BELIEVING IS SEEING!**

As I look back over my shoulder at the America I love and respect I can see the moral, spiritual—and yes, even the monetary—foundations of our nation crumbling around us. King David experienced the rise of the golden age of Israel. But he was concerned about the weak foundations. In Psalm 11:3, 7, David the psalm writer raised this dilemma to the heavens:

> If the foundations are destroyed,
> What can the righteous do? . . .
> For the LORD is righteous,
> He loves righteousness;
> His countenance beholds the upright.

Another psalmist of Israel raised the question of ignorance and blindness in the midst of crumbling foundations—the very essence of Israel's problems.

> They do not know, nor do they understand;
> They walk about in darkness;
> All the foundations of the earth are unstable. . . .
> Arise, O God, judge the earth;
> For You shall inherit all nations (Ps. 82:5, 8).

Another psalmist, Asaph, raised the question of how long God will contend with "stubborn hearts." He predicted what was to become of the Israel of that day:

> "But My people would not heed My voice,
> And Israel would have none of Me.
> So I gave them over to their own stubborn heart,
> To walk in their own counsels" (Ps. 81:11-12).

Why We Have Snubbed God

Why have we as Americans substantially turned our backs on God? Why have so many American hearts hardened on the subject of Right versus Wrong?

Because we have become addicted to "the things of the world" and thus to the ways of the world—a salient and sobering warning that runs throughout the Bible and this book.

And it is because we are so immature in so many ways, and most of all, in our spiritual understanding and in our personal commitment, personal behavior, and our personal ministry.

Tucked away in the longest of the psalms, Psalm 119, is the essence of the answer:

> Teach me, O LORD, the way of Your statutes,
> And I shall keep it to the end.
> Give me understanding, and I shall keep Your law;
> Indeed, I shall observe it with my whole heart.
> Make me walk in the path of Your commandments,
> For I delight in it.
> Incline my heart to Your testimonies,
> And not to covetousness.

Turn away my eyes from looking at worthless things,
And revive me in Your way.
Establish Your word to Your servant,
Who is devoted to fearing You.
Turn away my reproach which I dread,
For Your judgments are good.
Behold, I long for Your precepts;
Revive me in your righteousness (Ps. 119:33–40).

The authors of this book try to remember to back up every prayer request with this plea: Lord, if it be Your will. We have discovered that God knows what is Right and best in all matters. We are convinced that, barring a special work of our Lord—and He can do anything—there is one certain way to bring America back to our senses and down to our knees: a financial holocaust that wakes and shakes Americans to bow down in humility and then look up in prayer for divine deliverance in accordance with 2 Chronicles 7:14.

If My people who are called by My name will humble themselves, and pray and seek My face, and turn from their wicked ways, then I will hear from heaven, and forgive their sin and heal their land.

This is still the corrective prescription that best works to destroy the foundations of spiritual ignorance, spiritual apathy, and spiritual apostasy.

REVIVE US IN YOUR RIGHTEOUSNESS!
LORD, YOU HAVE SO RICHLY BLESSED
AMERICA, NOW WE PRAY:
GOD SAVE AMERICA!

Notes

Chapter One

1. Albert M. Wells, Jr., compiler, *Inspiring Quotations* (Nashville: Thomas Nelson, 1988), p. 9, no. 52.

2. Sam Donaldson, *Hold On, Mr. President!* (New York: Random House, 1987), p. 205.

3. *The New Open Bible* (Nashville: Thomas Nelson, 1990), p. 1379.

4. Richard C. Halverson, from a talk at The Cove, Asheville, NC, July 1984.

5. S. E. Ahlstrom, *Religious History of the American People* (New Haven, CT: Yale University Press, 1972), vol. 2, pp. 96–98.

6. Aleksandr I. Solzhenitsyn, *The Gulag Archipelago, 1918–1956: An Experiment in Literary Investigation I-II* (Perennial Library, Harper & Row, 1973), p. 168.

Chapter Two

1. Dr. Paul Johnson quoted in *Seize the Moment: America's Challenge in a One-Superpower World* by Richard Nixon (New York: Simon & Schuster, 1991), p. 24.

2. George Barna, *What Americans Believe: An Annual Survey of Values and Religious Views in the United States* (Ventura, CA: Regal, 1991), p. 85.

3. James Patterson and Peter Kim, *The Day America Told the Truth: What People Really Believe About Everything That Really Matters* (New York: Prentice-Hall, 1991), pp. 6, 25, 9.

4. *Ibid.*, pp. 26–27.

5. Barna, p. 14.

6. *Ibid.*, p. 27.

7. Carl H. Henry, editor, *Baker's Dictionary of Christian Ethics* (Grand Rapids, MI: Baker, 1973), p. 590.

8. Alexis de Toqueville, *Democracy in America* (New York: The New American Library, 1956).

9. Larry Burkett, *The Coming Economic Earthquake* (Chicago: Moody, 1991), p. 34.

10. *Ibid.*, pp. 96, 70, 61, 83, 172, 156, 122, 120, 114, 120.

11. *The State*, Columbia, SC, p. 1, 5 Feb. 1992.

12. *Ibid.*, p. 1, 6 Feb. 1992.

13. Committee on the Budget, U.S. House of Representatives, December 1991, *Restoring America's Future: Preparing the Nation for the 21st Century* (U.S. Government Printing Office, Washington, Serial No. CP-5), pp. 1, 3.

14. *The State*, Columbia, SC, p. 1, 8 Nov. 1991.

15. Barna

Chapter Three

1. Albert M. Wells, Jr., ed., *Inspiring Quotations: Contemporary and Classical* (Nashville: Thomas Nelson, 1988), p. 69, no. 862.

2. Russell Chandler, *Racing Toward 2001: The Forces Shaping America's Religious Future* (Grand Rapids: Zondervan Publishing House, and San Francisco: Harper, San Francisco, 1992), p. 90.

3. Dr. Armand Nicoli, Talk at Symposium, University of South Carolina, Columbia, SC, Jan. 1988.

4. Dr. Ken Magid and Carole A. McKelvey, *High-Risk Children Without a Conscience* (New York: Bantam, 1989), back cover.

5. *Ibid.*, p. x.

6. Nicoli, Symposium, University of South Carolina.

7. Tipper Gore, Talk at Symposium, University of South Carolina, Columbia, SC, Jan. 1988.

8. Walt Schreibman, quoted in *High-Risk Children Without a Conscience*, p. 245.

9. David Popenoe, *Disturbing the Nest: Family Change and Decline in Modern Societies* (New York: Aldine de Gruyter, 1988), pp. 57–79.

10. Oscar W. Thompson, Jr., poem in *Concentric Circles of Love* (Nashville: Broadman, 1981), p. 101.

11. Gary Smalley and John Trent, *The Two Sides of Love* (Pomona, CA: Focus on the Family, 1990).

12. J. Keith Miller, *Sin: The Ultimate Deadly Addiction* (San Francisco: Harper & Row, 1987).

13. *The State*, Columbia, SC, 24 Oct. 1991, pp. 1, 11.

14. Dr. Steve Farrar, *Point Man: How a Man Can Lead a Family* (Portland, OR: Multnomah, 1991).

15. Paul Lee Tan, *Encyclopedia of 7700 Illustrations* (Rockville, MD: Assurance Publishers, 1979).

16. Gary Smalley and John Trent, *The Blessing* (Nashville: Thomas Nelson, 1986).

17. Charles Swindoll, *Growing Wise in Family Life* (Portland, OR: Multnomah, 1988), pp. 134–147.

18. George Barna, *The Frog in the Kettle: What Christians Need to Know About Life in the Year 2000* (Ventura, CA: Regal, 1990), pp. 158, 229.

19. Ann Graham Lotz, Talk at National Exchange Club Convention, Washington, DC, June 1988.

20. Dick Woodward, *Anyway Love* (Williamsburg, VA: Mini-Bible College).

21. Dr. David A. Hamburg, *Today's Children: Creating a Future for a Generation in Crisis* (New York: Times Books, 1992).

Chapter Four

1. Wells, *Inspiring Quotations*, p. 43, no. 6.

2. Barna, *What Americans Believe*, p. 220.

3. *Ibid.*, p. 223.

4. Fisher Humphries, editor, *Laos: All the People of God* (New Orleans: New Orleans Baptist Seminary, 1984), p. 42.

5. Dr. George Gallup, Jr., *Religion in America: 50 Years, 1935–1985*, The Gallup Report, Report no. 236, May 1985.

6. *Ibid.*

7. Barna, *What Americans Believe*, pp. 232, 278, 299.

8. Dr. Lawrence Richards, *Richards' Complete Bible Handbook* (Waco, TX: Word, 1982).

International Children's Handbook (Dallas: Word, 1986).

Teacher's Commentary (Wheaton: Victor, 1987).

The Bible Reader's Companion: Your Guide to Every Chapter of the Bible (Wheaton: Victor, 1991).

9. B. P. Brooks, *The Bible: How to Understand and Teach It* (Nashville: Broadman, 1969), pp. 93–94.

10. Barna, *What Americans Believe*, pp. 232, 278, 299.

11. *Ibid.*, pp. 295–302.

12. James F. Engel, *Contemporary Christian Communications: Its Theory and Practice* (Nashville: Thomas Nelson, 1979).

13. J. Oswald Sanders, *Spiritual Maturity* (Chicago: Moody, 1962).

14. Dr. Avery Willis, Jr., *MasterLife: Discipleship Training* (Nashville: Sunday School Board, Southern Baptist Convention, 1980).

15. Dr. Avery Willis, Jr., *MasterBuilder: Multiplying Leaders* (Nashville: Sunday School Board, Southern Baptist Convention, 1982).

16. *Christianity Today*, 22 July 1991, p. 14.

17. *Ibid.*, p. 14.

18. J. Keith Miller, *Hope in the Fast Lane: A New Look at Faith in a Compulsive World* (San Francisco: Harper & Row, 1990).

19. J. Keith Miller, *A Hunger for Healing: The Twelve Steps as a Classic Model for Christian Spiritual Growth* (San Francisco: HarperCollins), pp. xii and 7.

20. Dr. Hans Kung, *The Church* (Garden City, NY: Image Books, 1976), p. 169.

21. Richard Eley, in a talk at The Cove (Asheville, NC, June 1984).

Chapter Five

1. Blaise Pascal, *Les Pensées* (New York: E. P. Dutton, 1958), p. 70, no. 241.

2. *National & International Religion Report*, Roanoke, VA: 20 April, 1992, vol. 6, no. 9, p. 1.

3. Lyle E. Schaller, *It's a Different World!: The Challenge for Today's Pastor* (Nashville: Abingdon Press, 1987).

4. B. A. Santamaria, *Western Australian*, Perth, Australia, 10 April 1989, p. 4.

5. Dr. Denton Lotz, *The Southern Baptist Educator* (Nashville) Sept. 1987.

6. Dean Kelley, *Why Conservative Churches Are Growing* (New York: Harper & Row, 1977), pp. ix–xx, 134–135.

7. Dr. George Gallup, Jr., *Religion in America: 50 Years, 1935–1985.*, p. 4.

8. Dr. Harold Burchett, *Spiritual Life Studies: Manual for Personal Edification* (Columbia, SC: Columbia Bible College and Seminary, 1980).

9. Dr. Os Guinness, a Talk in Greenville, SC, to South Carolina Baptist Marketplace Ministry Seminar, 27 Sept. 1991.

10. Richard J. Neuhaus, editor, *Different Gospels: The Meaning of Apostasy* (Grand Rapids, MI: Eerdmans, 1989), vol. 10, p. 132.

11. *Ibid.*, p. 134.

12. *Ibid.*, pp. ix, 133.

13. *Ibid.*, p. 9.

14. Marcus J. Borg, *Jesus the New Vision: Spirit, Culture and the Life of Discipleship* (San Francisco: Harper & Row, 1987).

15. Barna, *The Frog in the Kettle*, p. 22.

16. Barna, *What Americans Believe*, p. 27, 295–301.

17. *Ibid.*, pp. 277–280.

18. *Ibid.*, pp. 230–280.

19. Helen Smith Shoemaker, *I Stand by the Door: The Life of Sam Shoemaker* (Waco, TX: Word, 1978).

Chapter Six

1. Robert Flood, *The Rebirth of America* (Philadelphia: Arthur De Moss Foundation, 1986), p. 127.

2. Russell Chandler, *Racing Toward 2001: The Forces Shaping America's Religious Future* (Grand Rapids, MI: Zondervan, 1992), p. 90.

3. *Charlotte Observer*, 20 Oct. 1991, p. 1b.

4. *The Polling Report*, Washington, DC, 14 Oct. 1991.

5. *Ibid.*

6. *The State*, 6 Feb. 1992, p. 1.

7. Dr. Ronald H. Nash, *The Closing of the American Heart: What's Really Wrong with America's Schools* (Dallas: Probe Books: 1990).

8. Dr. Allan Bloom, *The Closing of the American Mind: How Higher Education Has Failed Democracy and Impoverished the Souls of Today's Students* (New York: Simon & Schuster, 1987), pp. 26–27.

9. Patterson and Kim, *The Day America Told the Truth*, pp. 26, 32.

10. Rev. Joseph Fletcher, *Situation Ethics: The New Morality* (Philadelphia: Westminster), p. 37.

11. Dr. Paul Johnson, *Modern Times: The World from the Twenties to the Eighties* (New York: Harper & Row, 1983), pp. 4–5.

12. C. S. Lewis, *The Abolition of Man: How Education Develops Man's Sense of Morality* (New York: MacMillan, 1947), pp. 39–63.

13. *Ibid.*, pp. 39–40.

14. Lewis, ibid., quoting St. Augustine, p. 26.

15. Dr. John P. Newport, *The Southern Baptist Educator*, Aug. 1989, pp. 4–5.

16. *Ibid.*

17. Nash, *The Closing of the American Heart*, p. 30.

18. Dave Breese, *Seven Men Who Rule the World from the Grave* (Chicago: Moody, 1990).

19. R. C. Sproul, *Lifeviews: Make a Christian Impact on Culture and Society* (Old Tappan, NJ: Revell, 1986).

20. *Ibid.*, p. 72.

21. Aleksandr I. Solzhenitsyn, *A World Split Apart* (New York: Harper & Row, 1978), pp. 47–49.

22. Magid and McKelvey, *High-Risk Children Without a Conscience,* pp. 261–262.

23. "A National Survey: Drinking Habits, Access, Attitudes and Knowledge" (Washington, D.C., U.S. Department of Health and Human Services, June 1991), U.S. Government Printing Office.

24. *The State,* p. 1d, 25 July 1991.

25. *Ibid.,* p. 1, 4 Jan. 1992.

26. *Ibid.,* p. 1c, 22 Dec. 1991.

27. *Ibid.,* p. 1b, 3 Jan. 1992.

28. *Ibid.,* p. 1, 10 April 1991.

29. *Raleigh News and Observer,* Raleigh, NC., 10/7–12/90.

30. National Commission on the Role of the School and the Community in Improving Adolescent Health. *Code Blue: Uniting for Healthier Youth* (Alexandria, VA: National Association of State Boards of Education; Chicago: American Medical Association, 1990).

31. *Imprimis,* Hillsdale College (Hillsdale, MI), Sept. 1991, vol. 20, no. 9, pp. 1–3.

32. Flood, *The Rebirth of America,* p. 103.

33. National Commission on Excellence in Education, *A Nation at Risk: The Imperative For Educational Reform,* Washington, DC: U.S. Government Printing Office, 1983), p. 9.

34. David Barton, *America: To Pray or Not to Pray* (Aledo, TX: WallBuilder Press, 1991), p. 109.

35. James D. Richardson, *A Compilation of the Messages and Papers of the Presidents, 1789–1897* (U.S. Congress, 1899), vol. I, p. 220.

36. President George Bush, quoted in Associated Press story in *The State,* Columbia, SC, 8 May 1992, pp. 1a, 16a.

37. William J. Bennett, "Moral Literacy and the Formation of Character," *Faculty Dialogue* (Spring/Summer 1988), no. 8.

38. *Ibid.*

39. Russell Kirk, *Introduction to Babbitt's Literature and the American College,* p. 7.

40. Bennett, *The De-Valuing of America: The Fight for Our Culture and Our Children* (New York: Summit, 1992).

41. *Ibid.,* pp. 37–38.

42. *Ibid.*

43. *Ibid.,* p. 26.

44. H. Wayne House, editor, *Schooling Choices: An Examination of Private, Public, & Home Education* (Portland, OR: Multnomah, 1988).

45. Kirk, *Enemies of the Permanent Things* (La Salle, IL: Sherwood Sugden & Co., 1984).

46. Patterson and Kim, *The Day America Told the Truth,* pp. 235–239.

Chapter Seven

1. *Inspiring Quotations,* p. 219, no. 2940.

2. Magid and McKelvey, *High-Risk Children Without a Conscience,* p. ix.

3. Dr. Stanton E. Samenow, *The Criminal Mind* (New York: Times Books, 1984), p. 20.

4. Dr. M. Scott Peck, *The Road Less Traveled: A New Psychology of Love, Traditional Values and Spiritual Growth* (New York: Simon & Schuster, 1978), p. 283.

5. Dr. Colin Wilson, *A Criminal History of Mankind* (New York: G. P. Putnam's Sons, 1984), pp. 495–670.

6. Evelyn Christenson, *Gaining Through Losing* (Wheaton: Victor, 1980).

7. Lawrence O. Richards, *The Teacher's Commentary* (Wheaton: Victor, 1987), p. 541.

8. Thomas J. Peters and Robert H. Waterman, *In Search of Excellence* (New York: Harper & Row, 1982).

9. *The Chicago Tribune*, 3 Nov. 1990, p. 1.

10. Lee Atwater in a talk in Columbia, SC, 25 Oct. 1990, excerpts in *The State*, 26 Oct. and 2 Nov. 1990.

11. G. Gordon Liddy, *Will* (New York: St. Martin's, 1980).

12. Dr. George Gallup, Jr., *Forecast 2000* (New York: William Morrow, 1984), p. 153.

13. Doug Sherman and William Hendricks, *Your Work Matters to God* (Colorado Springs: NavPress, 1987), p. 100.

14. *Ibid.*, p. 183.

15. Chuck Colson and Jack Eckerd, *Why America Doesn't Work* (Dallas: Word, 1991), p. 45.

16. Patrick M. Morley, *The Man in the Mirror* (Brentwood, TN: Wolgemuth & Hyatt, 1989), p. 274.

17. *Ibid.*, p. 276.

18. Pete Hammond, National Renewal Conference on LAOS Evangelism in the Marketplace, Toccoa, GA, 26–29, Sept. 1988.

19. Robert E. Slocum, *Ordinary Christians in a High-Tech World* (Waco, TX: Word, 1986).

20. Edward R. Dayton, *What Ever Happened to Commitment?* (Grand Rapids, MI: Zondervan, 1984).

Chapter Eight

1. Edward Gibbon, *The Decline and Fall of the Roman Empire* (London: Penguin, 1985).

2. Alexis de Toqueville, *Democracy in America*.

3. Josh McDowell, *Evidence That Demands a Verdict* (San Bernardino, CA: Here's a Life, 1979), p. 107.

4. Barna, *What Americans Believe*, p. 85.

5. C. S. Lewis, *Mere Christianity* (New York: Macmillan, 1943), p. 102.

6. Harry S. Dent, *Cover Up: The Watergate in All of Us* (San Bernardino, CA: Here's Life, 1986), p. 14.

7. Peck, *The Road Less Traveled*, pp. 304–305.

8. M. Scott Peck, *People of the Lie: The Hope for Healing Human Evil* (New York: Simon & Schuster: 1983), p. 81.

9. Erich Fromm, *The Heart of Man*, quoted in *People of the Lie* at p. 82.

10. *Ibid.*, p. 83.

11. *Ibid.*, p. 182.

12. Lewis, *Christianity and Culture*, p. 33.

13. *U.S. News & World Report*, 6 April 1992, p. 19.

14. Richard M. Nixon, *Seize the Moment: America's Challenge in a One-Superpower World* (New York: Simon & Schuster, 1992), pp. 292–293.

15. *Newsweek*, 2 March 1992, p. 32.

16. *Time*, 6 April 1992, p. 20.

17. John F. Kennedy, *Profiles in Courage* (New York: Harper & Brothers, 1955).

Chapter Nine

1. *Inspiring Quotations*, p. 44, no. 515.

2. *Webster's New World Dictionary of the American Language* (Nashville: Southwestern, 1968), pp. 829, 819.

3. This anecdote appears in numerous works, including "America's Bill of Rights at 200 Years," by former Chief Justice Warren E. Burger, printed in *Presidential Studies Quarterly*, vol. XXI, no. 3, Summer 1991, p. 457.

4. *Inspiring Quotations*, p. 87, no. 1111.

5. Quoted by Probe Ministries, Dallas, TX in radio broadcast dated 20 Dec. 1989.

6. A. James Reichley, *Religion in American Public Life* (Washington, DC: The Brookings Institute, 1985), p. 4.

7. Dr. Richard Pierard and Dr. Robert Linder, *Civil Religion and the Presidency* (Grand Rapids, MI: Zondervan, 1988), pp. 17, xiii.

8. Daniel G. Reid, editor, *Dictionary of Christianity in America* (Downers Grove, IL: InterVarsity), p. 282.

9. Reichley, *Religion in American Public Life*, p. 5.

10. *Ibid.*, p. 359.

11. *Ibid.*, p. 15.

12. *Ibid.*

13. Dr. Larry Richards, *It Couldn't Just Happen* (Ft. Worth: Sweet Publishing, 1987), p. 15.

14. *Ibid.*, pp. 26–27.

15. William Martin, *A Prophet with Honor* (New York: William Morrow, 1991), p. 353.

16. *Ibid.*, pp. 356–357.

17. Pierard and Linder, *Civil Religion and the Presidency*, quoted at p. 271.

18. Jimmy and Rosalynn Carter, *Everything to Gain: Making the Most of the Rest of Your Life* (New York: Random House, 1987).

19. *The Collected Works of Abraham Lincoln*, ed. Roy Basler, 9 vols. (New Brunswick, NJ: Rutgers University Press, 1953), 5.532.–37.

20. *Ibid.*, 7.23.

21. Francis B. Carpenter, *Six Months at the White House* (New York: Hurd and Houghton, 1866), p. 282.

22. Tom Wicker, *One of Us: Richard Nixon and the American Dream* (New York: Random House, 1991), quoting Harry Dent on p. 504.

23. Harry S. Dent, *The Prodigal South Returns to Power* (New York: John Wiley & Sons), pp. 121–156.

24. Wicker, *One of Us*, pp. 486, 504.
25. Richard J. Neuhaus and Michael Cromartie, editors, *Piety and Politics* (Washington: Ethics and Public Policy Center, 1987), pp. 377–378.
26. Richard J. Neuhaus, *The Naked Public Square: Religion and Democracy in America*, 2nd ed., (Grand Rapids, MI: Eerdmans, 1984), pp. ix–x.
27. Mark A. Noll, *One Nation Under God?* (San Francisco: Harper & Row, 1988), p. 72.
28. *Ibid.*, pp. 74–79.
29. Pascal, *Les Pensées* (New York: E. P. Dutton, 1958), p. 265, no. 265.
30. Charles Colson, *Kingdoms in Conflict* (Grand Rapids, MI: Zondervan, 1987), p. 291.
31. Reichley, *Religion in American Public Life*, p. 3.
32. *Time/CNN Poll*, December 1991.
33. Reichley, *Religion in American Public Life*, pp. 112–113.
34. Dr. Paul Johnson, *A History of Christianity* (New York: Atheneum, 1980), p. 516.
35. Dr. Paul Johnson, a 1986 speech at Dallas Theological Seminary, Dallas, TX.

Chapter Ten

1. Michael Scott Horton, *Made in America: The Shaping of Modern American Evangelicalism* (Grand Rapids, MI: Baker, 1991), p. 8.
2. Dr. Philip M. Steyne, *Gods of Power: A Study of the Beliefs and Practices of Animists* (Houston: Touch Publications, 1989), pp. 47–59.
3. Otto Friedrich, "New Age Harmonies," *Time*, 12/7/87.
4. Arnold Toynbee, *Reconsiderations, A Study of History*, vol. 12 (New York: Oxford University Press, 1961), p. 488.
5. Dr. Herbert Schlossberg, *Idols for Destruction, Christian Faith and Its Confrontation with American Society* (Nashville: Thomas Nelson, 1983).
6. Dr. Alvin Toffler, *Future Shock* (New York: Bantam, 1971); Toffler, *The Third Wave* (New York: William Morrow, 1980).
7. Alvin Toffler, *PowerShift: Knowledge, Wealth, and Violence at the Edge of the 21st Century* (New York: Bantam, 1991), pp. 20–21.
8. *Ibid.*, p. 376.
9. David Lamb, *The Arabs: Journeys Beyond the Mirage* (New York: Random House, 1987), p. 58.
10. John Bartlett, *Bartlett's Familiar Quotations* (Boston, Little, Brown, 1980), p. 138.
11. Dr. George Gallup, Jr., and George O'Connell, *Who Do Americans Say That I Am?* (Philadelphia: Westminster, 1986), p. 62.

Chapter Eleven

1. *Inspiring Quotations*, p. 214, no. 2855.
2. Dr. Paul Johnson, Speech at Dallas Theological Seminary in 1986.
3. Dr. John P. Newport, *Life's Ultimate Questions: A Contemporary Philosophy of Religion* (Dallas: Word, 1989), p. 5.
4. *Ibid.*, p. 32.
5. Gallup, *Religion in America*, p. 50.

6. Newport, *Life's Ultimate Questions*, p. 12.
7. Art by Charles Sookikian, 1983. Used by permission.
8. Gallup, *Religion in America*, p. 50.
9. Hugh Sidey, *Time*, 9 Sept. 1991, p. 18.
10. Patterson and Kim, *The Day America Told the Truth*, pp. 235–239.
11. *Ibid*.

About the Authors

Harry Dent has served three presidents and a U.S. senator. He has also been an attorney, newspaper reporter, businessman, and soldier. In 1981 Harry closed his law practice and began full-time Christian service. He has been director of The Billy Graham Lay Center, where his wife, Betty, also served, and chairman of the 1987 South Carolina Billy Graham Crusade.

Harry is now a Christian lay writer, speaker, and teacher. Harry and Betty have a lay ministry, "Laity: Alive & Serving," based in Columbia, South Carolina. Their ministry takes them around the country and the world each year to proclaim the gospel. They are members of First Baptist Church in Columbia. They have been married forty years and have four married children and seven grandchildren.

For more information on the Dents' ministry, write to:
Laity: Alive & Serving
1120 Glenwood Ct.
Columbia, SC 29204-3360